The Mindful
HIGH
PERFORMER

The Mindful
HIGH
PERFORMER

CHELSEA POTTENGER

murdoch books

Sydney | London

Published in 2022 by Murdoch Books, an imprint of Allen & Unwin

Murdoch Books Australia
83 Alexander Street, Crows Nest NSW 2065
Phone: +61 (0)2 8425 0100
murdochbooks.com.au
info@murdochbooks.com.au

Murdoch Books UK
Ormond House, 26–27 Boswell Street, London WC1N 3JZ
Phone: +44 (0) 20 8785 5995
murdochbooks.co.uk
info@murdochbooks.co.uk

A catalogue record for this book is available from the National Library of Australia

A catalogue record for this book is available from the British Library

ISBN 978 1 92235 194 4

Cover and text design by Amy Daoud
Cover photography by Yuki Design Studio

Typeset by Midland Typesetters, Australia
Printed and bound in Australia by Griffin Press

DISCLAIMER: The content presented in this book is meant for inspiration and informational purposes only. The purchaser of this book understands that the author is not a medical professional, and the information contained within this book is not intended to replace medical advice or to be relied upon to treat, cure or prevent any disease, illness or medical condition. It is understood that you will seek full medical clearance by a licensed physician before making any changes mentioned in this book. The author and publisher claim no responsibility to any person or entity for any liability, loss or damage caused or alleged to be caused directly or indirectly as a result of the use, application or interpretation of the material in this book.

Every reasonable effort has been made to trace the owners of copyright materials in this book, but in some instances this has proven impossible. The author and publisher will be glad to receive information leading to more complete acknowledgements in subsequent printings of the book and in the meantime extend their apologies for any omissions.

We acknowledge that we meet and work on the traditional lands of the Cammeraygal people of the Eora Nation and pay our respects to their elders past, present and future.

10 9 8 7 6 5 4 3 2 1

The paper in this book is FSC® certified.
FSC® promotes environmentally responsible, socially beneficial and economically viable management of the world's forests.

For Jay and Clara

CONTENTS

INTRODUCTION

'HIGH PERFORMER' MAY not be in the dictionary (yet), but I'll bet it's a phrase you've been hearing quite a lot lately. Often used to describe someone who deeply cares about reaching their full potential at work and in life, it's a person who loves setting goals, exceeding expectations and raising the bar pretty much wherever they go. While this may be exactly how you define yourself (or hope to become), high performers can be both their own strength and weakness if they don't act *mindfully*.

It doesn't matter whether you're an entrepreneur, parent, doctor, dancer, salesperson, student or practitioner currently immersing yourself in the art of crystal healing, the *way* you approach your daily tasks and life goals is going to have a direct impact on not only your productivity and success, but also your mental health. In this age of overflowing inboxes and constant connectivity, it's easy to get lost in the quest of being on a Forbes list or the notion that it's possible to tick 63 things off a to-do list in one day. It's easy to justify a fourth cup of coffee at 4 pm because you can 'just come down later with that well-earned glass of wine'. It's also easy to believe that if you work through the night just *one more time,* you'll get that promotion, meet your deadline or finish that freelance gig. I get it – sometimes you need to hustle and push yourself outside your comfort zone. But here's the thing: subsisting on caffeine, spiking cortisol levels and constant exposure to the blue light from the smartphone that's glued to your hand can only be sustained for so long. Before you know it, you're burning out and wondering if everyone is as aware of the twitch in your eye as you are.

I learned this the hard way: being a high performer doesn't have to hurt. Over the years, I've gone from a Division 1 basketball player in the United States to a Johnson & Johnson medical device sales representative to a working mother, business owner and keynote speaker. However, in 2015, I found myself suicidal and in a mental hospital.

To say I was shocked by this situation is an understatement. As a self-described high performer, the last place I thought I'd be nine weeks into motherhood and my maternity leave was somewhere with padded walls. It was about as far as I could have fallen from my previous schedule of *achieving* 24 hours a day, seven days a week. Something clearly had to shift.

As part of my recovery, I started studying psychology and devouring any and every book about neuroscience, mental health, productivity and gut health I could get my hands on. I radically shifted my priorities to put my mental health first, adopting habits and tools that made my daily performance not only more effective, but also infinitely more enjoyable. The process was so life-changing that I went on to found EQ Minds to help others reset their mental health, too. EQ is short for Emotional Quotient, which is your ability to manage your emotions to relieve stress, communicate effectively, empathise with others and sympathise with yourself. I've since had the privilege of working with many of the world's leading brands such as eBay, Google, Estée Lauder, CBA and Macquarie Bank to improve team wellbeing. In 2021, I shared the EQ Minds mental-health and mindfulness tools with over 95,000 people in the corporate world.

Now, you don't have to find yourself in a psych ward to benefit from what I'm going to share. While, yes, I am going to suggest tools that can help if you feel burnt out, anxious, depressed, stressed or even suicidal, this book is ultimately a guide to giving yourself a healthier, happier foundation so you can operate at a high-performance level without feeling overcommitted, overwhelmed, overworked or simply over it. It's about giving yourself the best possible chance to not only achieve your goals, but to do so while weathering the inevitable disruptions and stressors life throws at all of us.

Throughout your life, there's a high chance that you are going to be faced with adversity. Whether it's workplace bullying, a cancer diagnosis, a recession, a drought, the death of a loved one or a global pandemic, these are moments that push us out of our comfort zone. Like it or not, life is one helluva bumpy ride. That's just the way it is. The cliché speaks the truth: without darkness there cannot be light. You need the right mindset and mental torch to illuminate the dark times – not only to survive them, but also to think and act *triumphantly*. Without challenges, we wouldn't have change. Without change, we wouldn't have innovation or inspiring success stories. Resilient people don't discredit the trauma or negative things. They have simply worked out a way of dialling into the good and finding what they can learn from a particularly challenging situation to create a brighter future.

Just as some people are born with more athletic ability than others, some people are born with more innate resilience. You want to know the cool part? You can build and strengthen your resilience the same way you train to get more muscle and coordination to run faster, row harder or jump higher. All it takes is consistent exercise! While some of the exercises you need to do to strengthen your mindset are physical, like going for a walk or practising yoga, the majority of them are cognitive. (And good news: they're way easier than running 10 km or doing a HIIT class.) Neuroscience shows that it only takes 10 minutes per day of intentional cognitive training, like a gratitude practice and reflective journalling, to make healthy changes to your brain. That's even less time than it takes to listen to David Bowie's song, 'Station to Station'.

⌐ LET'S BREAK THE STIGMA ⌐

There is no shame in needing or wanting help. Did you know:

☐ According to the World Health Organization (WHO), one in five people is going through a mental-health crisis at any given time.

☐ 3.6 per cent, roughly 264 million people worldwide, have an anxiety disorder.

☐ 23 per cent of women between the ages of 40 and 59 are taking antidepressant medication.

No one is shamed for cancer or diabetes; likewise, no one should be shamed for depression, anxiety, panic disorders and other brain health issues. There's also no shame in not knowing how to help the ones you love to overcome a mental-health crisis. This book can help you empathise and act constructively.

Living your life to the absolute fullest requires grit and gumption, but it doesn't need to come at the cost of your health or happiness. Think of this book as a companion you can turn to whenever times feel tough or you need to supercharge your performance. You could be having an identity crisis, health scare or relationship breakdown. You could be anxious about public speaking or asking for a promotion. You could be rehabbing an injury or trying to face a fear of flying. Or you might simply be ready to recharge your happiness and resilience for the future. Whatever brought you here, this is your reminder that you have the capacity to strengthen your mental and physical health any time you want.

01
ABOUT ME
(NOT THE LINKEDIN
VERSION)

WHEN I ENVISIONED MYSELF entering motherhood, I imagined a brightly lit hospital room polluted with nothing but the fragrance of gifted flowers and, of course, a mother's natural instinct to love, care for and protect her young. While my hospital room was brightly lit and the aroma of one too many chrysanthemums did make the air feel a bit unbreathable, I couldn't shake the feeling that I didn't quite know how to love, care for or protect the little girl I was cradling in my arms.

The year was 2015. My husband Jay was 34, I was 33 and our daughter, Clara, was what any parent who has struggled with fertility would call a miracle. For five years, we did the *Two-week Wait to Yet Another Negative Pregnancy Test* dance. (By the way, I'd like to take a moment to say, *You're welcome,* to anyone who has shares in Church & Dwight, the manufacturer of First Response pregnancy tests.) Our specialists could never find anything physically wrong with us, but for some reason (which probably included my high-stress job, hard-socialising tendencies and extreme workouts), we couldn't get to the implantation phase of pregnancy. It wasn't until we BOOKED in to begin the IVF process that we finally saw two pink lines on our 43rd pregnancy test. Apparently, it's quite common for couples to fall pregnant after making the appointment because stress levels go down due to hope.

Once we received triple confirmation that we were, in fact, pregnant, I relished the waves of nausea and bouts of restless leg syndrome, embracing every opportunity to nail this pregnancy thing. From doing 20 reps of pelvic-floor exercises a day to devouring books, podcasts and both free and paid versions of pregnancy tracking apps, I was on a mission to add 'the perfect pregnancy' to my unofficial list of Life Accomplishments. The only thing I didn't do to prepare was read up on mental illnesses like postnatal depression and anxiety. (Because that would never happen to me, right?) Feeling confident and in control, I focused on the fact that each week my baby was growing to the size of a cucumber, eggplant or melon (instead of what was going on with me). To be honest, there's not a lot of time to think about your own hormonal changes and mental health when you're neck-deep in the obligatory pram research process. I also worked furiously on my birth plan. While I would have loved to have given birth naturally, due to two previous head traumas, our doctors were concerned that I would have a seizure or a vasovagal attack and faint while in labour.

When I was skiing in 2010 with Jay and his family, a snowboarder slammed into me, which left me lying facedown in the snow, unable to breathe. He sped off, but luckily, Jay's father found me only moments after it happened. To make the situation even more terrifying, I began convulsing from a vasovagal attack. This accident left me with a concussion and broken ribs. The next time I had a head injury was in 2013. I was running a bag of rubbish down the stairs of our apartment building when I slipped and whacked my head on the stairs. Immediately, I had another vasovagal convulsion attack. My brother and Jay found me because they had heard the crash. After being driven by ambulance to the hospital, I had numerous tests to determine the extent of my injuries. From the tests, everything looked okay. This was on a Saturday. I went back to work on Monday. While driving home through the Harbour Bridge Tunnel, suddenly, I couldn't breathe. My peripheral vision was narrowing. Fearful that I was going to black out and cause a 20-car pile-up, I managed to pull over onto the shoulder, crawl into the back seat and will myself to take breaths. Even though I couldn't see and felt like the tunnel was caving in around me, I could hear commuters zooming past, blissfully unaware that there was a woman in the foetal position who was either: A. having a panic attack or B. having her soul leave her body (which is what it felt like). I don't know how much time went by, but security arrived because by all appearances, my parked car and empty driver's seat very much resembled a bomb threat. I explained that I believed I was having a panic attack and just needed a moment. Kindly, they towed my car out of the tunnel and drove me home.

Because this incident happened within 48 hours of falling down the stairs, I went back to my neurologist for further testing. Nothing looked suspicious and he sent me on my merry way. Even though they couldn't find anything on my brain scans, something was clearly wrong because I could not get back in my car knowing I had to commute through the tunnel. Jay knew it, I knew it, my GP knew it. At last, I was referred to a psychologist who acknowledged that I was experiencing severe anxiety. Was it due to the head traumas? Maybe. Was it work stress? Maybe. The cause isn't the important part. It's your reaction. As someone who likes to feel like they're accomplishing something every minute of every day, I couldn't come to terms with suddenly having to deal with such a mind-f*ck of a diagnosis. In typical Chelsea fashion, I decided to try 'gentle' exposure therapy. After all, who has time for 'severe anxiety' that prevents you from being able to drive through a tunnel? It took six in-person sessions, daily cognitive exercises, and Jay driving me through the tunnel multiple times a day (which quickly resulted in $80 worth of tolls), but I was able to overcome my anxiety about having anxiety. (Hilarious, I know.)

But back to my birth plan prep. As a Johnson & Johnson Medical Device Sales Representative, I was frequently in and out of C-section operations and knew the surgeons and the materials, and that within 20 minutes of going into theatre, I'd have my baby safely in my arms.

This was a situation I felt very comfortable with. Unlike an emergency C-section, the experience and room can be set up in a really special and nurturing way. Jay and I chose James Vincent McMorrow's cover of the song 'Higher Love' to echo off the walls, I chose my favourite brand of sutures and, as February came to a close, we welcomed Clara into the world. When I first held her little pink body, heard her first cry and counted each eyelash – everything felt clear and right.

Oh, what a difference 72 hours can make. Three days into mother-hood, I knew that I had a secret I couldn't possibly let out. Everything was getting blurry: my mind, my heart, my soul. I didn't know how to love my baby. Actually, I didn't even recognise my baby. In hindsight, I can pinpoint when things started to go wrong.

Day One: Nothing but newborn cuddle bliss, love and oxytocin-coated euphoria.

Day Two: Extreme pain and miscommunication between nurses resulted in a double dose of Endone.

In short – I was off my face. Instead of looking like a new mum, I looked like a 19-year-old at Future Music Festival. As I laid in my bed with lockjaw, Clara laid on my breasts with no clue how to feed. Since I couldn't feel anything except my Endone high, I didn't realise that she was sucking and licking my nipples to the point of no return. Within 12 hours they had become raw, chapped, cracked and damaged. That evening, I began vomiting. Vomiting with a C-section scar is like sneezing after a vaginal delivery. (Not recommended.) Couple this with the mental image of me shuffling naked to and from the bathroom and you can see why I don't look back fondly on Day Two of motherhood.

Day Three: This was the day that I would be able to be transferred to one of those flash hotel hospital rooms. The only hook: I needed to prove that I was doing well mentally and physically. With nipple shields covering my nipples (which more closely resembled bullet holes), I plastered a smile on my face to win over the doctors and nurses as I winced through Clara's feeding attempts. 'Yep, totally getting this breastfeeding gig now!' Here's the thing: I really wanted a steak and a glass of champagne. Badly.

I was convinced that it was the gross hospital food preventing me from finding my A game. Luckily, I was given the all-clear, and Jay, Clara and I moved to the Crowne Plaza Hotel in Coogee. Our floor had ten other babies and their mothers and one nurse to handle our needs. As we got unpacked, I noticed my mind going to some strange places.

I wonder if I should jump off the balcony.

Whoa, that's a weird thought to have. Why was I having a thought like that? I told myself I was just tired. But then the nurse came in to talk to me about Clara's coccyx. Apparently, it looked like there was a little indentation near the bone and it was a sign of spina bifida.

Oh my God. My child isn't going to be able to walk.

The paediatrician came, debunked what the nurse said and reassured me that everything was completely fine. Clara was simply going to be a tall girl. That was all. This scare alone was enough to jolt my body with enough adrenaline to power Vivid Sydney. Little did I know, I was about to spiral into the depths of insomnia. Sleep became an elusive lover. The more I craved it, the less I got of it. And there was also the fact that I couldn't feed Clara and began to view her as my source of pain.

As someone who wouldn't be surprised to discover *See: Chelsea Pottenger* as the definition of 'Type A Personality' in the dictionary, I really didn't anticipate feeling these feelings or the need to keep them buried deep inside my sleep-deprived body. Over the years, I've heard a lot of women talk about how meeting their baby was like meeting a stranger. I appreciated their ability to be so vulnerable. Of course, they'd follow it up with how this feeling was brief then suddenly the world made sense. They knew their purpose. They knew their role. They knew their value. When I held Clara for the first time, I suddenly knew what they meant about it being like meeting a stranger. Taking in her chubby toes, long bendy fingernails and button nose felt like sizing up a passer-by in Centennial Park. But to my horror … the stranger feeling wasn't fading.

Unlike strangers you 'people-watch' in public parks, part of welcoming your little stranger into the world often involves breastfeeding them. Feeding my child breast milk was important to me for a number of reasons. While I was pregnant, I had read all about how it helps build a baby's immunity, promotes bonding and contains everything they need to thrive. Yes, I had read about some mothers struggling and the need for a lactation consultant, but deep down, I just assumed I'd nail it. Nope. When it came time to work out the actual mechanics of this supposedly 'natural act', *nothing* seemed to feel organic. Due to the damage done on Day Two, by the time my milk came in, I was starting from a bad baseline. I had blood coming through my milk ducts, which is confronting to see in the spout of a breast pump. Clara was crying, I was crying … no one was happy. Not even the nurse. Looking back, I feel like I wasn't given the opportunity to succeed. It was like society and the hospital staff viewed breastfeeding as the only right way. Formula was suddenly the F-word you shouldn't say. I don't know if this is because I'm a self-diagnosed perfectionist, but the fact that I couldn't do the one thing my body needed to do to help my baby grow was killing me. After all, I was the one who'd run to yoga, find my flow and run home. I was the basketball player who landed a full scholarship to play in the United States. I was the person who was named the 'Johnson & Johnson Salesperson of the Year' multiple times. I was an achiever, so why wasn't I achieving this? My descent into darkness started out slow. First, there was the self-doubt most parents have:

I'll never get a handle on this breastfeeding thing.

Will my body ever be the same again?

Will this baby ever sleep?

All in all, easy enough to push away. But as I approached the two-week mark, I was operating on just minutes of microsleeps, and my thoughts turned into a constant gnaw in my stomach.

I am a failure.

I'm going to run away if I have to attempt to breastfeed again.

I must be the only one who feels like this.

Of course, I couldn't tell anyone that, right? They'd send me to the loony bin, take my baby, and Jay would divorce me.

When Clara was three weeks old, we finally decided to supplement with formula. While this pacified her, the guilt and shame I felt for still not being able to breastfeed spiralled into debilitating anxiety. My already blurry world was now ringing. No, it was *actually* ringing. Every door creak, cough, every baby cry, pierced my ears and left my fog-filled head pounding. I would walk around the house with noise-cancelling headphones so I didn't have to hear my baby cry. To prevent fabric from touching my nipples, which were still extremely sore, my top was perpetually undone, and in all honesty, I looked like a dishevelled fembot from *Austin Powers* (if they shot breast milk out of cracked nipples, that is). After a particularly challenging evening, I asked Jay to move Clara down into the kitchen so I couldn't hear her. That night, I slept. Albeit for an hour. Maybe that's what we both needed? Space.

With that revelation, I unofficially ended my maternity leave and started showing up at work. I even booked a solo flight to go to Scotland to be a bridesmaid in my girlfriend's wedding. Making these decisions made me feel in control. While I couldn't feed my baby, I could do my job. I could be there for my friends. I also secretly thought that if I could just escape, maybe I could get myself on track and come back to be the mother I was meant to be. Of course, I created the ultimate veneer for colleagues, family and friends. My hair was perfectly groomed, my clothing immaculate, and when asked if I was liking motherhood, I expressed nothing but words of joy. At our six-week check-up, I told my doctor everything I knew she wanted to hear during the postnatal depression (PND) survey check, which to this day makes me think I'd be a fantastic actor. The only thing I was honest about was my lack of sleep. To help remedy this, my doctor prescribed me benzodiazepine sleeping pills. Blissfully unaware of just how addictive benzos are, I took one that night and slept for a glorious five hours. Hello, lover!

The next day, I felt like a completely different person. That night, I took another tablet and slept for five hours yet again. I knew it. I just needed sleep. The third night though, one tablet wasn't cutting it. The next night, I took two to ensure I'd get the same five hours. By the time Clara was nine weeks old, I was taking five benzos a night, but only getting between one and two hours of sleep. There was no denying that I was royally screwed.

There's no way out of this.

When at mothers' group, I'd plaster a smile on my face and make small talk with the women about nappy rash and name origins. As they'd try to connect over sore boobs and milk-stained clothing, I couldn't help but wonder if any of them would prefer to poke their own eyes out than be a new mother. I was also wondering if 11 am was too early to have a gin.

The thing is, I had people there for me. My mum came and stayed with us for the first six weeks. Jay was nothing but attentive, helpful and doting. His family are so far removed from dysfunction it's not even funny. My friends were asking thoughtful questions. But, for some reason, I was dying inside and was terrified for anyone to know it. I told myself that I just needed space and that once in Scotland, I'd have the chance to finally get it. With Clara now ten weeks old, our families assured me they would look after her as I waved goodbye en route to the airport.

Of course they'll do a better job of looking after Clara than I can.

She won't even miss me.

Maybe my plane will go down. That would be better for everyone.

Those are just a few of the thoughts that ran through my mind as I drove to the airport. As I was making my way onto the M1, the dull ringing in my ears escalated to fire-alarm levels. My vision started going dark. My chest was tightening. I knew instantly that I was having the same panic attack I had had in the Harbour Bridge Tunnel. I pulled over to lie down.

I can't even get to the airport.

I am such a burden on everyone.

Jay, Clara, my family and friends will be better off without me here.

The only way out of this is to remove myself from the planet.

This is a selfless act.

Jay will marry someone else. Someone amazing.

Clara will get a mother who isn't a failure.

As I regained my ability to breathe, see and hear, I made the decision to drive home, write a goodbye letter and take my own life. I knew Jay would be at his parents', so this was the right time. Now it's hard to think about how my mind was able to get to this point, but somehow it did. When I walked in our door, I was surprised to find Jay home. He looked equally surprised to see me standing there.

'Are you okay?' Jay asked.

•

In answer to this three-word question, which I hadn't been able to answer truthfully for ten weeks, I was finally ready to say 'No', I was not okay. Straight away, Jay called my cousin who is (fortunately) a psychiatrist who specialises in postnatal depression. She told me about St John of God Hospital's psychiatric program for mothers and that I needed to be admitted. After getting my GP to write a referral for me, I realised that I would never have known about this program if it wasn't for my cousin. To this day, I feel so lucky to have her in my life and will be forever grateful.

Clara and I were admitted the next day for a five-week stay for inpatient psychiatric help. I don't know if you've ever watched *Orange Is the New Black*, but I was really identifying with Piper Chapman at this moment. I couldn't help but laugh at the thought of my other mum-friends lining up to get their coffees for a playdate while I was lining up for meds.

When you're in a psych ward, there is an unwritten rule that you automatically try to work out if you're the craziest person there. While doing laundry I noticed a woman who had unbrushed hair and the type of uncut nails you'd see in the latest Guinness World Records. (They were starting to curl over!) And when I say 'unbrushed' hair, I don't mean bed hair or Nick Nolte's general appearance, I mean stray dog that needs a general anaesthetic and clippers to get rid of the matting. Surely this woman was the craziest person there.

'Hey you.'

I looked up from the washing machine I was loading. Crazy lady was talking to me.

'I'm trying to work out who's crazier, you or me,' she said matter-of-factly.

Gobsmacked that she was playing my game, I could hardly say she was the one winning the race before she added, 'I know I haven't brushed my hair for months on end, but your maternity jeans are on back to front.'

I looked down and, sure enough, the wide panel of elastic that should cater for a growing belly was sitting above my butt. We both burst into laughter. There I was – suicidal, addicted to sleeping pills, buttons mismatched and my pants on backwards. Maybe I was the craziest. But at least I had a new friend. And what a friend this woman was. Her name was Vanessa and she had been a high-powered lawyer before having her baby and slipping into a state of depression that left her unable to care for herself, let alone her baby. Together, we bonded over our desire to be first in line to get our meds. As once-upon-a-time goal setters, now that we were able to see the light at the end of the recovery tunnel, we wanted to see who could heal the fastest. The nurses hated the way we'd pace the hallways together and always sent us to the back of the line – some sort of punishment for our eagerness, I guess. We'd go through old photos and laugh about how hot and put-together we used to be. Often, we'd just hug and cry.

We also bonded over the fact that the hospital food was shit. Honestly, how can you be expected to heal when you don't have the right food to nourish you? As my energy levels increased, so did my brazenness. I quickly earned the title of ballsiest patient for receiving shipments of organic groceries at 2 am through the emergency exit door. (Sometimes you have to go rogue for good food.) Only once did the Director of Nursing sit me down to tell me organic food was not an emergency. (I disagree to this day. Will explain why later in the book!)

You're probably wondering where Clara was while I was popping the right pills, weaning off the bad ones and making friends with women who felt every bit as lost as me. While I wanted her to be with Jay, she was actually right next to me. One of the major issues I was dealing with was bonding with my baby. Every time I looked at her, I felt like a failure. Why didn't I feel all of those gushy feelings other mothers felt? In a counselling session, I was really surprised to hear the therapist tell me to try a 'fake it until you make it' approach. She said that I should just smile and sing to Clara, and in a few weeks my motor neurons would fire and I'd feel all of those amazing maternal feelings. Miraculously, this worked. (Or maybe it's not a miracle because there's literal science behind this.) The reason I was as low as I was stemmed from my desire to love my baby and be the best possible mother. When I didn't do things perfectly or how I had anticipated, I didn't ask for help. I didn't give myself grace or space. I was so rigid in my perfectionism that I'd inadvertently become everything I feared. It was only when I became vulnerable that I was able to ask for help and ultimately change the way I responded to how society had told me motherhood should be.

I don't know how things got so bad because I truly did have the most incredible support system. Friends and family members came to visit me every single day I was in hospital. Some friends even flew from Queensland. Without this support, I'm not sure I would have healed the way I did in five weeks. This showed me how important it is to invest in your friends and family because when times get tough (and they will), the saying is true: it takes a village to raise a child. It also takes a village to save a mother.

•

If you needed to have your appendix removed, chances are you'd take at least a week off to recover from the surgery. But what about your mental health? If you were struggling with anxiety or depression, would you take a week off to heal? Sadly, the answer is usually 'No'. That's because we can't see the mind's scars. There's also the stigma surrounding mental health that makes us want to bottle up our emotions, ignore physical warning signs and put on a performance that everything is totally and completely fine.

After I left the Mums and Bubs Unit, my psychiatrist suggested that I study psychology because she had a feeling that I would be really good at helping others. After experiencing firsthand that it is possible to go from contemplating suicide to being sane and joyful, I became passionate about protecting my mental health and helping others to do the same. Life is full of unexpected trauma, triggers and tests. That's why I left the corporate world, began studying psychology at The University of Adelaide and started EQ Minds. Today, I'm on a mission to share the tools and resources that saved my life so that you don't find yourself alone with thoughts that scare you.

So, let's get started. Over the next 12 chapters, we're going to go through the key areas you can start working on today to improve and protect your mental health, and be the high achiever you were meant to be.

02
ABOUT YOU

THE THING ABOUT achieving and maintaining a healthy brain and mind is that it's not a set-and-forget deal. It's something that needs to be worked on every day. Just like a car, your mental health needs to be monitored, adjusted, protected and serviced. Some improvements are easy, others might warrant a total overhaul. While throughout this book I am going to dive deep into neuroplasticity, goal-setting, routines, sleep, exercise, mindfulness, meditation and the potential need for medication, I want to get started with surface-level adjustments that can get you feeling and thinking better immediately. To begin: I need you to become aware of how you're currently feeling, thinking, reacting, eating, moving and sleeping.

I've spent a lot of time listening to my body, noticing my habits, identifying my triggers and learning when I need to make a change or ask for help. I encourage you to start listening and noticing how you're feeling throughout the day. If possible, try to keep a journal or update a note in your phone. Some people like having one journal, but others have different journals to track their sleep, gut health, general mood and goals. The moods we feel are usually correlated with an action we've taken – or sometimes with inaction. I have a friend who noticed she has crippling anxiety the day after having between three and five alcoholic drinks. She likes calling this 'hangxiety'. I have another friend who cannot sleep if he has coffee after 10 am. Without sleep, he gets brain fog. With brain fog, he can't be as productive as he needs to be to keep up with his workload. Cue: anxiety spiral. Personally, I have to eat organic food. My stomach is incredibly sensitive and if I don't ensure I stick to the foods that make me feel good, I experience both physical and mental fatigue, which gets in the way of my #workingmum life. By taking time to record and reflect in a journal, you're much more likely to stay aware of how your mind and body are performing, which will enable you to adjust your habits as needed.

I also suggest making an appointment with your doctor to ensure there's nothing physically making you feel exhausted or flat. A common issue, especially among women, is low iron. Another is low B12. And you could have a hormonal imbalance. Ask your doctor to order a blood test to rule out any deficiencies or underlying causes. You may also want to show the results to a naturopath or integrative doctor. (More on inner health and the importance of choosing the right health specialist in the chapters to come!)

Your doctor may also be able to refer you to a psychologist or cognitive behavioural therapist. Most people have experienced some sort of trauma in their childhood, whether they are conscious of it or not. This can be anything from losing a parent to sexual abuse. If you aren't able to work through these past experiences and find ways to manage them, it will be difficult to do the other work that needs to be done. We will spend quite a bit of time in Chapter 13: Your Support discussing the different types of therapy available as well as how to find the right therapist but, in the meantime, I simply want you to start being aware of and auditing how you're feeling. Don't worry: you're not being graded. I want you to start paying attention to your energy levels, emotions and habits. By gaining self-awareness, you'll be much more likely to notice when you need to take action. Do you have a journal handy? You can begin by using the prompts at the end of each chapter.

EXAMPLE OF A DAILY HEALTH JOURNAL

Date:

I woke up feeling:

At lunch I felt:

Before bed I felt:

The change I could make to feel better is:

YOUR ACTION PLAN

When people take the time to read a book about mental health, chances are they want to feel better YESTERDAY. As I mentioned earlier, your journey to a healthier brain will take time and work, but there are easy steps you can take immediately that can accelerate your progress and bring you back into balance. I'm not saying you need to cut out all triggers or adopt rigid routines *forever*, but in the beginning of the healing process and at certain points in your life, it can be a highly effective way to get back on track.

Get Yourself Checked Out:
- Get your blood work done.
- Have your hormones checked.
- Assess your gut health.
- Consider speaking to a therapist or counsellor.

Moderate Your Triggers:
- alcohol
- caffeine
- social media
- news
- emails
- toxic/overly demanding people.

Prioritise Your Sleep:
- Swap TV for a book to unwind.
- Leave your phone outside your bedroom.
- Take a day off work to learn a new relaxation technique.
- Miss a morning workout if it means getting the sleep you need.
- Invest in a comfy eye mask and ear plugs.
- Avoid alcohol and caffeine.

Nourish Your Body:
- Drink 2 litres of water a day.
- Spend 10–20 minutes in the sun every day to boost vitamin D.
- Find a probiotic that is right for your gut health.
- Limit your intake of processed foods.
- Take a long bath with Epsom salts.

Move Your Body:
- Go for a walk or run.
- Complete a yoga practice.
- Do an online workout video.
- Visit a gym.
- Spend time stretching.
- Go for a swim.

Acknowledge Your Emotions:
- Write in your journal.
- Listen to music.
- Do a meditation.
- Allow yourself time to cry or be angry.
- Write a letter to someone you're not ready to confront yet. (You don't have to send it.)

Self-care:
- Get a massage or facial.
- Read a book.
- Spend time in your yard or garden.
- Go see a movie or play.

Connect with Friends and Family:
- Hug someone.
- Compliment a friend.
- Go for a walk with a friend.
- Flip through photos and celebrate past times.

Connect with Yourself:
- Set an intention for the day.
- Write in a gratitude journal.

IN YOUR JOURNAL

Take a moment to reflect by answering the following questions:

- Do you wake up feeling happy and excited for the day?
- Do you experience an afternoon 'energy crash'?
- Do you get at least seven hours of sleep at night?
- Do you have more than ten alcoholic drinks a week?
- Are you having a bowel movement every day? (More importantly – is it solid?)
- How much caffeine do you have on a daily basis?
- Are you currently dependent on any prescription drugs (such as sleeping pills or stimulants)?
- Is there something specific that is affecting your stress levels?
- When was the last time you spent the day relaxing and not feeling guilty about it?
- When you think about the future, do you feel hopeful?
- Which key things from the action plan will you do right away?

03
YOUR MIND

DID YOU KNOW that scientists used to believe that the brain was fixed and that we would tap out on our neurological peak in our late teens or early twenties? In the 1960s, they discovered that our brains actually have neuroplasticity, which is a fancy way of saying our brains can change physically and be reshaped by our actions and our environment. It doesn't matter if it's your brain needing to relearn how to communicate with your hand to pick up a cup of tea after having a stroke or adopting a new way of thinking when faced with adversity, we have the capacity to form new neurological connections that allow us to achieve the impossible.

As someone who is all too aware of the shenanigans I got up to as an 18-year-old, to say I was thrilled to learn that I can redeem myself is an understatement because, let's be honest, being able to retrain the brain to recognise that clear bra straps aren't fooling anyone is a GIFT. Jokes aside, the truth is your brain is influenced by your genes as well as your environment, which means that we all have a brain that is entirely unique to us. They're like our fingerprints; no two are the same. But unlike the epidermal swirls that grant us access to our phones and restricted areas of office buildings, our brains can be taught to think, feel and act *differently*. While you don't have control over your brain's formation, you can control how it changes. Wild, right?

THE TRIUNE BRAIN MODEL

Chances are you've been out of your high-school biology class for a while now, so let's go back for a little lesson on the human brain. While you may be able to recall the basics like cerebellum, cerebrum and brainstem, I want to talk about the triune brain model, which was created by American neuroscientist Dr Paul MacLean in the 1960s. This model suggests that the brain is divided into three regions that are the result of evolution:

- Region 1: The primal brain (also referred to as the basal ganglia and reptilian brain)
- Region 2: The emotional brain (also referred to as the limbic system and paleomammalian brain)
- Region 3: The rational brain (also referred to as the neocortex and neomammalian brain).

The Primal Brain

The primal brain sits at the base of the brain and has been around for millions of years. It doesn't matter if you are an elephant, shark, caveman, cockatoo or human born after the Industrial Revolution, this is the part of the brain that ensures your body is functioning properly and *surviving*. From regulating body temperature to releasing hormones at the right time, it's the operating system that pretty much any animal needs for survival.

The Emotional Brain

The emotional brain is what makes mammals unique. While the primal brain may be telling you to drink water to stay alive, the emotional brain is telling you to mate for life, drink alcohol for pleasure and, of course, be afraid! Okay, so the *be afraid* part isn't quite as fun as the first two, but we need this part for survival because it's how we identify a threat. Eons ago, we needed to know if there was a carnivorous animal trying to snack on our legs while we were blissfully sleeping in a cave. These days, we don't have quite the same threats anymore, but unfortunately, this part of the brain still LOVES to go into overdrive and react as if getting cut off by another car is the same as needing to seek shelter during a lightning storm.

So what physically happens when the emotional brain senses a threat? Your emotional brain tells your body to start pumping hormones like adrenaline and cortisol that are silently screaming, 'Stay alive!' This triggers that fight-or-flight response. While, yes, we need this when we are actually in danger (like being a woman walking home alone at night), it isn't exactly helpful when the 'threat' is simply a confronting email. Senior Fellow of UC Berkeley's Greater Good Science Center and *The New York Times* bestselling author Dr Rick Hanson once said, 'The brain is like Velcro for negativity and Teflon for positivity.' Due to the way our brains are wired, it's not surprising that we opt to worry and gravitate towards dark and stormy thoughts instead of rainbows, sunshine and optimism.

The Rational Brain

The rational brain is the 'newest' part of our brain and what separates us from other mammals. It's responsible for our ability to think critically, respond rationally and behave productively. While the primal and emotional brain regions reach maturity rather quickly, the rational brain isn't fully developed until our twenties. Have you ever noticed that car insurance rates go down when you turn 25? Insurance companies know that until then, people are more likely to engage in high-risk behaviour.

So why does the rational brain not always feel so rational? Think about typical kid behaviour for a second. Have you noticed that the majority of children can chuck a tantrum out of left field? One minute, everyone is happily eating their breakfast cereal and talking about a morning walk, and the next minute a milk-covered spoon is flying through the air because (wait for it) a child just realised they were eating Cheerios and not Honey Nut Cheerios and even though the bowl is mostly finished, this IS A TRAVESTY that must be paid for by the entire family. The reason why this child lost their shit (so to speak) is because evolution hasn't fully solved the wiring issues of the brain. Basically, until you reach your mid-twenties, there's a weak signal between the emotional brain and the rational brain. Even once the connections are fully formed, when we're in a state of stress, the rational brain can go offline. This happens to adults because we, as a society, keep taking on more and more responsibilities, expectations and commitments. You know all of those looming deadlines that keep you awake at night? They're probably contributing to the strained connections between the thoughts, emotions and actions of your brain.

But Chelsea, can I strengthen the communication channels between my emotional and rational brain?

I am so glad you asked! The short answer is yes. To find out how, let's dive into the wild and wonderful world of neuroplasticity.

WELCOME TO NEUROPLASTICITY

Every time you learn something new (like what the most efficient driving route is to work or that pygmy marmosets are the world's smallest monkeys), your brain makes a new synaptic connection. Physical changes to your brain like this are what scientists refer to as neuroplasticity. Similar to adding a faster processor or spam-blocker to a computer, these connections literally change the way your brain looks, thinks and acts. Unlike when you're a child and are making endless new synaptic connections (like how many blocks you can stack before your glorious tower topples over, how to form words to communicate your needs, or that if you eat your chicken finger before you blow on it, you can and will burn your tongue), once you reach adulthood, your brain starts letting go of old connections to make room for new ones. I call this the 'one in, one out' information policy of the brain and it's probably why you can't remember the name of your best friend from Year 2.

While the brain changes when you learn new concepts or have something positive happen, it also changes when you go through a negative, stressful or traumatic experience. Studies have shown that stress can cause your brain to decrease its cognitive functions, impact your memory and even atrophy. Extreme trauma can lead to psychological disorders such as post-traumatic stress disorder (PTSD), acute stress disorder (ASD), dissociative disorders and depression. Even though the brain can be one of the most vulnerable parts of our bodies, thanks to neuroplasticity, there is always hope for healing, retraining and resetting.

Just like kale, pumpkin-spice lattes and nitro coffee, concepts like 'self-efficacy', 'growth mindset' and 'reframing' are on trend and something you've probably seen peppering your newsfeeds (if you follow personal development or psychology accounts). If you haven't heard of them, I'm here to tell you to get excited because they're better than kale, pumpkin-spice lattes and nitro coffee COMBINED. Why? They're all simple neuroplasticity techniques to bolster your mental health and give yourself a leg up in any area of performance. Let's look at each one in turn.

WHAT IS SELF-EFFICACY?

Self-efficacy is a social learning concept created by Canadian-American psychologist and academic Dr Albert Bandura. Essentially, self-efficacy is our judgement about ourselves and our ability to perform well in a particular area. It is the perception that we have about ourselves and what we believe we can or can't do. People with high levels of self-efficacy exert more effort and persist longer in the face of difficulties. That means they are more likely to surpass seemingly insurmountable barriers that may pop up in their personal or professional lives. People who are confident in their capabilities approach challenges as things to be mastered, rather than threats to be avoided. People with low self-efficacy tend to avoid challenges and take fewer risks.

According to Dr Bandura, the four components that build self-efficacy are:

1 personal attainment
2 social modelling

3 verbal persuasion

4 emotional state.

Personal Attainment

Take a moment to think back on a past accomplishment. This could be something like running a marathon, auditioning for a play or moving to a new country. Once you attained it, did you feel more confident about trying it again? Chances are YES! This is because success breeds success. When a baby is learning to walk, they inevitably fall down quite a few times. Through encouragement and determination, they keep going until they're confidently charging through the living room, favourite toy in hand. By achieving their past goal of walking, they're now more likely to find the strength and confidence to learn to run, jump and eventually leap. Attaining a personal goal is a key way to boost your self-efficacy.

Now take a moment to think about past adversity. This could be losing a client, failing a course or having travel plans cancelled. Now that you're on the other side of it: did overcoming it feel as hard as you thought it would? Are you less afraid of a similar situation happening again? When we talk about the personal attainment facet of self-efficacy, we're not just talking about huge personal or professional success. We're talking about any situation you had to face with perseverance, motivation and grit. Success raises self-efficacy whereas repeated failures lower it. By consciously reflecting on past successes, you can give yourself a reminder that you are capable of achieving big goals and overcoming adversity.

Social Modelling

Social modelling is drawing inspiration from the achievements of people whom you deem similar to you. The greater assumed similarity between you and them, the higher your motivation will be to persist. For example, let's say you've been considering applying to a vet nursing program. While you are incredibly passionate about animals and handle high-stress situations well, you know that science is not your strongest area when it comes to formal education. While mulling over your decision to apply, you learn that Becky Johnson, your friend from high school, who definitely failed molecular biology is now an actual veterinarian – and a great one at that! Looking back, you know you have a similar capacity ... perhaps she got extra tutoring help to do the course. After taking her out for a cup of coffee, you learn that yes, she did need to work extra hard through her course but was able to do so thanks to tutoring options and some really influential mentoring. Finally, you think, *If Becky can do it, so can I.* Application: submitted.

When we look at people with similar skills and competence to our own and see how they're facing challenges, we're able to get the confidence we need to achieve things on the same or greater level.

Verbal Persuasion

When someone you respect or admire tells you that you have the power to succeed and thrive, it can influence your self-efficacy. Do you have a friend, colleague or family member whom you turn to when you need someone to pump your tyres up, so to speak? Maybe it's a whole group of people who are your cheer squad. We'll talk more about social connections in Chapter 11: Your Connections, but it feels pretty wonderful to have people who are there for you, who believe in you and see your potential even when you can't.

It doesn't matter if this is someone telling you that everything will be okay after a break-up or someone pointing out that yes, you do have the talent to succeed in the stand-up comedy world, it's the act of someone *you* trust telling you to trust *yourself* that persuades you to become more resilient.

When I decided to leave the corporate world to study psychology and set up a mental-health company with the mission of creating healthier workforces, I was terrified for a number of reasons. For starters, what would happen to my income? I also worried about losing my identity as a goal-setting, target-meeting salesperson. Most of all, I was worried about failing. What if I couldn't help anyone? Cue: Chelsea's Cheer Squad. My husband assured me that we had been strategic enough with financial planning that I could take time off to retrain and not worry about lost income. My Johnson & Johnson friends all reiterated that they weren't going anywhere and couldn't wait to see me thrive in the space of mental-health advocacy. Most importantly, my mentor helped point out the reasons why my message would resonate with many people. I had lived through and survived a mental-health crisis, I am compassionate, I am smart and I was determined to do the things I needed to do to be an expert in this space.

Emotional State

Your emotional state is your mood. How you feel on a daily basis will greatly impact your judgements about your self-efficacy. If you are feeling positive about a situation and healthy in your daily life, your chances of reacting in a constructive manner to a setback will be much higher than when you're feeling depressed, anxious and exhausted. Have you ever heard someone say they're sick and tired of feeling sick and tired? It's hard to find the energy you need to be resilient in any situation if you're feeling under the weather or flat.

Keeping a balanced life, eating well, exercising, sleeping well, meditating, expressing gratitude and taking scheduled breaks are key for self-efficacy to make sure your stress levels aren't hijacking your potential to succeed.

WHAT IS A GROWTH MINDSET?

Do you know how many thoughts we have every day? On average, we are thinking 70,000 thoughts a day. Of those, 95 per cent are recycled thoughts that we had yesterday and 80 per cent are negative. Do you know how many decisions we're making every day? 35,000. I know. (And 226.7 of those are dedicated to food!) With so much happening in our minds at any given moment, it makes sense that we might slip into a sort of autopilot mode and just go with the flow. It also makes sense that we might gravitate towards feeling victimised, defeated and burnt out by work, relationships and life admin.

After all, questioning why you can't do something is a lot harder than simply coming to the (usually wrong) conclusion that *Nothing ever works out for me, anyway.*

American psychologist Dr Carol Dweck has spent a lot of time researching students' attitudes about failure. What she has found, as she described in her 2006 book *Mindset*, was that while some kids were excited by a challenge, others completely shut down and stopped trying after encountering even the smallest little hiccup. To record each person's attitudes and underlying beliefs about what they could and could not do, she created the terms *fixed mindset* and *growth mindset*. Today, these two terms are used widely by psychologists, teachers, coaches and parents, along with Dweck's philosophy that people should be praised for their progress, not their intelligence or accomplishments. For example, when you compliment a child for 'studying so hard' for a test versus saying, 'Gosh, you're so smart!' they're more likely to develop a growth mindset and face future problems with grit and motivation. They've made a link that working hard equals success. Not that simply being born smart equals success. This can be applied to adults as well. When you praise an employee for asking for feedback on a project, you're encouraging them to reflect, adjust and essentially do better next time versus feeling capped by their current skill set and approach.

Author and motivational speaker Tony Robbins likes to ask people to imagine that life isn't happening TO you, it's happening FOR you. When it comes to explaining what a growth mindset is, I always come back to Robbins' words because they essentially put the responsibility of attaining happiness and life-satisfaction into our own hands. In the same way you need to tend to a garden to make it grow, you need to tend to your brain. A number of people have the misconception that what we're given from our parents is what we're going to have for the rest of our lives. But if we all believed that, we'd never go and try to achieve things. Adopting a growth mindset allows us to challenge the status quo. It also allows us to choose to learn (and grow) from setbacks, losses and traumas.

In the world of psychology, when it comes to how we respond to challenges, mistakes or adversity, conventional wisdom says there are two types of people: psychological victims and psychological survivors. Psychological victims tend to have fixed mindsets while psychological survivors tend to have growth mindsets.

Psychological victims, as you'd expect, are often passive, pessimistic, victimised and live in the past. They're unlikely to give someone credit for working hard to achieve a goal and more likely to assume that it was luck or nepotism. (And, of course, neither of those are on their side!)

- They ask, *Why doesn't anyone help me?*
- They believe they can't help themselves.
- They don't feel like they have control of their fate.
- They feel like success is only for lucky people.

Psychological survivors on the other hand are people who are often described as active, optimistic and who look to the future with enthusiasm. They view successful people as role models and look for ways to emulate their behaviour.

- Instead of saying, *Why doesn't anyone help me?*, they ask, *How can I help myself?*
- They believe that through hard work, they can overcome any issue.
- They are still human, so they make mistakes, feel let down and grieve, which is healthy, BUT they continue to persevere.
- Instead of feeling threatened by their peers, they learn from their peers' actions.

I believe this second title needs to change because 'survivor' isn't adequate for what it takes for someone to achieve a growth mindset. I suggest: psychological victor. We don't win the game of life by surviving. We win by being victorious.

Thoughts Someone with a Fixed Mindset (aka a Psychological Victim) Has:

- *I didn't deserve it anyway.*
- *I'm not smart enough to do it.*
- *Someone else stole it from me.*
- *I should just give up.*

Thoughts Someone with a Growth Mindset (aka a Psychological Victor) Has:

- *What can I learn from this situation?*
- *What was a positive outcome from this situation?*
- *Even though I didn't get my ideal outcome, I do have …*
- *What can I do differently next time to increase my chances of success?*

Even though it might sound like I'm telling you to be a Positive Polly, I need to emphasise that it's okay to feel angry and sad when you experience a setback. Brené Brown talks a lot about toxic positivity and the way Instagram culture has put pressure on us to push our negative feelings aside and just meditate, yoga or infrared-sauna our problems away. Without negative feelings, we would not have positive feelings. They're what make us human. Having a growth mindset just means taking those feelings and then opting to be responsible with your emotions. Emotions direct our behaviour in important ways because they show us what we value. Negative emotions are normal and healthy and often have really big benefits. By approaching a setback with a wider emotional vocabulary and eventually finding the confidence to choose a growth-mindset action, you're breeding resilience. Every time you do this, your capacity for resilience gets stronger and stronger – just like a muscle.

WHAT CAN NEGATIVE EMOTIONS TEACH US?

☐ Grief can show us that we need someone's help or support.

☐ Anger can show us that we care passionately about something.

☐ Sadness can show us what we truly value.

☐ Apathy can show us what we don't truly value.

☐ Fear can show us just how powerful our imagination can be.

WHAT IS REFRAMING?

The concept of reframing has to do with how you can intentionally shift your mindset to one of gratitude, growth and resilience. How do we do this? Let's look at three techniques: choosing to focus on 'progress' and 'process' rather than end results, using specific language and asking, is this helpful or harmful?

Focusing on Progress and Process

According to American neuroscientist Dr Andrew Huberman, your body has two reward systems, each of which releases feel-good chemicals into your body. The 'progress' reward system refers to all of the things that you're grateful for in life: your family, a gorgeous sunrise, a truly well-made coffee. When you take a moment to express gratitude for these things, your body releases serotonin and oxytocin, otherwise known as the love hormones. The second reward system is that of 'process' – of pursuing a goal and celebrating your efforts. Did you know that dopamine (a type of neurotransmitter that enables us to feel pleasure among other things) is secreted when you're pursuing a goal? For example, you might get a burst of dopamine when you're training for a marathon and finally crack the 20-mile distance. Or when you've been working for months on your marriage and you get a big Oprah ah-ha! moment in therapy. Or when after spending more time in nature you discover that you're actually pretty good at surfing. Instead of solely focusing on end results (e.g. I got the job! I lost the weight! I graduated from the course!), focus on the process of whatever you're learning and doing.

By taking time to consciously acknowledge your progress and process, you can help signal your brain to release serotonin, oxytocin and dopamine. With these feel-good chemicals coursing through your body, you'll be more likely to persevere with your goal.

> ## TRY WRITING 'I'M ON THE RIGHT TRACK' ON A POST-IT NOTE AND PLACING IT SOMEWHERE YOU CAN SEE IT AND READ IT EVERY DAY
>
> If you came to my house, you best believe you'd find Post-it notes of affirmations in every room. This is because I'm using my growth mindset and intentional reframing to tap into my reward systems. I suggest placing your own notes somewhere you can see them daily (near your computer screen, on your fridge, next to your bathroom mirror) so whenever you feel motivation is waning, you can glance at this reminder and help signal your brain to release dopamine for motivation.

The Power of 'Get'

Raise your hand if you've caught up with a friend for coffee and rattled off a list of things you HAVE to do this week. As you were itemising phone calls that needed to be made, meals that needed preparing or a doctor's appointment that's been postponed one too many times, did you notice how negative they felt? It made tasks a burden. Let's try something. Instead of using the word HAVE, I want you to use the word GET.

Original: *I **have** to make my child's lunch every morning.*
Reframed: *I **get** to make my child's lunch every morning.*

By swapping 'have' for 'get' you're now able to add a whole list of positives to that statement. You're also able to see these 'tasks' as processes for your progress.

I get to choose the foods that nourish my child.

I get to thoughtfully prepare something for someone I love.

I get to make informed choices about the businesses I'm supporting.

Let's do another one.

Original: *I have to endure annoying side effects from the medication I'm taking.*
Reframed: *I get to endure annoying side effects from the medication I'm taking because:*

I get to know that the medication is working and my body is responding.

I get to know that I tried everything in my power to feel better.

I get to know that some medications are worth the side effects.

Since good things come in threes, let's do one more.

Original: *I have to look for another job.*
Reframed: *I get to look for another job.*

I get to choose a job that aligns with my values.

I get to learn what opportunities there are for someone with my work ethic and skill set.

I get to have another experience to learn from.

It's interesting how much the word 'get' changes the way a statement feels, isn't it? Now let's talk about my other three letter word: *YET*.

The Power of 'Yet'

The power of YET is another product of Dr Carol Dweck's growth mindset research and work. These three simple letters are the first step someone with a fixed mindset can take to start thinking with a growth mindset.

Fixed Beliefs:

- *I can't speak publicly.*
- *I can't overcome my grief.*
- *I can't pay off my mortgage.*

By adding yet to your fixed beliefs, you're adding hope and the possibility of growth. The next thing you need to do is ask yourself (or a trained professional) what can be done to help you turn that *can't* into a *can.*

Fixed Beliefs + the Power of Yet:

- *I can't speak publicly … YET.*
- *I can't overcome my grief … YET.*
- *I can't pay off my mortgage … YET.*

What Can You Do to Help Yourself Achieve Your Goals?

- *I can join Toastmasters International.*
- *I can speak to a therapist to gain the tools I need to manage my grief.*
- *I can speak to a financial adviser.*

Look at that. Now we have attached an action to the outcome, and there is a way forward. We have to continually confront the logic of our negative thoughts because often they're outdated beliefs that just keep us stuck. It's all about changing your language and lens to shift your mindset. This word, 'yet', is arguably the most important for every leader and professional to utilise in overcoming setbacks.

Is This Helpful or Harmful?

In 2014, resilience researcher Dr Lucy Hone's life dramatically changed when she lost her 12-year-old daughter in a tragic car accident. She went from a resilience expert to a grieving mother. Being a parent, I can't even imagine what this would feel like. She had to put all her resilience research to the test, to get through one of the biggest traumas a parent could ever experience. One of the most effective techniques Lucy found was asking this question: Is this helpful or harmful?

When going through any sort of adversity, we begin picking up habits, asking questions or taking actions to cope. It could be opting for a glass of wine to unwind after the workday. It could be staring vacantly out the window and picking apart every detail of a conversation you had with someone a week ago. It could be constantly checking someone's social-media profiles to see what they're wearing, eating and doing for the holidays. (More on the price of comparison later!) This is normal and makes sense. However, sometimes these habits, questions and actions aren't beneficial. Dr Hone found herself looking at pictures of her daughter and would be overcome by pain and grief. This is when she started asking herself, 'Is this helpful or harmful?' In this case, spending so much time with the images of her daughter wasn't helping her heal. While they might be fine to revisit later, at that moment, it was actually a harmful exercise.

Here are some examples of how you can bring the question, helpful or harmful?, into your life:

- Is the way I'm thinking about this relationship helpful or harmful?
- Is this glass of wine helpful or harmful?
- Is staying up late to watch TV helpful or harmful?
- Is my thinking pattern about the promotion helpful or harmful?
- Is incessantly following the news helpful or harmful?

By questioning your thoughts, behaviours and mindset, you are putting yourself back in control for the day. Just like I want you to become more aware of how you're feeling, I want you to start noticing your thoughts. Take the time to decide if they are helpful or harmful. Next, see if they need to be reworded. Then try to attach an action that aligns with a growth mindset.

WHEN HAVING A GROWTH MINDSET HELPS YOU HEAL
by Jay Pottenger, Chelsea's Husband

I've always been sceptical about mindfulness and meditation, but in 2012 I learned that there's nothing like some life adversity to prove a sceptic wrong. Given my 6'4" frame and decades of sports injuries, it wasn't shocking when I blew out two discs in my lower back while deadlifting in the gym. What was shocking was my new reality: instead of facing my wife, friends and work, I was facing the ceiling due to my inability to walk, stand or even sit.

While it was my back that was technically the busted part of my body, my mind and mood were in pieces. As someone who focuses on physical health and activity and spent a lot of time exercising or being active, my new reality really knocked me around. Even though I knew how lucky I was to not be in a worse condition and had a huge amount of support from family and friends, I still felt isolated and unlucky. These days were dark, but I wouldn't say I was depressed. If anything, I just felt like I was a burden on Chelsea. Even though it was easier to be a miserable prick, I had to work extra hard to lighten her load (and my mood) if we were going to get through this time. Having seen my dad successfully recover from surgery and armed with mindfulness tools, I faced my recovery head on.

First, I shifted from thinking, *I have to do rehab today*, to *I get to do rehab today for a brighter future*. I journalled my gratitude, nourished my body and reached out to my friends for support.

Since I'm conveniently married to Chelsea, who used to work in the medical world, we got in contact with Neuroscience Australia, which accepted me into a study that was researching if subjects could rewire their mindsets ➔

towards their pain and underlying injuries. It turns out, my brain was so used to receiving pain messages that it had rewired the response to expect pain, even though the injury was no longer painful. It was communicating what it expected, rather than what it was. Extreme cases are like what happens in phantom limb pains. Even though the back injury had healed, my brain had not.

I love Jay's story for a lot of reasons. For starters, he approached his recovery with optimal self-efficacy. From using his dad's own recovery as a social model to using his growth mindset to find the motivation to try new ways to heal, he really blew me away. Perhaps the most interesting thing about his recovery is how his brain had become rewired to feel pain because of his injury, even though the pain wasn't actually there anymore. This is neuroplasticity at work, people! One of the most fascinating therapies I've ever heard of is mirror therapy. Commonly used with stroke victims to restore both fine and gross motor skills, it essentially involves placing the arm, hand or foot that you can control next to a mirror so that it looks like both of your sides can do the motion. While studies into why this is so effective are still being conducted, it's thought that mirror neuron activation deserves the credit for its success.

IN YOUR JOURNAL

Take a moment to reflect by answering the following questions:

- Can you think of someone in your life who has contributed to your self-efficacy? Who was it and what actions did they take to influence you?

- Describe a time when you overcame adversity. Write down everything that happened and the emotions you felt. What did you learn from the experience? How can you use this as a basis for growth?

- Write down three things you can't do. Now go back and add YET to the end. Now write down actions you can take to help you achieve these things.

- If you have a series of thoughts you keep repeating throughout the day, write them down. Next, ask yourself: Is this helpful or harmful? about each of them.

04
YOUR PURPOSE

IT'S ALL WELL and good that we have the power to change the way our brains operate, but what's *driving* you to do the work? What makes you happy? What gives you energy? What do you love? What would you do even if you didn't get paid? If I asked you to shut your eyes and imagine your perfect day, what would the view be? What would you be doing? Who would be around you? Not sure yet? That's okay!

Identifying and understanding your purpose will bring you clarity on your values, passion, life's work and boundaries. Your values are what will reward you, your passion is what's going to fuel you, your life's work is what will allow you to help others, and your boundaries will allow you to help yourself. By gaining a clear understanding of these four areas, you will be able to set goals, form habits and adopt routines that will enable you to live your optimal life and protect your mental health.

WHAT ARE YOUR VALUES?
Your values are the things that you believe are important in the way you live, work and show up in this world. They determine your priorities and

help measure whether you're fulfilled by your life. When your behaviours match your values, life is good. But when your behaviours don't align with your values, it can make your daily existence difficult.

For example, let's say one of your values is family. You know that life-talks around a dinner table, belly laughs in the backyard and memorable road trips are what feed your heart and soul. BUT you work 70–80 hours a week, you rarely take holidays and, when you do, you're glued to your email. As a result, you feel internal conflict and stress because you know deep down that your behaviours are not aligning with what you truly value.

Maybe you are a law student who values financial security and progressive social policy BUT you keep going out mid-week and are finding yourself too tired and hungover to do the work you need to do to pass your exams. As a result, you're feeling overwhelmed by your workload and unsure if you have the capacity to create the career you set out for. Or maybe you're someone who deeply values the environment BUT you end up taking a job at a notorious fast-fashion chain because the salary package seemed 'too good to pass up'. As a result, you're still not happy because you're now contributing to the negative impact mass-produced clothing has on both land and oceans. My guess: the future of the world's health means more to you than money.

When I talk to people about what their values are, they tend to say things like 'family' and 'giving back' because that's what's socially accept-able. Yes, those are wonderful values to have, but I like to push people to be as authentic as possible when describing what they really value. If becoming famous lights a fire under you, I want you to own that you value fame. If you want to be able to jet off to an exotic location in your private plane, recognise that you value financial abundance. If you want to spend a large portion of your time reading in private, accept that you value education and calmness. It's okay to want what you want – be it bottles of French champagne or volunteering to help underprivileged children – but to achieve it, you need to do what affords these things in your life.

WHAT DO YOU VALUE?

- □ family and relationships
- □ financial abundance
- □ financial security
- □ sustainability
- □ social change
- □ travel
- □ exercise/movement
- □ arts and culture
- □ education
- □ nature and adventure
- □ philanthropy and giving back
- □ fame
- □ freedom
- □ legacy
- □ stability and contentment
- □ calmness
- □ connections
- □ faith

When you know, own and protect your values, you can make decisions about how you want to live your life. Values-based decision-making is particularly important for answering questions like:

- Do I want to accept the promotion?
- Do I want to start my own business?
- Do I want to sell my business?
- Do I want to pay for a gym membership?
- Do I want to go travelling for a year?
- Do I want to have children?
- Do I want to invest in property?
- Do I want to live near the beach or mountains?
- Do I want to stay close to my family?

By answering questions like these honestly you can make choices that make you feel proud and happy. Making values-based choices isn't always easy. Often, fear of missing out on an opportunity or letting someone down clouds your judgement. But remember: you need to do what's right for you, because when you honour your own purpose, you are able to contribute to the world in an authentic and meaningful way.

I recommend taking time to write down three to five values in your journal. Then begin to process why they are important, how they make you feel and why you want to protect them.

But Chelsea, what happens if my values change?

As your circumstances change and you get more life experiences, your values may well change, too. What I valued as a 20-something with few mental-health issues is vastly different from what I value now. I used to care deeply about hitting financial targets, creating a strong network of friends and living in a fast-paced city. If I wasn't working hard and playing hard, I wasn't being true to what I valued, which was financial abundance, connection and travel! But then I turned 30, and suddenly the idea of starting a movie after 9 pm seemed overwhelming. Couple that with my postnatal depression, career change and (lest we forget) a global pandemic, and now my approach to life ensures I protect my new values of family, peace, calm and inner harmony. What were some of the values-based decisions I had to make? I swapped life in Sydney for life in a small coastal town. I structure my work calendar to allow for (and prioritise) my rest and recovery. I put energy into select friendships. I have a digital detox every Sunday.

⌐ HOW HELPING MAKES YOU HAPPIER ¬

People ask me all the time: 'How can I get happier?' I always say, 'Go and help someone else who can never repay you, and your happiness bucket will overflow.' Of course, there is neuroscience behind my reasoning. When we help others by giving our time, energy and/or money, the same part of your brain that is stimulated by food and sex is activated and you feel pleasure! I'm not saying you should give up trying to accumulate money or fame and focus on being a civil servant if that's not where your passion lies. What I am saying is, ➔

> giving of yourself, especially when it is in a way that's
> connected to your passions, will fill you up. As the Chinese
> proverb says: If you want happiness for an hour – take a
> nap. If you want happiness for a day – go fishing. If you want
> happiness for a year – inherit a fortune. If you want happiness
> for a lifetime – help someone else.

THE PASSION BEHIND YOUR PURPOSE

What do you make time for in your life? What do you unintentionally channel a lot of energy into? Is it communication? Exercise? Volunteering with animals? Do you get paid for it? When you think about your passion, I want you to think about it holistically. From what you eat to how you move your body to the way you speak to people, what is the driving force behind every action you take? For some people, they might turn their passion into a career. For others, they might channel their passion into their friends, family, hobby or community service.

One of my friends is a painter and it is clearly her passion. She is so laser-focused on her work that she knew there would be no other job for her than painting. It took a lot of hard work, and after dedicating 10 years to making it a reality, she now makes a living from her painting. Her partner, on the other hand, is passionate about barbecues, fishing, camping and travelling. While these are the things that he knows he values and would like to do 24/7, he is completely content to go to work as a coalminer so that he has the money and time off to do the things he actually enjoys. It's okay to have a job to pay your bills and have passion for your family, sport or side-hustle. Ultimately, you want to choose to expend energy on activities, projects and people that put your passion to work and showcase your strengths and talents.

What Are Your Strengths and Talents?

This can actually be the most difficult question to answer because we, as humans, aren't great at giving ourselves compliments. (Insults, doubts and insecurities? Yes. Compliments? Not so much.) By knowing what you bring to the table, you can start thinking about how your skill set adds value to people's lives (yours included).

Just like when identifying your values, it's really important that you are your authentic self when determining your strengths. I suggest taking time to journal a list of your strengths and talents. If you find yourself experiencing writer's block, reach out to a trusted friend or colleague.

You might discover that:

- You're incredible at building a network.
- You have a natural talent for getting people to donate to a cause.
- Your discipline and grit are why you always meet or exceed sales targets.
- You stay calm and have excellent conflict-resolution skills.
- You aren't afraid to fail, learn and try again.

Read back over your list every day as a reminder of what your strengths are.

STRENGTHS AND TALENTS REQUEST TEMPLATE

If you have trouble asking for help identifying your strengths and talents, here's some wording you could use to reach out to a friend, family member or colleague:

Hi, I'm in the process of working out my goals.
This isn't easy for me to ask, but can you tell me
three words or phrases that best describe my talents
and strengths? I really value your opinion. Please
keep it short as I don't want to take up too much of
your time. Thank you!

YOUR LIFE'S WORK

Understanding what you're passionate about, knowing your strengths and staying true to your values is what's going to drive what you do career-wise. When I say 'career' I don't necessarily mean something that's paid, which is why I'm going to use the term 'life's work' from now on. For some, your passion, strengths and values make you want to stay home with your children and that's wonderful. You could want to stay home to create art. You could be someone who is happy in your job because you value financial security but channel a lot of your passion and strengths into a community project. As a high performer, anything you choose to do, you want to do well. On the flip side, you may decide to change your 'life's work' at various points in your life. This could be because your values have changed, you've been made redundant or you're simply looking to shake things up. Whether it's becoming a stay-at-home parent or changing industries, it's imperative that you're clear on the what, why, how and when of manifesting your ideal work.

If you've ever worked on or read a business plan, you've probably seen a company's mission statement. Designed to show potential investors and employees who the company is, how they add value and why they're needed in the world, this statement is simple, powerful and usually fewer than 50 words. Every time you want to get clear on how you want your life to be, you need to use your values, passion, life's work, boundaries and goals to write your own mission statement. (Don't worry – you don't need to show anyone!) One of my favourite motivational speakers, Adam Leipzig, has a great set of questions for helping you discover and articulate who you are, what you do and how your life's work helps others.

1. Who are you?
2. What do you love to do?
3. Who do you do it for?
4. What do those people want or need?
5. How do they change as a result of what you do?

Here's mine: I empower and educate people to know they have the power to change their mental health. As a result, they suffer less and their behaviour influences others to change their mental health, inadvertently causing a social-ripple effect so everyone in the world can live healthier lives.

BOUNDARIES

I love boundaries; they're vital for keeping you fresh and thriving so you can achieve your purpose. I firmly believe that we need boundaries in every aspect of our lives to ensure we don't become burnt out, exhausted or taken advantage of. I used to find it really difficult to say 'No'. It didn't matter if it was a colleague asking me to go to coffee so that they could pick my brain, or a friend asking me to attend a party on a Friday night after a hectic work week, I'd always say 'Yes'. Part of it was not wanting to let someone down and the other part was because I was reluctant to admit that I needed some me-time. I felt this constant pressure to be there for everybody else.

WHY PEOPLE ARE AFRAID TO SAY 'NO'

☐ fear of being rude

☐ fear of conflict

☐ fear of missing out on an opportunity

☐ desire to conform

☐ desire to actually help someone

☐ desire to be well liked.

If you keep helping others without regard for yourself and your own welfare, you may end up sacrificing your personal goals, your time with your loved ones and your physical and mental health. If you say 'Yes' every time – it's an opportunity cost. While each request might feel like a small amount of time, when you add them all together, they're going to impact your long-term goals and health. When you get comfortable saying 'No', it means you can say 'Yes' to the things that really excite you and you stay aligned with your goals.

The Benefits of Saying 'No':
- It protects your mental health.
- You can tick things off from your own list.
- It creates space for you to say 'Yes' to the things you love.

There are multiple ways you can say 'No' without being rude, creating conflict or missing out on an opportunity.

Tips for Saying 'No':
- Soften the blow by thanking them for thinking of you.
- Tell them what's on your plate. (If this is your boss making a request, you can share what's already on your list and then ask if what they're requesting should be prioritised.)
- Explain it's not 'No' forever.
- Change your perspective. For example, instead of thinking, *I'm not letting my colleague down by saying 'No'*, try reframing it to something like: *I'm making space for someone with more time and passion to take on this task.*
- Role-play saying 'No' with a friend.

If a friend gets offended when you say 'No', it might be time to assess that particular relationship. There is a bit of cosmic accounting when it comes to friendship. To look after your mental health, ensure you're surrounding yourself with positive people who appreciate open and honest communication as well as boundaries.

THE 'NO' EMAIL TEMPLATE

Thank you for the opportunity and for thinking of me. I am very grateful that you asked. Currently, I'm at full capacity with my workload. For the benefit of my work, health and family, over the last month I've had to decline new opportunities and projects, creating more space.

While I really would like to collaborate and respect the work that you do, I have to pass this time. Hopefully, we will get a chance to talk somewhere further down the line. I promise anything I have for you then will be a lot more insightful than it would be now.

Now that you're thinking about what your purpose is, it's time to put your plan into action. In the next chapter, we're going to work on the fundamentals of goal-setting so you can start adopting the routines needed to feel purposeful, useful and grateful every day.

IN YOUR JOURNAL
- Write down three to five things you value and why.
- Write down your strengths and talents.
- Write down your life's work mission statement.

05
YOUR GOALS

ONCE YOU'VE GAINED clarity around your purpose, it's time to create your goals. A goal is simply a future desired result that you then imagine, visualise, plan and commit to achieving. Articulating and progressing towards meaningful goals not only sets you up to excel in any area of life, but also fills you with a sense of purpose, which is key for overall mental wellbeing.

While your goals may be something like 'volunteer with a local charity', 'pay off a credit card' or 'run a marathon', I want you to focus on the overall feelings you're chasing as well as why those goals are important given your purpose, values and life's work. I recommend examining your goals yearly and not being hard on yourself if something gets derailed due to unforeseen circumstances (like a global pandemic) or a change of heart. While there is plenty of time in your life to achieve what you want to achieve, now is the time to chase the feelings you want to feel because research shows that when you are striving for something significant, you become happier.

In the same way each of us has our own favourite way of arranging groceries on a checkout conveyor belt, everyone is going to have their own way of setting their goals. (But surely, you put the heavy stuff on first and keep all the cold things together, right?) While you are more than welcome to do what works best for you, I'm going to detail the process I have found most effective and it starts with S.M.A.R.T. thinking, a mnemonic tool to help set goals and objectives created by George T. Doran.

So what is a S.M.A.R.T. goal? S.M.A.R.T. is an acronym for: Specific, Measurable, Attainable, Relevant and Time-bound. The more specific, measurable, attainable, relevant and time-bound your goal is, the more likely you'll be able to achieve it. I like writing my goals in this format because it prompts me to be super clear about what the outcome is, why I want it and how I'm going to achieve it.

For example, let's say my goal is to become a keynote speaker. Using the S.M.A.R.T. approach, I could break down my goal as follows:

- **S**pecific: Become a professional keynote speaker.
- **M**easurable: Take a public-speaking course and book at least three events in the next 12 months.
- **A**ttainable: As my speaking engagements increase, I'll hire people to help write my speeches.
- **R**elevant: It's aligned to my life's purpose of empowering people.
- **T**ime-bound: I will start pitching my speaking services on 1 July.

So how do you set your own goals and then start achieving them? Let's walk through the three steps of effective goal-setting:

1. Determine how you want to feel and let it become your theme for the year.
2. Set S.M.A.R.T. goals in all the main areas of your life.
3. Create new habits and reward progress.

STEP 1: Determine How You Want to Feel and Let It Become Your Theme for the Year

Have you ever noticed that you choose to wear, eat, drink or do something because you're trying to chase a particular feeling? You put on clothes to feel powerful or comfortable, you eat to feel nourished or satisfied, you drink to feel hydrated or stimulated and you do something because you want to feel valued or rewarded. When setting your goals and looking at the year ahead, you need to start with an idea of the feeling that you most want to experience. Do you want to feel:

- vibrant?
- abundant?
- energetic?
- successful?
- balanced?
- capable?
- motivated?
- content?
- accomplished?
- purposeful?

Limiting Beliefs

Before you can figure out what your goals are, you need to make sure you don't have any limiting beliefs stopping you from dreaming, thinking and acting in line with your purpose. A limiting belief is something that you believe to be true that stops you from achieving your goals. It could be about yourself, other people or even the world. These beliefs can keep you from seeing different opportunities and your own special talents, and stuck focusing on the negative aspects of your life.

Limiting beliefs come from many different places, including your family members, friends, teachers, coaches, social media, society and even your culture. They are formed by repeating certain thoughts inside your mind and are typically created during childhood from interactions with the people around us. That's why it's so important for parents to shape their children with beautiful positive language and to instil a growth mindset (remember 'get to' instead of 'have to'?).

By applying growth-mindset thinking to your limiting beliefs, I guarantee you'll find ways to overcome the barriers you've been creating. For example, let's say your limiting belief is: *I'm too time-poor to exercise and meditate.* Now let's use growth-mindset thinking to ask the right questions needed to find a solution:

- Do you have the capacity to wake up an hour earlier to exercise or meditate?
- Can you bring your lunch to work and eat at your desk so your lunch break is free for you to exercise or meditate?
- Do you have any daily time-stealing habits (checking social media, chatting with co-workers or reading non-urgent emails) that could be nixed? Collectively, this might free up an hour!
- In the evening, could you swap some of your TV-watching time for meditation time?
- If applicable, is there someone who could watch your kids while you take a moment to exercise or meditate?

STEP 2: Set S.M.A.R.T. Goals in All Seven Areas of Your Life

When working on your goals for the year, it's important to address the following seven key areas for a full and balanced life.

- health and wellbeing
- relationships and family
- finance
- community and environment
- education and learning
- holidays and fun
- spirituality and purpose.

I recommend choosing one overarching goal and two small goals for each key area while keeping in mind your theme for the year. Yes, that's seven big goals and 14 smaller goals.

If you don't yet have clarity around your values in these areas, don't fret! I have some prompts to help you start ideating and visualising how you'd like to feel. After finishing this chapter, take some time to journal your responses to these questions. I have also included sample statements to show you how you can express your goals.

Once you've narrowed down your three goals for each area, I recommend putting them in the S.M.A.R.T. format in your journal. I also recommend doing these over a few sessions or even a few weeks. While some areas may be easier to gain clarity on, others might require a bit of soul searching.

Health and Wellbeing

Your health and wellbeing should be your number-one priority because we are no good to anyone else if we are not healthy ourselves. This area includes things like exercise, nutrition and mental health.

Prompts to help you discover your health and wellbeing goals:

- When you wake up, how do you want to feel?
- How do you want to exercise?
- What are your nutritional choices?
- Do you need to address digital overload?
- What is your stress-management technique?
- What is your sleep like?

Examples of statements you can write in your journal:

- This year I want to feel _____.
- I will be exercising ____ days per week.

- I will sleep ____ hours per night.
- I will improve my nutrition by _____.
- My stress-management tool is ____.

Which of your statements is most important? Highlight the one that calls to you the most. For example, *I'm improving my health.* This will be the overarching goal for this area. The next two might be: *I'm exercising three to five times a week. My stress-management tool is painting.* Now write them in the S.M.A.R.T. format.

⌐ HEALTH AND WELLBEING GOAL EXAMPLE ⌐

Specific: Eat whole and organic foods.

Measurable: Keep a food diary.

Attainable: I've found a great blog with shopping lists and recipes.

Relevant: It's aligned to my life's purpose of keeping my energy up for my family.

Time-bound: I will start today.

Relationships and Family

Did you know that the five people you spend the most time with will have a direct impact on your wellbeing, your outlook and how happy you are? Did you know that to increase your mood by 45 per cent, you have to surround yourself with positive people? Emotional contagions are real, so choose your friends and relationships wisely.

My mum taught me this when I first got a mobile phone. (Remember those bricks that Nokia called a phone?) Every spring, she'd flurry through the house doing the obligatory clean-out. Once our pantry and wardrobes were thinned out, she'd then say, 'Now spring-clean the contact list in your phone!' She'd tell me to let go of anyone who was negative or toxic. For years I would do this and I'm proud to say that I haven't had to delete anyone's number for about 15 years as I'm much more mindful about who I let into my life.

Equally as important as letting go of people is investing in the relationships that matter. Sociologist Dr Nicholas Christakis writes and speaks about emotional contagions and explains that we need to be connected to two people for happiness. He also teaches that when you start spending time with exceptional people, you'll attract more exceptional people.

Prompts to help you discover your relationships and family goals:

- What does your ideal relationship look like?
- How do you show people you care about them?
- Who are the five people you choose to spend quality time with?
- What is your love language? (Get the book *The Five Love Languages* by Gary Chapman!)
- How are you being kinder to yourself so you can be kind to others?
- What does relationship success look like to you?

Examples of statements you can write in your journal:

- I will go on _____ date nights per month.
- I will meet new people by _____.
- I will add spice into my sex life by _____.
- I will see a therapist to _____.
- I will communicate honestly by _____.

Finance

To live our dreams, we need to have financial goals in place. This isn't just about material wealth but creating the best future. People shy away from wealth because they think it's greedy, but I look at it as an enabler to do things for other people in this life.

I also want to point out that money is a key cause of stress and has been linked to relationship breakdowns, insomnia, social withdrawal and even suicide. It's common for people to avoid addressing their money concerns and take a reactive approach to their personal finance and wealth creation. When setting your finance goals, I want you to adopt an abundance mindset and trust that there is enough money for you to earn. You deserve prosperity and you absolutely have the capacity to spend your money in a way that aligns with your values.

Prompts to help you discover your finance goals:

- What does financial freedom mean to you?
- How much money do you want to earn?
- How much money do you want to save?
- How could you earn extra income?
- How can you further your financial education?

Examples of statements you can write in your journal:

- I will address my debt by _____.
- I will become more financially literate by _____.
- I will seek financial advice by _____.
- I will change my mindset on my personal finance by _____.
- I will set myself up for financial security by _____.

Community and Environment

I've mentioned this before, but I'll say it again: when you do something for someone else (without expecting anything in return), your brain releases serotonin. Generosity breeds generosity, which is why I always tell people to get out of their own head and go do something for someone else, for animals or the Earth. For example, you could swap your disposable coffee cups for a re-usable coffee cup. You could organise a neighbourhood rubbish pick-up. You could help an elderly neighbour with their bins. You could volunteer at your child's school or the local library.

Taking care of your community and environment ensures you're taking care of the world around you and protecting it for the future. With that said, you need to remember to protect yourself as well. If sitting on a charitable committee is too much emotionally and physically, then you can set other goals that don't demand as much of your time, energy and brainpower.

Prompts to help you discover your community and environment goals:

- Which charity could you be involved with this year?
- How are you taking care of the environment?
- How are you helping people in need?
- What is the legacy you want to leave behind?
- How do you want people to remember you?
- How can you become more involved in the community?

Examples of statements you can write in your journal:

- I will volunteer _____ number of days with _____.
- I will reduce my impact on the environment by _____.
- I will keep up with social issues such as _____.
- I will donate _____ to _____.
- I will empower others to give back by _____.

Education and Learning

Remember our old friend, neuroplasticity? When we engage in hobbies and commit to lifelong learning, we make synaptic connections in the brain, which is the key to maintaining high-level cognitive function. Other benefits of continuing your education and expanding your skill set include new personal and professional opportunities, the chance to expand your network and, of course, an anti-ageing effect on the brain.

For some, education and learning goals might be getting a Master of Business Administration degree. For others it might be learning how to play chess or a specific style of dance. Continuing your education doesn't necessarily mean spending large sums of money on tuition or a new hobby. There are plenty of free online courses, podcasts, books and YouTube videos that can help you learn or practise something new.

Prompts to help you discover your education and learning goals:

- What are you listening to?
- What books do you want to read?
- What particular topics do you want to explore?
- Who would you like to be mentored by?

Examples of statements you can write in your journal:

- I will invest _____ hours to continue my education.
- I will read _____ books per year.
- I will challenge myself by _____.
- I will ask _____ to mentor me.
- The hobby I'm going to take up this year is _____.

Holidays and Fun

Research shows that investing in fun and regular holidays can dramatically improve your mental and physical wellbeing. Did you know that when we are waiting to go on a holiday, we are much happier with our life as a whole and experience fewer negative feelings? Other studies show that regular breaks lower blood pressure, result in greater energy and strengthen your immune system.

Often the word 'holiday' equates to 'exotic and expensive' in some people's minds. I'm here to tell you that you don't need to fly overseas to reap the benefits. Grab your tent and go camping. Go somewhere without wi-fi that allows you to connect with yourself, your friends and nature. On Sundays, my family goes off the grid. We don't turn on any technology, wake up with the sun and have the whole day without looking at screens. It's mostly spent outside and honestly feels like two weeks away.

Prompts to help you discover your holidays and fun goals:

- What is your favourite holiday destination?
- Are there any short trips you can take?
- How are you creating more balance in your life?
- How can you explore where you live?
- How can you surprise a person with a trip or event?
- How often are you taking scheduled breaks?

Examples of statements you can write in your journal:

- I'm contributing _____ amount of dollars per month to my holiday fund.
- My dream destination this year is _____.
- I'm exploring where I live by _____.
- On staycations, I like to _____.
- I integrate rest into my life by _____.

Spirituality and Purpose

Discovering your spirituality, purpose and faith is a deeply personal journey that gives meaning to your life. Usually, we are taught our parents' beliefs growing up, but it's important to go on your own journey and challenge the ideas that have been presented to you. For some, this area of your life may include meditation, for others it may be weekly church services. The key to setting goals in this area is surrendering your need for concrete answers and accepting a series of transformative experiences.

Prompts to help you discover your spirituality and purpose goals:

- What do you value?
- What do you love to invest your energy in?
- How are you connecting to your spirituality or faith?
- What makes you feel safe and secure?
- What makes you feel passionate?
- How do you help others?

Examples of statements you can write in your journal:

- My purpose is _____.
- I'm making a difference by _____.
- I feel safe and secure because of _____.
- I'm expanding my capacity to grow spiritually by _____.
- I'm connecting with myself and a higher power by _____.

STEP 3: Create New Habits and Reward Progress

Once you have your 21 goals written in S.M.A.R.T. formatting in your journal, it's time to start achieving them. How are you going to do that? By creating new habits and rewarding progress, of course!

⌐ FORMING HABITS (THAT STICK!) ⌐

Research shows there are key markers when it comes to forming habits.

☐ Day three is when your energy starts to wane.

☐ Day 21 is when your short-term memory starts to hold on to habits and goals.

☐ Day 66 is when your reptilian brain forms long-term habits.

Treats and Rewards for the Brain

One of the things I've found helpful is setting realistic expectations around habit formation. While some changes and new routines will be easy to adopt, others will require a bit more brainpower, which is why I like to pepper a few rewards along the way to my ultimate goal.

For example, let's say that my fitness goal is to run a half-marathon by the end of the year. On day three of my training, I will book in a massage to help repair and nourish my body. On day 21, I will reward myself by buying a kettlebell. On day 66, I will reward myself with new activewear or running shoes. In your journal, look at your goals and see where and how you can reward yourself for your effort and progress.

Pre-commitment and Accountability

If you have a Facebook account, chances are you've seen someone post a link to a fundraising page because they're running a marathon. While their goal is probably to reach their fundraising target, this simple act is actually DOUBLING their chance of achieving their aim. This is because when we publicly state that we're going to do something, our innate need to not let people down drives us to stick to our word.

If you don't want to make a public claim about your goal, that's totally fine, but you might want to consider getting an accountability partner. This could be your spouse, parent, work colleague, personal trainer or friend. Just ensure it's someone who is going to believe in you, celebrate your wins and offer a fresh perspective. Never share your dreams with small-minded people.

Intrinsic Motivation – Finding Your Why

You may have heard some people talk about finding your 'why'. This is because your why is what identifies the reason and value driving you to do things like: get out of bed, go to work, make time for mindfulness, sign up for a new class, spend 20 minutes stretching or donate money to a charity. When you're clear on why you're doing something, it's easier to find your intrinsic motivation.

What intrinsically motivates you to achieve your goal? Your answers may look like this:

- Reaching my sales target means I can afford to go on a holiday with my family.
- Losing 10 kg means I qualify for surgery.
- Getting my degree in accounting means I can have a side-hustle that allows me to reach my financial goals.
- Planting a vegie garden allows me to affordably eat organic food.

Visualising Your Goals

Researchers at Harvard University found that visualising an activity had the same effect on the brain as actually doing it. In their study, Group A was made up of people actually playing a piano, and Group B was people visualising that they were playing a piano. For both groups, the region of the brain connected to the finger muscles changed to the same degree, regardless of whether they struck the keys physically or mentally. How fascinating is the fact that the brain processes imagination as if it's real?! Welcome to the amazing world of visualisation.

The power of visualisation is something more and more people are tapping into. Elite athletes use visualisation in their training, while stroke patients are encouraged to use it as part of their recovery. According to research, patients who did visualisation as well as their physio exercises recovered faster. And remember when I talked about mirror therapy? Essentially, the act of visualising your leg, arm, finger or neck doing something is practice as far as the brain is concerned.

But Chelsea, I'm not recovering from a stroke. I want to know how to practise visualisation for goal-setting.

Sorry! You know I love the science stuff. When it comes to using visualisation as a tool for achieving your goals faster, I want you to focus on making visualisation part of your daily routine. I also want you to focus on visualising both the process of achieving your goals and the outcome. There are two types of visualisation; both serve a purpose, and for the greatest impact you'll need to use process and outcome visualisation together.

Process visualisation is visualising things like the training you'll need to do to strengthen your muscles in order to complete your goal of rock climbing, the books you need to read to pass your medical-school entrance exam or the conversation you have to have to end a relationship that has run its course. You'll visualise the feelings attached to making progress and how your why is driving you.

Outcome visualisation includes visualising things like how you'll feel when you achieve your goal of crossing a finish line, catching a wave, earning a promotion or landing a volunteer position abroad. You'll visualise the feelings attached to that success, how you'll celebrate, and what this accomplishment means for future you.

When you're visualising your goals, it's important that you always use your own perspective. By this I mean, you need to see it through your eyes, as if you're experiencing it. For example, don't try to visualise your whole body on a surfboard catching a wave. Visualise what you would see if you were on that board. Imagine how your thighs would be feeling, what the board would feel like against your feet. Can you smell the salt in the air? Can you reach out and drag your fingertips through the water? When visualising your goals, I want you to use all of your senses and try to imagine how things look, feel, smell, sound and taste. I also want you to try things like creating soundtracks that help you get in the right frame of mind. If I'm visualising myself giving a keynote speech that requires high energy, I listen to music that I know pumps me up and matches the emotion I want to feel. If I'm visualising my goal of spending more time outside, I listen to a calming nature soundtrack.

In the world of cognitive therapy, emotion precedes thought. When you feel something really deeply, you achieve a level of belief associated with that. Think about when you're watching something upsetting on TV, but you don't get that worked up because you know it's not real. When you're visualising, you need to be able to tie so much emotion to what you're envisioning that you truly believe that it's real. However, sometimes what we produce in our minds can only come from what is already stored there. It can be hard to imagine something if it's never happened to you. For example, if you want to learn how to play tennis, but you've never played tennis before, you may have a difficult time visualising that experience because you don't have much to draw on. You may need to watch a YouTube video, visit a tennis club and watch people play or find a tennis player and ask them about the sport to broaden your exposure and your brain's capacity to start visualising yourself playing tennis in detail.

VISUALISATION CHECKLIST

☐ Visualise the process through your eyes.

☐ Visualise the outcome through your eyes.

☐ Use your senses to enhance your visualisation experience.

☐ Use music or visual aids to help attach emotions to your visualisation.

☐ Increase your exposure to what you're trying to visualise.

Vision Boards

I'm not going to lie: vision boards are hands down the most fun part of goal-setting (if you're someone like me that is, aka someone who loves glue sticks, photos and getting psyched about the future). When you see visuals of your goal multiple times a day, it stays top of mind, which will help you to stay motivated and achieve your goals faster. Where attention goes, energy flows, which is why I always look at my goals before I start my day. It's a nice reminder for me to know what to say 'Yes' or 'No' to!

Recently, I've been really into printing my photos on a website that does Polaroid-style prints and then writing my goal in the white space at the bottom. However, there are loads of other options. Some people love using online design and image tools like Canva or Pinterest, while others prefer a more traditional corkboard style. Don't forget you'll need to include imagery and inspiration for goals in ALL of the key areas of your life.

Regardless of how you decide to make your board, I always recommend making it a fun activity. You can put on music, light a candle, pour a herbal tea or glass of wine, or burn invigorating essential oils. Be sure to include emotive colours, images, quotes and photos. It's also beneficial to have yourself in the photograph. For example, let's say that one of my goals is to go skiing in Japan next year. I'll print a photo of me skiing and then write Japan and the year on it or next to it. Once complete: make sure you look at it every day. Twice a day. (Or more!)

Where are you going to see your vision board regularly? Try putting it on your:

- computer screen background
- phone background
- bedroom wall
- digital calendar as a recurring reminder
- diary.

Now that you've completed writing your goals for the year and started formulating a plan on how you're going to achieve them, in the next chapter, it's time to talk about routines.

IN YOUR JOURNAL

■ Make two columns. In the first column, write down all of your limiting beliefs. In the second column, write down possible solutions.

LIMITING BELIEF	POSSIBLE SOLUTIONS
I don't have the right experience to go for the promotion I want.	• Are there any courses I could take to gain the skills needed for the promotion? • Are there any books or podcasts I could find to help me upskill and gain confidence? • Can I find a mentor to help me prepare?

■ Identify your one major goal and two smaller goals for each of the key areas in your life and use the S.M.A.R.T. format to write them down, including your 'why' for each goal. The seven key areas are:

- health and wellbeing
- relationships and family
- finance
- community and environment
- education and learning
- holidays and fun
- spirituality and purpose.

06
YOUR MORNING ROUTINE

LET ME GUESS ... your morning routine often looks like:

- Wake up.
- Reach for your phone.
- Cycle through emails, social media, news and texts.
- Get up and use the toilet.
- Brush your teeth.
- Make yourself a coffee.
- Shower and get dressed.
- Head to work while munching on a piece of toast.

Before I had postnatal depression, that's exactly what my morning routine looked like. The reality is, when we pick up our phones before even fully opening our eyes, we don't give ourselves a chance to have a great day. Nothing derails us faster than a stressful work-related email, a murder on the news, not enough comments on our socials, or the unspoken comparison game we play with others. There's a reason why it's called doomscrolling. When I was finally ready to heal after having Clara, my morning routine was one of the first things I set out to change.

According to a Facebook-sponsored study done by IDC Research, 80 per cent of all respondents reached for their phone within the first 15 minutes of waking. That number climbed to 89 per cent among people aged 18–24. A similar study at Nottingham Trent University found that the average 18–33-year old checks their phone an astounding 85 times per day.

In a study investigating the effect of the emotional content of television news programs on mood and the catastrophising of personal worries, results showed that 14 minutes of watching negative news results in an increase in anxiety and has an impact on our mood. (Duh!)

I don't know anyone who learns about a national disaster on the news, does a fist pump and then shouts, TODAY IS GOING TO BE A GREAT DAY. The reality is, these stories never make us feel good, yet we are addicted to looking at them. A lot of us are addicted to our phones and televisions, and it's bad for our health. While there is very much a time and a place for catching up with friends, family and current affairs, it's not something you should be doing before you've even had a chance to put your feet on the floor for the day.

MORNING RITUAL AUDIT

Take a moment to journal the things you do before heading to work or starting your day at home. Place a Y next to the activities that give you energy and an N next to the ones that deplete you.

MORNING RITUAL AUDIT EXAMPLE

- ☐ Scroll through social media.
- ☐ Check work emails.
- ☐ Drink water.
- ☐ Watch the news.
- ☐ Have breakfast.
- ☐ Get ready.
- ☐ Commute to work.

Which of the things that deplete you could you remove entirely? (The answers are social media, work emails and news!) What about the things that deplete you, but you can't really change? Could you reframe your thoughts around the way they make you feel? For example, try changing your inner monologue from *I have to commute to work* to *I get to spend an hour in the car listening to my favourite podcast.*

Remember Dr Lucy Hone's strategy of asking yourself, *Is this helpful or harmful?* When examining your morning routine, take a moment to ask yourself if each ritual is enriching your life or negatively impacting it. For example, does reading the news *really* help you start your day? If you're a journalist or specifically following industry news, then probably yes. But if you're someone who doesn't really need to know all the details before work, I suggest limiting your exposure. This will help you stay more mindful and focused.

MAKE A HEALTHY MORNING ROUTINE

Throughout my journey to adopt sustainable high-performance habits, I've read a lot of research, listened to gurus from around the world and road-tested numerous routines in an effort to live my optimal life. While not every day goes to plan, I have been sticking to some version of the following routine for a few years now and love how calm I feel when I wake up, how focused I am when I start my day and how grateful I am when I end it. Please don't feel like you need to do every single one of these things but know they're always there for you to try.

My typical day starts at 6:30 am. These are the simple rituals I have embraced:

- Wake up naturally if possible or use an alarm that's not on my phone.
- Don't check my phone when I first wake up.
- Practise 30 seconds of gratitude before I get out of bed.
- Set an intention such as: *Today is going to be a beautiful day.*
- Make the bed.

- Brush my teeth with my non-dominant hand.
- Drink a tall glass of water.
- Take a probiotic for my gut health.
- Get sunlight onto my skin and eyes.
- Do some sort of movement or energy work.
- Take a cold shower.
- Practise meditation.
- Review my vision board and goals for the day.
- Eat breakfast.

You're probably thinking, *Okay, Oprah, that's a lot before 8 am*. I know, I would have thought that, too. But I swear these rituals don't take as long as you think. AND once you do start to form these habits, you'll feel so much better and energised for the day that you may find yourself waking up earlier to give yourself even more time for intentional self-care! Still suspicious? Let me make my case for starting the day with self care.

Waking Up (Without Your Phone)

It's pretty hard to avoid the cycle of checking your messages, missed calls, social-media notifications and news apps when your phone is your alarm clock. If you're someone who needs an alarm to wake you up, I suggest leaving your phone in the kitchen and getting a clock for next to your bed. If you're someone who knows they have little self-restraint, I also suggest either filing apps deep in your phone or deleting them entirely. You don't have to keep them deleted, but if your intention for the day is to stay focused on a work goal, it's best to get rid of any potential distractions. You can always treat yourself to an hour of unin-terrupted Instagram time in the evening.

Gratitude

Gratitude blows my mind. Essentially living in a state of appreciation of what you value, gratitude can help you acknowledge, embrace and celebrate what and who you have in your life. The more I look into the research of gratitude, the more I realise it totally rocks. The real power of actively expressing gratitude is that it makes you focus on what is working in your life. Happy people understand they are fortunate in some part of their life – whether it is their family, their health or simply the sun shining on their face.

The best things about cultivating gratitude are that it doesn't cost any money, doesn't take much time and is scientifically proven to have numerous benefits. Gratitude researcher Robert Emmons has found links between gratitude and wellbeing. His research confirms that gratitude effectively increases happiness and reduces depression. Other research shows that people who are truly grateful experience fewer aches and pains. They're also more likely to take care of their physical health and attend regular check-ups that likely contribute to longevity. According to a study done in collaboration with the University of California San Diego, having a focus on gratitude increases the activity of the parasympathetic nervous system and decreases inflammation markers, which is important because inflammation is a precursor to loads of illnesses. Perhaps the least surprising: when we express gratitude for our friends, family and colleagues, we sleep better at night, have higher self-efficacy and are generally happier humans.

Gratitude and Sleep

If you are struggling to sleep, research shows that if you spend 15 minutes before bed journalling about things you are grateful for, it will reduce negative thoughts, which helps you sleep better. After doing this for a few weeks, check in and notice if you are having better-quality sleep.

Gratitude and Relationships

Dr Martin Seligman is considered the guru of positive psychology. He says that writing and sending (or reading) a gratitude letter to someone you care about, such as a teacher, mentor, child, friend or partner, dramatically improves life satisfaction scores and happiness as well as decreases symptoms of depression.

One way I practise gratitude is by writing Clara a love letter every year on her birthday. I use an amazing online company that posts them to our mailbox and even puts a gorgeous stamp on the back so I know what year we are up to! I always include three things I have especially loved about Clara in the past year and am grateful for. When this card arrives in our mailbox, I place it in a keepsake box that I will give to Clara when she is 21 years old. She will then have 21 love letters from me to her on her 21st birthday. That surely has to beat a pair of new shoes?! I thought about giving it to her on her 18th, but I'm 99 per cent sure she may not care as much then. Even writing the card alone gives me a serotonin and oxytocin hit.

Gratitude and Your Mood

Gratitude also helps us overcome worry or negative emotions we might carry with us during the day. Try being pissed off and grateful at the same time. Or angry and grateful simultaneously … it's impossible! That's because, according to neuroscience, we can't focus on positive and negative feelings at the same time.

Neuroscientist Alex Korb says that practising gratitude is like taking your brain to the gym. Just as when you go for a run you get a 'runner's high', it's the same thing with gratitude. You get a release of dopamine, the reward chemical, which makes us want to hunt down that feeling again, and we begin to make it a habit. Once you start seeing things to be grateful for, your brain starts to look for *more* things to be grateful for and it becomes a recurring cycle.

Scan this QR code to access the EQ Minds Morning Meditation for Positive Energy.

IDEAS FOR PRACTISING GRATITUDE

☐ Silently or audibly express your gratitude before getting out of bed (instead of checking your phone!).

☐ Keep a gratitude journal at night (instead of doomscrolling!).

☐ Write a love letter or thankyou card to a friend, child, client or spouse.

☐ Post inspiring quotes around your office, kitchen or bedroom.

☐ Write little daily gratitude notes and keep them in a gratitude jar.

☐ Commit to a gratitude month photo series where you capture a photo each day of things that make you happy.

☐ Watch inspiring videos.

☐ Wear an elastic band and whenever you notice a negative thought, snap the elastic band and replace the thought with one about what is going right in your life.

☐ Do a guided gratitude meditation.

☐ Express gratitude to a friend in specific terms.

☐ Conduct acts of kindness for your neighbours or strangers.

☐ Experience gratitude through volunteer work.

☐ Silently or audibly list things you are grateful for while you:
  • wait for the kettle to boil
  • are stuck at the traffic lights
  • get ready to eat a meal
  • are in the shower
  • sit in a waiting room.

Set Your Intention for the Day

If you've been rolling out of bed and starting your day with a sigh and a sense of dread, I want you to commit to setting an intention for your day. One of the most insightful things I've learned from my research is something Dr Daniel Amen speaks about in his book, *The End of Mental Illness.* According to Dr Amen, we should start our day by opening up the curtains and saying, 'Today is going to be a good day!' Sounds so simple, right? Even a child could do it. (And yes, they should.)

As soon as you wake, before you check your phone, try saying 'Today is going to be a good day' out loud when you are opening up your blinds. When you focus on the positive, your brain will start to uncover all the reasons it's going to be that way and stimulate the happy chemicals. Dr Amen explains that where our attention goes, our energy flows and by making that simple declaration, you're setting a positive tone for the day. According to Dr Amen, when we have a happy, hopeful or empowering thought, our brain immediately releases serotonin, oxytocin and dopamine. When we have these happy chemicals coursing through our veins, our breathing slows and our muscles become more relaxed.

Setting an intention is like drawing a map of where you want to go. It becomes the driving force of your higher consciousness. Make sure your intention has a positive tone. If your intention is to be happy, then try to say something like, 'Happiness is my natural state.' Try to avoid, 'My intention is to not be miserable today.'

Change Your Morning with These Daily Positive Affirmations:
- I am thankful for all that I have.
- Everything happens for a good reason.
- I accept myself just as I am.
- Today I choose to be confident.
- I believe in me and have confidence in myself.
- I am in control of my thoughts, feelings and choices.
- I deserve a happy heart and to live at ease.
- I am living in total abundance.

- I am proud of myself and all that I have accomplished.
- I know good things will continue to come into my life.
- I deserve the best and accept the best.
- I am grateful for all new experiences.

Make Your Bed

One day, my mentor sent me a video by Admiral William McRaven called 'If you want to change the world, make your bed'. Funnily enough, my mum drilled bed-making into me from the age of five because that was good manners. Unbeknown to mum, she was gifting me one of the keys to a happier life.

Why Making Your Bed Is Important:
- You start off your day with a win.
- It reinforces in life that the little things matter.
- Doing the little things right sets you up to do the big things right.
- If you have a bad day, you will come home to a bed that is made.
- Research shows that making your bed helps with productivity and emotional wellbeing.

Brush Your Teeth with Your Non-Dominant Hand

Given the nature of my personality, in periods of idle and quiet time, my mind has a tendency to run counter to mindfulness. I sometimes get too swept up thinking about the future or multi-task in ways that pull me away from my present experience. When I'm running on autopilot, I tend to forget things like my keys, computer bag or water bottle because I'm not paying attention. Studying mindfulness has made me realise the significance of cultivating conscious, non-judgemental awareness.

While we will talk about mindfulness in Chapter 9: Your Mindfulness, I want to touch on a few of the benefits here so you can see how to incorporate it into your morning habits, such as brushing your teeth.

Studies show that practising mindfulness calms the mind, improves brain function, helps you focus and reduces stress. It makes people happier, less irritable and more engaged with others. One highly effective way to practise mindfulness is through meditation; however, a task that is simpler in the morning is brushing your teeth with your non-dominant hand. I brush my teeth with my left hand to jolt myself out of internal chatter and stay in the moment. It also trains my brain to do tricky tasks while stimulating a different part of my brain. This tool will help you to avoid falling into mechanical thoughts and actions. It will also leave your mouth feeling fresh and clean!

Hydrate

When we sleep, our bodies are hard at work repairing muscles, recharging our immune system and shedding toxins. One of the best things you can do to help your body complete its night-time detox cycle is to drink a tall glass of water when you wake up. This helps flush out toxins and hydrate our bodies. Hydration is also important first thing in the morning because our bodies lose a lot of water while we sleep through breathing and sweating.

Did you know that our brains are 80 per cent water? That means if we want to fire up our brains to operate at top functionality, we need to be well hydrated. Even if we are mildly dehydrated, it can have an impact on our mental health – making us feel anxious, tense or even depressed – as well as thwarting our energy. So, grab a tall glass of water before you reach for your morning coffee.

Take a Probiotic and Prebiotic for Your Second Brain

Have you ever noticed that when you're feeling a strong emotion, it's almost as if it's happening in your stomach? *I feel sick to my stomach. I have butterflies in my stomach! I feel like I've been punched in the gut.*

I'm going to give you a gutful about gut health in Chapter 10: Your Gut Health, but here's a little appetiser: your enteric nervous system is the boss of your gastrointestinal tract. Consisting of hundreds of millions of neurons, it's responsible for your body's motor functions, blood flow and mucosal transport (e.g. the tissues that produce mucus, such as the digestive, genital and urinary tracts) as well as controlling immune and endocrine functions. It's also the maestro of peristalsis, the contraction that moves your poo closer to the exit!

Often referred to as the body's 'second brain', your enteric nervous system is connected to your (actual) brain by the vagus nerve. It's also responsible for making 90 per cent of our serotonin and 50 per cent of our dopamine. Serotonin is vital for positive moods and good energy, while dopamine fuels our motivation, sense of reward and general feelings of happiness. For a long time, scientists thought these were only manufactured in the brain, but it turns out they also come from our gut! Because the gut acts as a home base for neurotransmitters, you can see how mental-health conditions like depression and anxiety emerge when there is a problem in the gut. There is a tremendous overlap between irritable bowel syndrome (IBS) and depressed mood and anxiety.

For decades, doctors did not understand that the root of a patient's anxiety or mood swings could be a gastrointestinal issue. It's now clear that when you have damaged gut bacteria, you can suffer from reduced serotonin levels, which then alters your mood.

Probiotics have been shown in clinical studies to decrease inflammation – which improves gut health – and they are even more effective when taken with prebiotics. Experts suggest looking for products you can take daily that contain both lactobacillus and bifidobacterium strains and over 3 billion live organisms.

Safely Get Some Sun

Thanks to skin cancer, the sun has been having a lot of well-deserved bad publicity lately, but it's something we should be actively seeking out in order to maintain our body's circadian rhythm. Designed to tell our bodies when to produce cortisol and when to produce melatonin, our circadian rhythm is directly impacted by our eyes' light consumption, especially blue-light wavelengths. These wavelengths are found in natural sunlight as well as artificial lighting and screens (e.g. smartphones, tablets, computers and TVs). While blue-light wavelengths are great because they help us feel alert, energetic and ready for the day, when you're exposed to them for too long (like sitting in front of a computer screen until 9 pm at night), your body doesn't get the signal to make melatonin. I'm going to talk more about circadian rhythms in Chapter 8: Your Sleep, but for now I want you to focus on exposing your eyes to sunlight first thing in the morning so your body knows to start scaling back on producing melatonin and ramping up cortisol.

But Chelsea, you just said I could get blue-light wavelengths from staring at my screen. Do I actually have to go outside?

Yes, you actually have to go outside and here's why: the lux, which is the unit of measurement of light level intensity, is better.

- A dark room has a lux score of 0.
- An artificially lit building has a lux score of between 500 and 1000.
- Outdoor sunlight can have a lux score of between 30,000 and 110,000 (2000 on a cloudy day).

Let's say you're living in London and travelling to work before sunrise and from work after sunset. You go from your flat to the tube to the office and back home again. If you're not stepping into sunlight once the sun is up, you're missing the part of the day that is designed to kick off your body systems. With that being said, many of you would argue London isn't a very sunny place or that this simply isn't possible for people who live in places like Iceland and Alaska. (Touché.) In that case, you can buy light boxes that are specifically designed to replicate outdoor sunlight. (Not the best option, but it beats the alternative!)

Now, I'm not saying you should go outside and stare directly into the sun. You'll burn your retinas out! I simply mean step outside in the morning and expose your eyes to the sunlight so your body knows that it's time to kick into gear. Below are a few ways I like to get sunlight into my eyes in the morning:

- Go for a morning walk without sunglasses.
- Exercise outdoors without sunglasses.
- Have my morning coffee on the balcony without sunglasses.

Build Your Energy and Move Your Body

The amount of research showing just how beneficial it is to move your body (especially in the morning) is staggering. Another way I begin building my energy is by doing breathing exercises every morning. I'll talk more about movement in Chapter 7: Your Movement and Energy.

Benefits of Regular Exercise:
- improved oxygen levels in the brain
- healthier muscle to fat ratio
- improved sleep
- decrease in depression.

Have a Cold Shower

Remember the ice-bucket challenge that raised awareness for ALS (amytrophic lateral sclerosis)? Apparently, they were onto something! Research shows that cold-water therapy does a great job at resetting your nervous system and improves mood, increases alertness and has the extra benefit of helping to manage inflammation. When I read this research, I gently dipped my toe into this practice. First, I started with a three-minute warm shower and 30 seconds of cold at the end. Then, over the course of a week, I gradually increased the cold. In the winter, I revert back to a warm shower at the start and only the last 30 seconds cold. If it's a possibility for you, you could go for an ocean swim or take a dip in an unheated pool in the morning.

Your Morning Meditation

According to a 2013 study, over time, meditation can shrink the size of your amygdala, which is the part of the brain responsible for stress and anxiety. This gets me really excited because if your amygdala is less reactive, you become less stressed and live more in the moment. Science also shows that meditation improves the size of your hippocampus, which is your brain's memory centre. (Hello, morning performance!) So even as we are ageing and getting a little saggier or developing more wrinkles, we can still stay super sharp in the brain.

In Chapter 9: Your Mindfulness, I will go deeper into how meditation can be a game-changer for anxiety, depression and productivity, but, for now, try thinking about spending 10 minutes a day in a meditative state.

But Chelsea, I have small children.

I hear you. With a young child, sometimes I don't get my morning meditation in, so on those days I schedule a non-negotiable 10-minute timeslot in my diary to meditate. This is usually either at 10 am or 3 pm. I literally book it in like I have an appointment.

Focus on Your Goals

Mornings can be the best time for productivity, which is why I always focus on the tasks that matter most to me. Begin each day by revisiting your goals and vision board so that you can set a clear intention. This will allow you to stay focused on the things that you value and keep you intrinsically motivated throughout your day.

Here's my biggest tip: I don't deplete my willpower on menial tasks. I do the big deep-thinking work first as I'm a lark and most productive in the morning. I don't even check emails until 10 am. If I allow the small tasks to creep in, I tend to get derailed and lack the clarity I need to achieve the meatier work. Always take the time to plan your day and list the things that matter most to you in order of importance. Remember, this includes your own mental health and self-care!

Eat Breakfast (or Don't)

Unless I'm fasting (which I will talk about in Chapter 10: Your Gut Health), I typically start my day with a brain-friendly meal and coffee. This could be something like:

- egg and avocado on gluten-free bread (I'm gluten intolerant)
- paleo granola, coconut yoghurt and blueberries
- smoothie
- boiled egg, spinach and toast
- apple with almond butter
- zoodles (zucchini spiralised and topped with organic herbs).

Disclaimer: everyone's diet will look different depending on the needs of their gut health.

I want to reiterate that my morning routine does remain fluid and flexible, and I don't do each of these things every morning! The last thing we want is for your morning routine to cause stress if you aren't ticking off all these items on the list. Start with one simple change that will benefit your mind and body, and be guided by what feels good for you.

IN YOUR JOURNAL

- Write a list of the things you do before heading to work or starting your day at home. Place a Y next to the activities that give you energy and an N next to the ones that deplete you.
- Every morning, write down and answer the following journal prompts:

  - What is the one thing I can do today that will have the largest return on investment (financially, professionally or personally)?
  - What am I doing today for self-care?

07
YOUR MOVEMENT AND ENERGY

ONE OF THE easiest ways to start feeling, thinking and sleeping better is to be physically active every day. This could be a walk, yoga class, swim, bike ride, run, stretch class, tai chi session, horseback riding, surfing, basketball or dancing while you do the dishes.

LIMITING BELIEFS

While what you choose to do may depend on your personal preferences, financial position, injury history or time constraints, I want to spend the first part of this chapter getting rid of any limiting beliefs you may have. (And then we'll dive into the good stuff!)

I Don't Like to Exercise

Let's talk about the word 'exercise'. It has eight letters, indicates doing some sort of activity that's intended to strengthen the mind and body and, for a lot of people, can trigger negative emotions. I get it. Society puts so much pressure on us to look a certain way that we've come to equate 'exercise' with high-intensity training designed to give us Instagram abs. That's why I'm not going to use the word (all that much) in this chapter. Instead, let's use the word 'movement' because it doesn't matter what athletic hobby or physical activities you're into: you simply need to be moving. Sweating might make you anxious and any sort of elevated heart rate might make you instinctively want to seek shelter, but here's the thing: movement is way too beneficial not to power through. While it might be the definition of 'unenjoyable' while you're doing it, just remember that reward comes *after*.

I Don't Have Enough Time to Exercise

If you've found time to spend 30 minutes sending videos and memes to your besties, you have enough time to exercise. You just haven't made it a priority ... YET! We talked about this briefly in Chapter 5: Your Goals, but if something means enough to you, you can and will make time for it. Look at your day and identify where you could be more efficient. Can you wake up earlier to go for a walk? Could you take your gym gear to work and hit the gym during your lunch break? How about swapping your afterwork drink for an afterwork yoga session? Instead of spending your Saturday hungover in bed, how about you book in a walking date with a friend? You can also always ask your employer for flexibility with your start and finish times. For example, I have a friend who loves doing a 7 am boxing class but is supposed to get to work by 8:30 am. She spoke to her manager and got permission to come in at 9 am and leave at 5 pm instead of 4:30 pm. When it comes to your health, it never hurts to ask.

I Don't Have Enough Money to Exercise

If you had enough money to buy a takeaway coffee today, you have enough money to exercise. You just don't value exercise ... YET! I totally get that gyms and classes can be really expensive. But the thing is: you can run, walk, practise yoga (and maybe swim) effectively for free. You can also tap into the endless workout videos on YouTube (although you might have to put up with the distraction of an ad or two if you don't pay for their premium subscription).

Ways to Save $$ and Put It Towards Your Fitness:

- Do a quick check of your phone, internet and electricity to see if you're getting the best deals.
- Instead of having multiple streaming services, could you consolidate to just one or two?
- Decrease your alcohol intake (grog is expensive!).
- Sell a few wardrobe or home pieces.
- Do your nails at home.
- Use a refillable water bottle to avoid buying drinks when you're out.

I'm Too Tired to Exercise

We talked about the word 'exercise', now let's talk about the word 'energy'. While some people are referring to calories when they use the term energy, I'm talking about a different kind of energy that is called qi (pronounced *chee*) in Chinese medicine. Your qi is your vital energy and to keep it flowing well you need to tend to it.

For many years I thought that movement was what gave me energy. While I often finished a morning run feeling invigorated and energetic, I was actually experiencing the morphine-like effects of endorphins coursing through my veins as well as a hit of dopamine. Not to mention a surge in cortisol! In reality, I was expending my body's energy. Recently, I've begun researching the Chinese practice of qigong, which translates to 'energy work'. I have come to understand that you must work on building both your energy *and* your body's movement in order to maintain optimal physical and mental health. Just like movies and popcorn, energy and movement are better together.

How You Can Build Your Body's Energy:

- Let the sun's rays touch your eyes and skin first thing in the morning.
- Connect with the ground by standing barefoot outside on the grass or dirt.

- Practise breathing techniques. (I really like the exercises from the Wim Hof Method.)
- Gently move your body and warm up your joints by doing a morning tai chi ritual.
- Spend 10–20 minutes meditating.

THE BENEFITS OF MOVEMENT

Alright, now that those pesky limiting beliefs are out of the way, let's talk about the science behind movement. From strengthening your muscles to increasing your lung capacity to enhancing your cognition, the benefits of moving your body are enormous. While, yes, I want to make sure you're moving every day to increase your physical performance, I also want you to move for both your physical and mental health.

Engaging in Regular Physical Activity:
- helps prevent and heal age-related diseases
- can prevent or reduce the symptoms of anxiety
- enhances your cognition
- keeps your bones and joints strong
- improves mobility
- can prevent or reduce the symptoms of depression.

Movement and the Body

It's wild to think about but moving your body regularly has been shown to keep your chromosomes healthy. In a study investigating ageing and the benefits of exercise, researchers found a correlation between the shortening of telomeres, which are the protective structures found at the end of a chromosome, and age-related diseases. Physically active people had longer telomeres, regardless of the intensity of exercise they did. This is important because shorter telomere length is associated with shorter lifespans.

In another study, researchers found evidence that regular physical activity can help prevent several chronic illnesses (such as cardiovascular disease, diabetes, cancer, hypertension, obesity, depression and osteoporosis) and even premature death. For something that's really not difficult to add to your day AND is proven to prevent your body from slipping into a diseased state, movement is a no-brainer, right?

Movement and the Brain

Speaking of the brain … when you move your body, you're not just working towards stronger muscles and better-fitting clothing, you're also taking your brain to the gym. While there is strong evidence that regular physical exercise can directly impact your mood and decrease symptoms of anxiety and depression, there's a whole lot more to exercise than mental health.

Cognitive Benefits of Movement:

- enhanced long-term memory function
- improved cognitive flexibility, aka the brain's ability to switch between tasks
- increased thinking speed
- improved executive functions (these are essential for decision-making, problem-solving, prioritising, maintaining your attention span and controlling impulses).

Movement and Disease Prevention

Your brain is made up of white and grey matter. As we age, this matter can atrophy, break down and become covered in plaque. While deterioration can negatively impact brain functions like cognition, memory capacity and executive functions, it can also make us prone to both grey-matter disease and white-matter disease, which can put us at risk of neurodegenerative diseases like various dementias, Parkinson's, multiple sclerosis (MS) and Guillain-Barré syndrome. It can also result in an increased chance of having a stroke. In a study on balance training and brain matter, researchers found localised increases in motor cortical thickness after one hour of practice in a complex balancing task, proving that physical movement can improve our brain health.

Ways to Increase Both Grey and White Matter While Reducing Your Risk of Neurodegenerative Diseases (aka tips for becoming a real-life Benjamin Button):

- Practise balance exercises: Try surfing, box jumps, single-leg yoga poses, single-leg weights, stability ball work.
- Learn something new: All your brain needs is 30 minutes per week of learning time to make new synaptic connections. That's just three 10-minute segments a week!
- Take up juggling: It's a great way to create neuroplasticity and increase grey matter.
- Sleep well: Sleep is when your brain gets a deep clean so make sure you're not skipping any Zs. If you sleep poorly your brain shrinks.
- Practise mindfulness and meditation: When you consciously relax and dial into your breath, you're able to get your brain to fire the wavelengths required for repair and growth.
- Mix up your running: For example, change your route or change your terrain to challenge your brain. (Be careful that you don't roll an ankle or twist a knee!)
- Play a musical instrument: This is a great sensory experience for your brain and a mood enhancer.
- Eat a diet rich in 'good' fats (particularly great for white-matter health).
- Immerse yourself in nature: Connecting with the outdoors heightens your senses, can help reset your body's clock and provides fresh oxygen to the brain.

Sitting Is the New Smoking

It wasn't all that long ago that humans used to stay low to the ground when hunting or foraging. Moving in a lateral squat was necessary for reaching things on the ground efficiently as well as staying out of sight of predators and prey, and is why our hips evolved as ball and socket joints. Today, however, we are spending more time than ever sitting and tend to bend over only briefly to pick something up when needed. The result: our hips have become hinged. Furthermore, it's making us unhealthy. When you sit for prolonged periods of time, you increase your risk of type 2 diabetes, cancer and premature death. You're also at risk of decreasing mobility in your back, hips and legs, and may even reduce your lung capacity.

Ideas to Help Reduce the Amount of Time You Sit During the Day:
- Invest in a standing desk.
- Take a break from sitting every 90 minutes.
- Take a walking meeting.
- Walk while on the phone.
- Use the stairs instead of the elevator.
- Invest in an activity tracker to keep you motivated.

How Much Do I REALLY Need to Be Moving?

We all have the one friend who seems to live in activewear and bounces between HIIT classes and philanthropic fun runs! While that may be you, it's okay if it's not. According to a report from the World Health Organization, adults between the ages of 18 and 64 should:

- do at least 150–300 minutes of moderate-intensity aerobic activity or at least 75–150 minutes of vigorous-intensity aerobic activity every week
- ensure they're doing muscle-strengthening activities at moderate or greater intensity that involve all major muscle groups on two or more days a week
- minimise the amount of time spent in prolonged sitting positions.

At the end of the day, doing any physical activity is better than doing none. If you currently do no physical activity, start by doing some, and gradually build up to the recommended amount. In no way do you need to train like an Olympic athlete to feel the benefits of movement.

Injury Prevention and Recovery

As an ex-athlete who played Division 1 basketball in the United States at Oral Roberts University, there was rarely a day I didn't move. (Side note: both Jay and I got scholarships to play basketball in the United States. While I was at one of the country's most devout Christian schools, he was living his best party life at the University of Massachusetts Amherst. I'm not bitter at all.) Throughout my teens and early twenties, my daily runs, swims, weights sessions and basketball practices taught me the power of being uncomfortable physically, mentally and socially, and my capacity to push myself to limits I could never have imagined.

In my first year at university, my team secured a position at the illustrious NCAA tournament, where the top 64 teams in America go head to head. While it's thrilling enough just to get to play at this level of competition, the media, crowds of 10,000 and fanfare are absolutely wild. I was on cloud nine and positive that my dream of playing in the WNBA (just like my childhood friend, Lauren Jackson) would come to fruition. But then I fractured my sacroiliac joint while lifting weights. Through rest and multiple cortisol injections, I managed to get mobility back by the following season. Believe it or not, I was the *least* injured on my team, so even though I wasn't fully recovered, I had to play. (That time in my life reminds me so much of *Varsity Blues*.) During my first game back, a player tapped my ankle on a rebound, which made me lose my footing and fracture my hip. This time, I was told I'd need to sit out for another six to 10 months. Determined to heal and stay competitive, I started lifting again as soon as I could. Well, wouldn't you know: I stress-fractured the same hip again. I remember sobbing to my mum on the phone about my injuries, pain and desire to play. That's when she said to me, 'Chelsea, you're 19. I want you to be able to run around with your kids when you're 35. Perhaps the universe is channelling you in a different way.'

While I now know my mum was 100 per cent right about the universe inadvertently showing me what my true purpose is, I came back to Australia pretty banged up. Working out the way I was used to wasn't going to cut it anymore. I needed to scale things back, take it easy and focus on the type of movement that had high results, but was low impact. Over the years, I've also experimented with lots of injury prevention and rehab activities.

Activities You Can Try for Injury Prevention and Rehab:
- Deep-tissue massage: Getting regular deep-tissue massages can help eliminate knots, improve flexibility, decrease stress and even boost your serotonin levels.
- Foam rolling: If getting a professional massage isn't an option, having a foam roller on hand can be a great way to achieve myofascial release, which is a fancy way of saying you're reducing the amount of adhesion of scar and soft tissue on the muscle.
- Cold-water therapy: Credited for reducing muscle soreness and inflammation, cold-water therapy (such as an ice bath or cold shower) can also boost your body's immune system and encourage mitochondrial health.
- Infrared-sauna therapy: A lot of people swear by infrared-sauna therapy because they say it improves circulation, aids in quicker recovery times post workout, helps prevent injury, reduces stress and can improve sleep.
- Magnesium-salt tanks: Aka sensory-deprivation tanks, magnesium-salt tanks have so much magnesium in them that you float your pain away! In all seriousness, they can help reduce the symptoms of anxiety, help relax your muscles and reduce pain.
- Cryotherapy: Particularly great for those recovering from an injury or experiencing chronic pain, cryotherapy exposes you to extremely cold temperatures to reduce inflammation and swelling. By temporarily reducing nerve activity, you may also experience less pain.
- Hyperbaric-oxygen chamber: Designed to double the amount of oxygen in the body, hyperbaric chambers may help reduce

inflammation in your muscles, joints and even brain. They're also thought to help heal stubborn wounds quicker.

Pain can be a huge reason why we choose not to move, but I promise that both your mind and body need you to find a way.

SET YOURSELF UP FOR SUCCESS

Adopting a workout routine isn't easy, which is why you should be gentle on yourself and ease into it. The last thing I want you to do is go out and spend a week's wage on activewear only to leave the tags on. Or worse, watch your gym debit your card every month even though you only set foot in the place once.

STEP 1: Start with Incidental Exercise

While I want you to work up to a big walk, weights session or core workout, start with your daily life and see where you can increase physical activity in your daily routine.

For example, you can:

- take the stairs instead of the elevator
- do some gardening
- take a walking meeting instead of a sitting down for a coffee meeting
- stand up to read your book or sit on a balance ball
- increase your steps by parking further away from your destination
- hang your washing out instead of using a dryer.

STEP 2: Find Something That You Enjoy Doing

Sometimes you need to find something that doesn't feel like 'exercise' to get over mental hurdles. Whenever I ride my bike or go for a surf, I know I'm technically 'exercising', but to be honest, it mostly gives me a holiday-mode feeling. Jay and I started doing salsa dancing recently. With all the laughing and dancing, we rack up an hour of movement without even realising we're doing it. If you're someone who loves the gym or group fitness, just remember that it's important to keep variety in your workout in order to reduce injury and also so you don't get bored!

STEP 3: Get the Added Benefits of Nature

A study done by the University of Exeter shows that we lower our stress levels and blood pressure as well as improve our immune system, mood and self-esteem when we immerse ourselves in nature. You can achieve it in just two hours a week of nature-time, so let's hit two birds with one stone by moving outside! We'll chat more about this in Chapter 11: Your Connections.

STEP 4: Schedule It into Your Calendar

Consistency versus intensity is the number-one way to get results. It is better to work out each day for 30 minutes rather than once a month for five hours. Create a plan that will keep you motivated with the right mix of interesting movements as well as rest days. I suggest writing a schedule. What are you going to do every day from Monday to Sunday? Which days will you rest? Keep in mind, not every day is going to be a day of HIIT or pounding the pavement. Some days will involve a casual walk, an ocean swim or a slow bike ride to your local café.

STEP 5: Factor in Recovery and Rest

Speaking of rest days, something that I find helpful is having active recovery days. Active recovery helps you recuperate (physically and mentally) from your more intense workouts. The intention of this day is to keep active, improve your flexibility and repair your muscles. If you came to my house, our lounge room at night looks like a physiotherapy clinic. We have foam rollers, lacrosse balls, a massage gun, yoga mats and stretch bands. While Jay and I watch a movie, we do myofascial release using this equipment. Myofascial release, which is essentially applying pressure to your muscles to achieve flexibility and reduce pain, also helps us avoid injury and maintain our training regimes. You can think of it like replacing the oil in your car. Basic maintenance helps keep your body running for a long time. If this is your first time hearing about foam rolling or lacrosse balls for myofascial release, check it out on YouTube.

My Favourite Active Recovery Day Activities:
- a walk with a friend
- yoga
- foam rolling
- massage
- swimming in the ocean.

MY WEEKLY MOVEMENT SCHEDULE

MON	TUE	WED	THUR
30 min weightlifting	60 min surfing	30 min weightlifting	60 min surfing
30 min walk with a friend	20 min bike ride	30 min bike ride	30 min walk
15 min foam rolling	15 min stretching	15 min foam rolling	15 min foam rolling

FRI	SAT	SUN
30 min weightlifting	Family hike, surf or bike ride	Active recovery with one of these:
30 min bike ride		• walk
1 hr deep tissue massage		• sauna • float tank.

STEP 6: Challenge Yourself

While you need to start gently and let your muscles gain strength and endurance over time, it's important to focus on increasing your intensity and output. This means if you've started off by walking 1 km at a time, you can look at 2 km next month. If you started by running 5 km in 35 minutes, you'll want to aim for 30 minutes. Same goes for the weight you're lifting or the difficulty of yoga, Pilates or dance moves.

Try to train for four weeks at a given level before you up the ante. Adding challenge is an art and takes many forms. Having a coach, personal trainer or an app like 'Couch to 5k' can help you increase your movement in a safe and sustainable way.

STEP 7: Set S.M.A.R.T. Movement Goals and Reward Yourself

As we talked about in Chapter 5: Your Goals, remember to reward yourself along the way to a big juicy goal! For example, you could sign up to do a half-marathon. Adopting a new movement routine can be difficult mentally, physically and logistically. Since we know the best way to stick to goals is by making them S.M.A.R.T., make sure you can identify achievable markers along the way to a reward. For example, if you're training for an endurance walk, once you've hit 20 km in training, reward yourself with a Camelbak to make it easier to stay hydrated, or moisture-wicking socks. I always try to check in and congratulate myself on days three, 21 and 66 of any new venture.

STEP 8: Plan Ahead

There's a good chance that you're going to need to work out early in the morning, and there's nothing harder than trying to think about how you're going to clothe your body and find your keys at 5 am. My advice: lay out your clothes, gym towel and water bottle the night before. In fact, I've heard about people sleeping in their activewear so they don't have the excuse of needing to get dressed.

STEP 9: Get a Gym Buddy

An accountability partner will make it so much easier to wake up, show up and bring your A game! Research says we are two times more likely to follow through with something when we've committed to the plan with another person.

STEP 10: Do NOT Get Hung Up on Weight

Even though I'm a huge fan of journalling and tracking progress, I never track my weight. Here's why: society has conditioned us to weigh a 'certain amount' even though it might not be right for our height, age and genetic makeup. Also, muscle weighs more than fat so, if you start a new gym class and see the number on your scale rising, it's most likely due to you getting stronger. However, this is a mind-f*ck for a lot of people (especially women), and something I just think we should all ignore. Chase the feeling movement brings to your life, not the number!

STEP 11: Articulate Your Why

When Clara was five, we both noticed her pants were looking a little small. When I said, 'I think we need to get you some new pants!' she replied, 'Yeah, I'm too strong for these pants now.' In a word, I was shook. And proud! I loved her positive language and I encourage you to understand your WHY and adopt a mantra such as:

- I'm moving to feel strong.
- I'm moving for my mental health.
- I'm moving for my brainpower.
- I'm moving so I can keep up with my kids.
- I'm moving to connect with nature.

STEP 12: Dress for Success

There's nothing like being too cold or having a blister say hello to make you want to throw in the towel! I'm not saying go out and buy a bunch of fancy activewear, but make sure you're investing in high-quality shoes, socks and clothing that will keep your body supported and protected.

IN YOUR JOURNAL

- Identify any limiting beliefs that may be holding you back from moving.
- Examine your current movement routine. Are you factoring in enough time for rest and recovery?
- List movement activities that also promote mindfulness.
- Who is someone you could ask to be your movement buddy?
- If you haven't already, set three to five S.M.A.R.T. goals that you can work towards over the next six to 12 months.

08
YOUR SLEEP

IS THERE ANYTHING better than the type of sleep that results in a drool-marked pillowcase? As someone who suffered from insomnia along with my postnatal depression, I do everything in my power to protect my sleep. I know firsthand just how quickly your mindset can go south if you're operating on a drug-induced two-hour micro nap, which is why I'm going to spend this chapter talking about what happens to your brain and body when you sleep, tips for creating an optimal sleep environment, substances and devices to avoid, as well as what to do if you're someone who can't fall asleep or finds themselves waking frequently.

For something that is a biological necessity and a state our bodies are programmed to be in, it's surprising how difficult it can be for us to fall and stay asleep. Research shows that 35 per cent of adults don't get enough sleep daily and are sleeping less than six hours a night. Due to the pressure we feel to be constantly 'on' and our dependence on things such as caffeine, screens, alcohol and bingeable Netflix series, we are losing sleep and it's causing us harm.

NOT ALL SLEEP IS CREATED EQUAL

On average, we spend a third of our lives asleep. Divided into cycles consisting of five stages, sleep is a crucial part of our body's way of processing information, detoxing our organs and repairing our muscles. While you may have heard of REM, the rapid-eye-movement stage of sleep (not the band), I want to dive a little deeper into why it's important and how it relates to the other stages of non-rapid-eye-movement (NREM) sleep.

What Is a Sleep Cycle?

A sleep cycle is the amount of time it takes your brain to go through the five stages of sleep. The duration of a sleep cycle varies from person to person, but on average, a full sleep cycle lasts roughly 90 minutes. Have you ever woken up an hour after falling asleep and found it super difficult to figure out what's happening? That confusion is because you're in mid-sleep cycle and your brain is in the middle of changing the wavelengths it's sending out. You'll feel particularly groggy if you're in the middle of the REM stage.

In a perfect world, we would go from sleep cycle to sleep cycle without waking up, but as your body (or a crying child) will tell you, sometimes that's not always possible. It could be because we are dehydrated and our body is signalling us to get water. It could be because we have high levels of the stress hormone cortisol, and not enough melatonin to tell us to stay asleep. It could also be because your room is too bright. Whatever the culprit may be, I will give you some tools and tips to help you ensure you're completing multiple sleep cycles every night. But first, let's talk about sleep stages.

Stage One

Have you ever found yourself falling asleep (in bed, at school or at work) and your body does a little twitch-jolt thing? (Fun fact: it's called a myoclonic jerk.) Welcome to the first stage of drifting off to sleep. In Stage One, your brain's beta waves, which are the wavelengths that keep you alert and able to think about your day and future, are slowly being replaced by alpha wavelengths. These allow your mind and body to relax and begin to tune out the world around you. While you're still easy to rouse, you're getting closer and closer to theta wavelengths. Theta wavelengths allow your brain to start drifting into an imaginative or dream-like state.

Stage Two

By Stage Two, your brain is active with theta wavelengths, but being periodically interrupted by high-frequency waves called sleep spindles. Sleep spindles are the way our brain processes and files information from the day in order to build both our short- and long-term memories as well as our cognitive ability to recall them.

Stage Three

In Stage Three, you're going from a sleep you could be easily awakened from to a deep sleep where your brain fires delta wavelengths. While sleep spindles are still occurring, it's happening less and now the prefrontal cortex is lighting up. Interestingly, this is a difficult stage to be woken up from (unless you're a parent hearing your baby cry).

Stage Four

I love Stage Four because this is a deep sleep that allows your brain to fire delta wavelengths like they're going out of style. Your body's temperature drops, your muscles become increasingly relaxed and your parasympathetic nervous system is slowing everything right down. Now it's time for repair work to begin!

Stage Five

While the NREM stages one to four are vital for our body's performance, it's actually not the sleep that matters most. If you really want the magic to happen, you need to make sure you're getting at least a total of one-and-a-half hours of REM sleep per night. This is the stage where the majority of your dreams occur and your eyes are darting from side to side and up and down. Why they move, scientists still aren't 100 per cent sure. It's quite interesting that they are able to move because the other muscles in

---

⌐A NOTE ON ALZHEIMER'S ⌐

One of the main culprits often linked to dementia diseases like Alzheimer's is a build-up of beta amyloid, a waste product from the energy used when brain cells are communicating. During sleep and, in particular, the slow-wave stages, your brain is actually self-cleaning and working to remove the build-up of beta amyloid plaques!

your body are paralysed at this point. The biggest thing that's happening during this stage is your brain is consolidating memories from your day and making important synaptic connections so you can easily recall them later.

How Bad Is Sleep Deprivation?

Back in my corporate life, we all used to put the executives on pedestals who'd fly in at 2 am and still rock up to work at 7 am. We had unconsciously adopted machismo attitudes that somehow pushing our bodies to operate while experiencing sleep deprivation was to be admired. In reality, it was reckless and unproductive.

Remember when I was talking about sleep spindles and REM and how important they both are for memory consolidation? That's because they're two major parts of getting information to your brain's hippocampus. Located deep in the temporal lobe of our cerebral cortex, the hippocampus helps regulate your memory, your ability to learn, to process and express emotions and to find motivation to do, think, feel and act. If you don't get adequate sleep, your brain is unable to perform the functions needed to make you cognitively fit during the day. Recalling information, responding rationally to stress and finding energy to jump through the hoops of life-admin will be extremely difficult.

One of the most common misconceptions is that if you've left your prep to the last minute, 'pulling an all-nighter' will help you do better on a test, deliver a presentation or nail a best-man speech. Research shows this couldn't be further from the truth. If you get less than six-and-a-half hours of sleep, you're going to consolidate 40 per cent LESS information than you would if you simply gave yourself eight hours. Sleep deprivation blocks your brain's capacity for new learning, so you're better off resting your brain so it can recall the information you do have the next day.

The Joys of Sleep Deprivation:
- fatigue
- brain fog
- delayed cognition

- reduced attention span
- decreased ability to make informed decisions
- difficulty recalling information
- anxious thoughts, depression and psychosis
- increased risk of Alzheimer's
- premature death.

CAFFEINE, ALCOHOL AND SCREENS, OH MY!

If I had three guesses as to why people are struggling to sleep, I'd say: too much caffeine, too much alcohol or too much screen time. Don't worry! I'm not about to tell you to give those three things up. I just want to take a moment to talk about how they can affect your sleep and how you can make small adjustments to protect those precious Zs.

Caffeine

It may be the Australian in me; I do love a good coffee. Caffeinated, of course. The issue is that caffeine is a stimulant that tells your body to give you a spike of cortisol and adrenaline. As someone who loves the buzz of her morning flat white, this is all well and good until I experience a mental-health crisis. At the end of 2020, I found myself spiralling with anxiety. I will talk more about this in Chapter 13: Your Support, but I essentially had to go back to square one and figure out how to get my mind and body back on track. This meant taking six weeks off caffeine in an effort to minimise anxious feelings, calm my nervous system and increase my chances of achieving deep sleep. (Don't worry, I'm fine now and back on the flat whites.)

It's no secret that caffeine tends to contribute to a person's restless nights in bed. Most people don't realise that it takes between four and eight hours for caffeine to be eliminated from your system and, for those who are sensitive to caffeine (who experience hyper-arousal), it can take longer. I only allow myself one shot a day and never have it after midday. As enticing as it sounds to have a piccolo post dinner, I politely decline because I know it will disrupt stages three, four and five of my sleep.

Alcohol

Our society has made alcohol a very popular sundowner. From winding down with a glass of red to meeting up with workmates for happy hour, it's marketed as a magical tonic designed to take the edge off. But let's be honest: ONE glass might take the edge off, but research shows that two or more alcoholic drinks depress your brain, impair your ability to reach the REM sleep stage and dehydrate your body, which makes it difficult for your body to complete its nightly detoxification. (Not to mention all the times you have to get up to pee!)

While alcohol may make it easier for you to fall asleep, it often results in rebound insomnia. This is when you fall asleep quickly, but then wake up frequently to use the toilet, drink water, sweat, have panicked thoughts or check that you made it home with your phone. My rules for drinking are no more than two drinks per night and they must be consumed three hours before going to bed. I also recommend having three or four (or more!) alcohol-free nights a week. Good-quality sleep gives your brain a deep wash and is responsible for your mojo, the bounce in your step. Alcohol can obliterate this.

WHAT ABOUT SMOKING?

Nicotine is another central-nervous-system stimulant and disrupts sleep just like caffeine. Although smokers may experience relaxation when they smoke, the overall effect of nicotine is stimulating and incompatible with sleep (causing increased heart rate, blood pressure and concentration). Heavy smoking around bedtime may also lead to conditioned awakenings at night, when the person wakes up and immediately craves a cigarette. Avoid smoking at least one hour before bedtime and upon night awakenings (that includes vaping).

Screens (and Artificial Lighting)

I briefly touched on this in Chapter 6: Your Morning Routine, but when you look at your phone, backlit e-reader, tablet, TV or computer, you're looking at blue-light wavelengths that tell your brain it's daytime, which prompts your pineal gland to switch off its melatonin production and tell your adrenals to start making cortisol. By scrolling through your Facebook feed at 11 pm, you're basically telling your brain to 'Look alive out there!'

In order to maintain your body's circadian rhythm, you should avoid all screens and even limit your exposure to artificial light at least 30 minutes before bed. Try using a dimmer or low-wattage light bulbs in your bedroom. You can also look into getting blue-light-blocking glasses to wear indoors after sundown.

MAINTAINING YOUR CIRCADIAN RHYTHM

Did you know that your eyes are part of your brain? I don't mean that they're attached, I mean they are a literal extension of your brain and share the same tissue! Your neural retina, about as thick as a credit card, is one of the key ways your brain absorbs the environment. By being able to sense light (and danger/safety), your brain can then determine when to produce hormones like cortisol and melatonin. Before screens, this was a really simple and useful way for us to know when to be awake and alert and when it was safe to retreat and sleep. But thanks to synthetic lighting (and the fact that we're not fighting for our lives in the wilderness anymore), our brains are having a bit of trouble knowing when to switch on and switch off.

There are two types of people in the world: larks and night owls. Larks are the early to bed, early to rise, don't-you-dare-ask-me-to-go-to-dinner-after-8-pm people. Night owls are the love-a-snooze, thrive in the evening, sure-let's-start-a-movie-at-9:30-pm people. To maximise performance, if you're a lark, you need to be off the screens and preparing for bed no later than 9 pm. If you're a night owl, the magic time is about 10:30 pm. To help maintain this cycle, it's important to get up at the same time every day, open your curtains, go for a morning walk (without sunglasses), sit near a window or have your morning tea or coffee outside. If you're unable to access sunshine, get a light therapy box. All you need is about two to 10 minutes in the morning to signal to your body that it should start making cortisol. After the sun sets, ensure you're limiting your blue-light exposure and, of course, turning off screens at least 30 minutes before bed.

Helpful Tips for Minimising Artificial Light Exposure:
- Wear blue-light-blocking glasses indoors after the sun has gone down.
- Turn off half of your home's lights by 8 pm.
- Swap out your cool white light bulbs for warm yellow ones.
- Invest in dimmers.
- Cut off all technology use 30 minutes prior to bed.
- Read a paperback book by lamplight instead of an e-reader.
- Install blackout curtains.
- Cover lights on your TV, alarm clock or AC unit.
- Wear an eye mask.

Start by Creating Your Optimal Sleep Environment

After years of getting neck injuries and leg cramps from trying to sleep in planes, trains and cars, I have a huge amount of gratitude and respect for my bedroom. While, yes, my bed is a million times more comfortable than an economy seat, it's actually the air quality, temperature, lack of external noises and lack of light that have positively impacted my sleep quality the most. Your bedroom needs to be an oasis and inviting for sleep.

My bedroom is both technology and clutter-free because I want to go to bed and wake up feeling grateful, purposeful, on-track and rested. Does my phone, TV or computer promote any of those things? No, not really. What you look at before you go to sleep has an impact on what your brain is wiring into your subconscious mind. Instead of getting lost in the abyss of TikTok videos, I have a visual representation of my goals on the back of my bedroom door. I also have affirmations written on Post-it notes and artwork that inspires me. As for clutter, it is triggering, not calming. By keeping your bedroom neat and tidy, your brain will have an easier time relaxing.

Where possible, it's really important you don't use your bedroom for work, eating, watching TV, talking on the phone or serious conversations. When you do these things, your brain associates the space with wakefulness rather than sleepiness. You need your bed to be associated with sleep so your brain maintains this connection. Reading a book (that's not for work or school) is allowed because of the calming and relaxing effect it has on your mind and body. Sex is the other activity that is allowed in the bedroom because it can help you physically and psychologically relax.

Remember when I said we are asleep for approximately a third of our lives? This not-so-little statistic is why I'm a big advocate of investing in bedding. Everyone is going to have their own preference, but having the right mattress, topper, pillow, sheets and comforter can make a huge difference.

⌐ THE EXCEPTION ⌐

I get it. We are living in a time where everything is on our phones, including our meditation apps, ambient soundscapes, alarm clocks and wellness trackers. You can have your phone in your room if you promise not to spiral into a cycle of social-media or email checking and news-reading. If you need sound to get to sleep, download the track prior to going to bed, switch your phone to airplane mode and adjust your screen's backlight to be low and in night mode.

Air Quality

If you have piles of damp towels, shoes strewn about and activewear hanging from the foot of your bed, chances are it's going to smell pretty funky. Your bedroom needs to feel cool, calm and clean.

So, first things first:

- Open a window.
- Use a fan to circulate air.
- Use a humidifier or dehumidifier depending on your needs.
- Pick up dirty clothes off the floor.
- Opt for low-VOC furnishings (volatile organic compounds can off-gas from paints, carpeting and wood).
- Invest in an oxygen-releasing plant such as a peace lily, aloe vera or mother-in-law tongue.

Temperature Check!

If you're in the perimenopause or menopause stage of life, pull up a chair because this section of tips is going to be a game-changer. Rooms that are (or feel) extreme in temperature will disturb your sleep. Studies have shown that rooms with temperatures above 24°C (75°F) increase awakenings, reduce deep sleep, cause more body movements (like throwing a leg out of your bed) and negatively impact the overall quality of your sleep. At the same time, your body's temperature also affects how well you drift off and stay asleep. In order for your body to get the full signal that it's time to produce melatonin, it needs to sense that it's darker *and* cooler! To sleep deeply, your body temperature needs to drop by 1°C.

Tips for Maintaining an Optimal Sleeping Temperature:
- Do your best to get an indoor room temperature between 19–22°C (66–72°F).
- Invest in a cooling mattress pad. Many brands have technology that allows you to choose your sleep temperature and help regulate the surface temperature of your mattress.
- Have a warm Epsom salt bath two hours before bed. (As well as your body absorbing magnesium, the warm water will result in a rebound effect of cooling down your body's core temperature, which helps you fall asleep.)

- Splash your face and hands with cool water.
- Try wearing minimal clothing but put socks on your feet before you go to bed. The socks entice the blood from your body's core to move to your feet, allowing the brain and body to drop in temp. Just remember to kick the socks off before you go to sleep.
- In hot weather, use a clothes horse covered with a wet pillowcase in front of a fan to blast cool moist air onto you.

Quit Making All That Racket!

While we all have that one friend who can fall asleep in the middle of Mardi Gras, the majority of us need a quiet space to unwind and drift off to sleep. Every time you hear a car horn, a neighbour's dog or your snoring partner, your brain will go on alert and pull you out of sleep. This is because our trusty limbic system needs to assess whether the sound is a real threat or not. Unfortunately, your ability to eliminate noise depends on your circumstances as well as how comfortable you feel making these changes.

Tips for Reducing Noise:

- Use a white- or ambient-noise machine. If you live by a train station or a busy inner-city street, the 'raindrops' or the 'ocean waves' can drown out the external noises and hopefully keep you in a deep sleep.
- If your neighbour's dog barks incessantly, could you have a constructive conversation with them about the impact the dog is having on your sleep, and is there anything you can do to help them?
- Living with a snorer? Get your partner checked for sleep apnoea.
- Invest in high-quality ear plugs.

HOW YOUR MOVEMENT AND DIET AFFECT YOUR SLEEP

The way you move your body throughout the day can increase your total sleep time as well as the quality of your NREM and REM stages. And, of course, a good night's sleep dramatically improves your fitness the next day. Regular aerobic exercise can improve sleep, but the benefit depends on an individual's physical fitness, the amount of energy used and the timing of the exercise. In physically fit people, aerobic exercise improves sleep patterns by increasing deep sleep. If you're not used to exercise it can lead to lighter sleep to start with. For example, running a marathon will affect sleep differently from jogging for 30 minutes. Exercising just before bedtime interferes with falling asleep because it stimulates the production of cortisol and adrenaline – not to mention you need to cool down to produce melatonin. It's best to avoid vigorous exercise within two hours of bedtime.

Food also plays a big role in how well we sleep. Hunger can cause wakefulness, while eating can make you sleepy. Unfortunately, it's not as simple as having a light snack before bed or gorging yourself for a marathon sleep session. Like most things in life, you need to find the right balance. A light snack before bed may help you fall and stay asleep, whereas a heavy meal may disrupt sleep because your digestive system has to work overtime. Thirsty? It may be difficult to fall asleep, but drinking too much near bedtime can interrupt sleep by waking you to pee. It all depends on the timing, type and amount of food you eat and fluids you drink.

Foods to Avoid Before Bed:
- Chocolate: High levels of caffeine and sugar can make it hard to relax and fall asleep.
- Cheese: Contains high levels of the amino acid tyramine, which makes us feel alert.
- Ice-cream: The sugar and fat will send your digestive system into overdrive.
- Apples: These are an energy food that may make your blood sugar spike.
- Caffeinated tea: Caffeine is a no-no!
- Alcohol: While it may help you fall asleep, it can also wake you up.
- Deep-fried food, dodgy takeaway food, cheap wine (if you know, you know). These can cause heartburn.

Foods That May Help You Fall Asleep:
- Proteins: Things like eggs, meats, legumes, dairy and tofu contain an amino acid called tryptophan, which converts into melatonin.
- Oats: Eating a small warm bowl of oatmeal can help increase your melatonin and encourage relaxation.
- Almonds: While almonds have loads of antioxidants and are known for reducing inflammation, they also contain magnesium, which can improve sleep.
- Herbal teas: Teas like chamomile, peppermint and lemongrass can help you relax.

CREATE A SLEEP ROUTINE

One of the best ways to train your body to sleep is by sticking to the same routine, even on the weekends. Regardless of the number of hours you slept the night before, try to get out of bed at the same time. A regular rising time is the best way to keep your sleep/wake schedule in line with your biological clock and to overcome your sleep disturbances. Easier said than done! You might need to engage an accountability partner, set two alarms or even leave your curtains open for the sunlight to come in and wake you up. Just remember, this should only be temporary while improving your sleep patterns.

Sleep Rituals

A huge part of my sleep routine is my sleep ritual. Just as you make a plan for your day, it helps to make a routine before you sleep. I try to stay as consistent as possible and start approximately 30 minutes before my scheduled bedtime. These habits serve as a cue for your mind and body that you are settling down for the night and are ready for sleep.

Things to Try in Your Routine:
- Take a magnesium supplement or try an Epsom salt bath.
- Have a hot shower.
- Brush your teeth.

- Splash water on your face and hands (or do your skincare routine).
- Have a gentle stretch for five to 10 minutes. (I'm a tall unit that needs to stretch often. Remember when I said my lounge room looks like a physio's office?)
- Chat with your partner.
- Practise 30 seconds of gratitude.
- Write in your journal.
- Read a book (that isn't on your tablet or phone).
- Meditate (A guided sleep meditation will drift your brain waves down from the beta brain wave of thinking down to the theta brain wave. This is an easier transition into the delta brain wave of sleep. Scan the QR code below to check out our guided sleep meditation.)

Try not to get too rigid with your night-time routine. This should be a relaxing period. If you find yourself worrying about your routine, you are probably overdoing it so just scale a few things back.

Scan this QR code to access the EQ Minds Blissful Sleep meditation.

HOW TO FALL ASLEEP OR GET BACK TO SLEEP

There are a lot of reasons why we might struggle to fall asleep or prematurely wake up. It could be the temperature in your room, thirst, hunger, the need to pee, noise or something a little more difficult to correct: stress. It comes as no surprise that if you are experiencing stress in your life, chances are you are tossing and turning at night. The stress may be related to your relationship, job, finances, children or your health. When the stress goes away, the majority of people's sleep starts to return to normal. However, some people, those who are predisposed to insomnia, continue to have sleep problems. (If that's you, don't worry, we'll talk about insomnia and professional help later.) When we are worried or stressed, our minds struggle to calm down and cortisol levels can stay high. Have you ever laid down to fall asleep and spiralled into negative self-talk about previous conversations, money or your never-ending list of things to do? Same. Below are a few ways you can reduce your stress before bed and help unwind your mind.

Take Time to Decompress

Every evening we need time to unwind and decompress from the day to perform our best the next day. This will look different for everyone, but I recommend scheduling a minimum of one hour of relaxation time in the evening. It is imperative you carve out time for this, otherwise it will likely fill up with work. The activity can be anything that helps you relax, such as doing a puzzle, reading, listening to music, socialising with friends, listening to a podcast, stretching, taking a bath or meditating. Protect your evenings. This is why learning to say 'No' is critical.

Do a Mind Dump

In your journal, dump all of your thoughts onto the page and don't stop writing until you are finished. This exercise allows you to get everything out of your memory centre, so you can either let the thoughts go or process them another time.

Some journal prompts are:

- What on your to-do list is making you anxious?
- What is on your mind?
- What are your biggest fears about not getting enough sleep?

Take a Few Things Off Your Plate

In your journal, write down everything you have coming up in the next week. Sometimes this alone will shock you by seeing just how much you have on your plate. Next to each item, write down what you can outsource. Be creative here. This exercise shouldn't take you more than an hour and can buy you incredible amounts of time. And if you're sitting there thinking you don't have an hour to do this, I'm going to argue that you need it more than anyone else. Lightening your load will drastically lower your stress levels and help you sleep better. Time is our most precious resource. Choose the things that nourish you, give you energy and that are the highest value for you right now. This may change over time, so do this task based on where you are today.

Tips for Going Back to Sleep:

- Avoid clock-watching: Frequently checking your phone or clock during the night can wake you up and reinforce negative thoughts like, *Oh no, it's only 1 am and I'm done for the night.* Instead, put your clock facing away from the bed so you aren't tempted to keep looking at it.
- Trust that by lying still, your body is still getting much-needed rest.
- Reverse it: Think about what you did in the day, but in reverse order (e.g. *I turned off the light, I set my alarm, I lay down …*)
- Use the 1000–0 Technique: There is a reason why the majority of guided sleep meditations get you to count backwards from 1000 to zero. It gives your brain the opportunity to focus on something specific so you aren't thinking about two things at once, and it's boring enough to make you drift off to sleep somewhere along the countdown.
- Don't lie in bed awake for a long time: If you're still awake after 20–30 minutes or you are feeling anxious, get up and do something relaxing until you feel sleepy again. Just remember: no screens! You could do something like reading by lamplight.
- If the sensation keeping you awake is hunger, have a warm piece of toast.
- If it's thirst, your body could need help detoxing. Keep a glass of water next to your bed.

TO NAP OR NOT TO NAP?

This sounds cruel, especially for people who are suffering from insomnia, but naps aren't your friend. When you nap, it undermines all the hard work you have been doing. If you suffer with insomnia, napping disrupts the natural sleep/wake circadian rhythm and interferes with your sleep that night. As hard as it is, staying awake all day will help you feel sleepier that evening and will increase your chance of sleeping through the night.

Please note: if you are feeling exceptionally tired, to the point of exhaustion, and it will be detrimental to operating equipment or driving a vehicle, you should take a nap. You should also seek professional help from your GP or at a sleep clinic.

Tips to Help Avoid Napping:
- Try doing something active when you feel yourself getting tired in the afternoon.
- Take a cold shower to awaken your senses.
- Try a guided meditation to recharge yourself without slipping into a deep sleep.
- Schedule a catch-up with a friend, in person or on the phone.
- Run errands and keep yourself busy.

INSOMNIA AND SEVERE SLEEPING STRUGGLES

When I had insomnia, I honestly thought no one could ever under-stand the severity. People with insomnia or poor sleep habits usually have unhelpful thoughts. Sometimes we are aware of these thoughts and thinking patterns and other times they occur automatically because we have been caught up in feedback loops. The more we keep thinking about something, the more it is wired into the brain.

Cognitions (a scientific term for thoughts, beliefs, expectations and interpretations) flow through our minds almost all of the time during our waking hours. Sometimes we are aware of these cognitions, but often they occur in an automatic way, almost like a mental reflex in response to a stimulus around us. Whether we are aware of them or not, our cognitions often determine how we feel – and our feelings impact our actions. For people with insomnia, unhelpful thoughts often lead to negative feelings, which can interfere with sleep. Below are common types of negative thinking and examples of how to actively reframe them.

- All-or-nothing thinking: This is when you view situations in black-and-white terms and as entirely good or bad. This thinking style has the reality of missing the grey zone, because the world is far more complex than this.
  - Instead of thinking: *If I don't sleep well tonight, I will never be able to sleep well ever again,* try saying to yourself, *If I don't sleep tonight, I'm just going through a phase and I know I will sleep well again soon.*
- Over-generalising: This common type of unhelpful thinking is about seeing a pattern based on a single event or being too broad (typically negative) with the conclusions we draw. In this thinking pattern, insomnia is viewed as a never-ending pattern.
  - Instead of thinking: *My sleep is always rubbish – nothing is going to work for me,* try saying to yourself, *My sleep is rubbish this week – however, with the right tools and consistency of good habits I will be able to enjoy sleep again.*
- Catastrophising or exaggerating: When we blow things out of proportion, we give events more weight than what they really deserve.
  - Instead of thinking: *If I don't get enough sleep tonight, I won't be able to work tomorrow,* try saying to yourself, *If I don't get enough sleep tonight, I will be able to make it through tomorrow. I have had a restless night before and was able to be productive at work.*
- Jumping to conclusions: When we jump to conclusions we are trying to fortune-tell the future. When you try to guess what will happen to you in the future, you become caught up in these feedback loops and it can cause anxiety. There are many variables that cause diseases, not just a severe lack of sleep.

– Instead of thinking: *If I don't get over my sleep problems, I will get early-onset dementia,* try saying to yourself, *I'm going to live in the moment and deal with the night as it comes.*

- Selective attention: With selective attention, you only pay attention to certain types of information. Perhaps it was a warm night, or you didn't unwind properly, or there could be other variables for you not sleeping. Try looking at the overall picture before drawing conclusions and making judgements.
  – Instead of thinking: *I can only go to sleep if my room is completely quiet. Last night there was noise on the street, and I knew I wouldn't be able to sleep,* try saying to yourself, *I didn't sleep that well last night. There could have been a few reasons. Tonight I'll try the white-noise app so outside noises don't disturb me.*

The Sleep-restriction Technique

The sleep-restriction technique is a very important part of recovering from insomnia for many people. To try it, reduce the amount of time you spend lying in bed so it matches the time you are actually asleep. For example, if you typically spend nine hours in bed, but you are only sleeping six hours, then you are spending three hours awake in bed. Spending lots of time awake in your bed typically leads to more sleep disruption.

⌐ RECORDING YOUR SLEEP ⌐

If you're suffering from insomnia or poor sleep, take a moment now to identify how you are going to record your sleep. This could be good old-fashioned pen and paper or a digital sleep-tracking device. Over the next week, make a note of things like how long you laid down for and how many hours you were actually asleep. From there, you can start restricting your sleeping window to the hours you spend sleeping.

Sleep restriction works by pulling together the total amount of sleep obtained in one period and then makes you more tired the next night, to achieve greater time asleep.

WHEN TO SEEK PROFESSIONAL HELP

Sometimes you need the big guns and, as you know, I'm a huge fan of taking a deeper look into what's happening in my mind and body. If you have been practising everything from this chapter for three or more weeks and you're still struggling to sleep, or you feel like there is something physically preventing you from falling asleep, I highly recommend seeing your GP, or an integrated doctor, and getting your blood tested to check the levels of your magnesium, cortisol, iron and vitamin D.

I have also found working with cognitive behavioural therapists to be highly beneficial. They have numerous techniques designed to break bad habits and address anxiety. Ask your GP for a referral to see a psychologist. You could also ask them about doing a sleep study.

IN YOUR JOURNAL

- Start keeping track of the quality and length of your sleep. How are you feeling when you lie down at night and wake up in the morning?
- Can you identify anything that may be disrupting your sleep?
- Create your own pre-sleep routine using the steps in this chapter as a guide. Make a list of the things you currently spend time on that you could cut back or replace with a more relaxing habit.

09
YOUR MINDFULNESS

I WANT YOU to take a moment and think about a typical day in your life. From the moment your feet hit the floor in the morning to the time your head hits the pillow at night (and you finally put down your phone), how much information do you think you receive and process? How many new faces do you see? How many names are you trying to remember? How many little fires are you trying to put out? How much sleep are you operating on? How long did you spend scrolling through a newsfeed peppered with updates from high-school friends and political news stories? How many times do feelings of guilt or fear wash over you? How many breaks do you take? How much are you reflecting on the past? How much are you worrying about the future? How much are you expressing gratitude for your present moment?

Mindfulness is a word we are hearing more and more, but a lot of people don't *really* understand what it means and how it can help our performance. I often get asked if it's meditation. While, yes, meditation is a major part of mindfulness, it's not the full equation. Mindfulness operates on multiple levels. Meditation is the groundwork and maintenance you do in order to become and stay more powerful than your thoughts.

The second part of mindfulness is putting what you practise during meditation into action in everyday life to move, breathe, work, love, eat, drink, speak and, most importantly, *think* mindfully. As we continue to live in a world with the number of stimuli growing exponentially, we can easily feel like our unconscious mind is overloaded to the point of (almost) no return. By practising and mastering mindfulness, you'll not only program your brain's cruise-control mode to keep you in the present moment, but also put yourself back in the driver's seat.

If you haven't mastered a mindful approach to the day or set a clear intention, so much of what you do can feel reactive. Of course, things will come up that you never could have anticipated, but instead of a knee-jerk response that can leave you feeling anxious, out of control, agitated, worried, short-tempered or depressed, having a mindful brain can help you proactively make decisions that will allow you to be in control and in a state of acceptance. Life will always send something your way that has the potential to throw you off kilter – be it work, health, family, friends or community. Mindfulness is what's going to help keep you steady.

⌐ BENEFITS OF PRACTISING MINDFULNESS ¬

- ☐ helps you find clarity in a world full of distractions
- ☐ helps you make values-based decisions
- ☐ helps you calmly and rationally respond to thoughts that may otherwise be distressing
- ☐ helps you transition to and from the different moments in your day
- ☐ increases your compassion for yourself and others.

MEDITATION IS THE NEW MEDICINE

Okay, so it's actually probably the *oldest* medicine. For several thousand years (dating as far back as 500 BCE), cultures around the world have used meditation for spiritual, secular and medicinal purposes. As meditation started making its way into Western culture in the twentieth century, scientists began doing studies and quickly realised what they'd been missing out on.

Research has shown that consistent mindfulness practices (like meditation) can change the way your brain physically looks and how it communicates. As I mentioned earlier in the book, in a study looking at mindfulness, scientists saw a decrease in the size of the amygdala, which is your brain's stress centre and alarm system. With a smaller, less reactive amygdala, you're more likely to remain calmer in stressful situations and more in control of your emotions and actions. Another study showed an increase in the size of the hippocampus, which is your brain's memory centre. When you have a larger, better-performing hippocampus, you're more likely to have more mental stamina, a quicker reaction time and improved memory and learning skills. More research has shown that meditation can even help your brain become better at focusing. When looking at a group of meditators versus non-meditators, scientists saw differences in the part of the brain responsible for spontaneous thought. The meditators had more stability and were able to focus better. This has obvious benefits when working to a deadline, having conversations or trying to learn something.

One of my favourite studies on the power of meditation measured its effects on your hormones compared with running. You've heard of a 'runner's high', right? Well, a study looking into the effects of running and meditation showed that meditation has the power to make your body release the same feel-good, high-energy hormones as running. I'm not saying you shouldn't go for a run, but I am saying that you don't have to pound the pavement every day to get the runner's high! (Your knee joints will thank you.)

While your mindset will benefit from meditation, your heart is going to love it, too. In 2017, the American Heart Association published a study that concluded consistent meditation can reduce cardiovascular risks and blood pressure, help prevent a second heart attack or stroke, improve psychological and physiological reactions to stress and strengthen brain pathways responsible for self-regulation and healthy habit changes. More and more, we're seeing doctors prescribe meditation for their patients.

⌐ MINDFULNESS AND PAIN ⌐

In a study looking at mindfulness and pain, mindfulness practitioners were able to reduce discomfort by 22 per cent and anticipatory anxiety by 29 per cent during a mindful state. Scans of the participants' brains showed that there was a decrease in activity in the lateral prefrontal cortex and increased activation in the right posterior insula during stimulation of pain, and increased rostral anterior cingulate cortex activation during the anticipation of pain. If you're someone who is recovering from an injury or experiencing chronic pain, mindfulness and meditation could help!

MINDFULNESS: WHERE TO BEGIN

Mindfulness begins with gaining control of your unconscious mind and then consciously deciding to acknowledge, ignore or react to your thoughts, feelings and emotions. I'm not going to lie; it's easier said than done. Remember in Chapter 3: Your Mind when I said that you have over 70,000 thoughts a day? Well, the first few times you try to gain a clear mind, they may hit you like a hurricane! Don't worry, you will learn very quickly how to weather these types of thought storms.

Meditating 101

Meditating is a practice used to focus your mind on something (or nothing) for a designated period of time. The act of meditating can be done lying down, sitting up, with eyes open or eyes shut, alone or in a group. It can be led by a coach, soundtrack, prompt or be self-guided. The meditations themselves can also be really different. For example, you may choose to do a meditation designed to help you welcome your thoughts, and then bid them farewell. This type is intended to help you gain control of your emotions and decision-making process. Other types of meditations could be for grief, body awareness, mindful eating, relationships with others, loving-kindness, gratitude, sleep, focus, productivity or to connect with your higher self.

In a perfect world, I'd love for everyone who has a busy mind to meditate for a minimum of 10 minutes a day, but alas, the world is not perfect. It's also not a realistic starting point, which is why I recommend beginning with a daily three-minute meditation. The main goal here is consistency; if you can consistently commit to working on your mindfulness, it will eventually become a habit. Once you've well and truly owned this habit, I guarantee you will love it so much it will become not a chore, but a daily practice you look forward to.

How to Meditate and Tips for Success

Find a Time

When it comes to meditating, I try to fit it in wherever I can. Sometimes it's in the morning before my house begins to stir, sometimes it's when I'm taking off or landing on a flight, and other times it's when I'm walking or preparing for bed. I'll even do it in the back of an Uber! The main point is that I want you to fit it in when you can. Remember, three minutes is all you need.

Find a Vibe

If you're planning to meditate at home, I recommend setting up a little meditation space in your bedroom or spare room. You could have a cushion, blanket, salt lamp, candles, essential oils … really anything that will help make your space and mind feel calm. If, like me, you're someone who is always on the move, may I suggest investing in noise-cancelling headphones? They really help me focus. I also carry a small bottle of one of my favourite essential oils. (My go-tos include lavender, frankincense and chamomile.) Taking a deep inhale of essential oils before beginning my meditation creates a zen space by anchoring me to my senses. It also allows me to associate certain smells with meditating, which is great for building (brain) muscle-memory.

⌐ ON NOISE ⌐

Silence is great, but sometimes we don't have the luxury of having somewhere quiet to sit. If you can find a secluded place on your balcony or in a nearby park or away from people at the beach then that's great. If you can't find a quiet place, use the noise as part of your meditation practice. Just like when we learn to observe our thoughts in meditation, you can learn to observe the sounds – without passing any judgement, letting them pass you by like leaves down a babbling brook.

Find an App (and Voice!) That Works for You

While you can absolutely meditate without any sort of guide, music or ambient noise, you may find it beneficial to explore a mindfulness app (which I will talk more about shortly), website or track that can help you stay focused and connected to your breath. It's important to find an auditory style that you enjoy and don't find irritating. (Nothing will distract you more than someone whose voice grates on you.) Hot tip: if using a guided track, download the meditation and then put your phone on airplane mode.

Take a Seat

Start by sitting cross-legged on the floor or upright in a chair (or on the train, in the back of a car or on a park bench!). Some prefer to lie down, but I find sitting with a tall spine and upright posture helps me avoid drifting off to sleep. Next, either place your palms on your legs facing down (to feel grounded) or facing up (to feel lifted, abundant and inspired). You can also place them in a *gyan mudra* position, which is where your thumb and index finger connect to form a circle.

Relax Your Pose

Take a few moments to scan your body to identify where you might be holding any tension. Do a big shoulder roll: lift up your shoulders, then pull them away from your ears, tucking your chin slightly so your neck is long and your spine is straight, and relaxing your tongue so it lays in the bottom of your mouth, not pressing against the roof. Gently close your eyes; you don't want to feel any squeezing of the eyelids or furrowing of the brow. (If you feel that this is too uncomfortable, you can gently gaze downwards at a spot on the floor.)

Expect Your Mind to Wander

If you get distracted, that is completely normal. A big part of meditating is identifying when the distractions happen and then consciously bringing yourself back to your breath, mantra or meditation guide. Look at it this way: every time you successfully bring your attention back to your practice, you're basically doing one bicep curl for your brain!

Where to Find Meditations

As I mentioned before, you can simply shut your eyes and focus on your breathing anytime, anywhere (if you're not operating any sort of machinery!). However, a lot of people love using an audio track to help guide them through their meditation. This could be music, ambient noise or a person speaking. The great news about living in a world full of so many movers and shakers is that we have a lot of websites, apps and audio tracks to choose from. There are loads of free or donation-based options including YouTube and Medito. Just be aware that with sites like YouTube, if you don't pay for a premium subscription, your meditative state may be disrupted by a pesky advertisement.

As an accredited mindfulness and meditation coach, I've recorded numerous meditations that you can listen to via my website, EQ Minds, as well as on InsightTimer. Choosing the right platform(s) and voices to listen to is a highly personal decision. I won't be offended at all if my voice isn't for you! Below is just a surface-scratching list of the different digital meditation platforms to start exploring.

Websites:
- EQ Minds
- YouTube.

Apps:
- InsightTimer
- Medito
- Calm
- Headspace
- Smiling Minds
- Buddhify.

Scan this QR code to access the EQ Minds Guided Meditation platform.

TRANSITIONS

Have you ever hung up from a more-than-frustrating phone call with someone, and silently mouthed (or said out loud) 'F@*k!', and then had to go straight into a meeting with a new team member you're supposed to be excitedly welcoming on board? I have, and I know just how easy it is to carry the anger and frustration you felt on that phone call into your next meeting for the day. In fact, I know how easy it is to carry it all day long and even bring it into bed with you at night.

Meditation
CHEAT SHEET

1

FIND YOUR GUIDE
If you're new to meditation, start with a guided practice. Find a voice you like.

2

COMMIT THE TIME
Find a time that suits your life. Schedule it into your calendar and commit.

3

CREATE YOUR VIBE
Create a space that you find relaxing: use cushions, blankets, essential oils etc. If you are travelling, pack your noise-cancelling headphones.

4

TAKE A SEAT
Do the Seven-point Posture Check on page 130.

5

START
The best time to start is NOW.

6

EXPECT YOUR MIND TO WANDER
It happens to us all. You are training the brain to recognise the thought and bring the thought back.

7

REFLECT
Do an internal check. How do you feel now compared with when you started?

8

PRACTISE
Nothing is perfect at the start. You have to train your brain to find the space between your thoughts.

Meditation
SEVEN-POINT POSTURE CHECK

1 SIT

Get comfortable. Sit cross-legged on the floor or upright in a chair.

2 SPINE

Sit up with a tall spine and upright posture to help avoid drifting off to sleep.

3 SHOULDERS

Do a big shoulder roll to create space between your shoulders and your ears.

4 HANDS

Place your palms on your legs facing down to feel grounded or facing up to feel lifted and inspired.

5 CHIN

Tuck your chin slightly so your neck is long and your spine is straight.

6 JAW

Relax your jaw. A little movement from side to side or opening and closing it gently can help you relax.

7 EYES

Gently close your eyes. You don't want to feel any squeezing of the eyelids or furrowing of the brow.

We have transitions all day long and it's very easy to take whatever energy you've absorbed from one event into another. Let's start with the most common (and avoidable) negative transition: you wake up in the morning and pick up your phone. Like always, you navigate to the news and see that the world is still enduring a global pandemic. Next, you open your work group-chat and it's not good. Your offsider totally just threw you under the bus. Obviously, the world sucks, work sucks and today is going to suck. Look at that: before you even had a chance to mindfully make your day great, you started Transition #1 off with some super negative energy.

What's next? You're at work and you've already had it out with your offsider. You discover their betrayal really wasn't intentional; it was the result of a series of miscommunications. Even though it's resolved, you're still frustrated AF when you meet up with your partner for a lunch date. You haven't had time for yourselves in a few weeks, and while they're excitedly trying to tell you about a work win they had, all you can think about is your own work's communication channels and processes and how flawed they are and if only those were better, you wouldn't have been publicly shamed in the work group-chat … 'You're not even listening to me,' your partner says. Oh great, now you think your relationship sucks, too.

I think you get where I'm going with this. The negative or positive energy you draw from the different experiences you have affects the next experience and the next. If you don't consciously let go of the negative vibes (or, at the very least, compartmentalise them for later), you can unintentionally project negativity onto others. (And then, *no one* is happy.) This is why I always take a moment to decompress after a difficult phone call, meeting, workflow session or life chat. By taking a moment to do some deep breathing and conscious letting-go, you're giving your brain a little micro-shower and actively practising mindfulness!

BREATHWORK

One of the best ways to cleanse your brain, recharge your body and calm down when you're feeling panicked is by doing breathwork. When we get engrossed in our to-do lists, daily schedules, interactions with others and ever-changing emotions, we lose track of the flow of life. The way we breathe is strongly linked to the way we feel. When we are relaxed, we breathe slowly; when we are stressed, we breathe more quickly. We also tend to alternate between shallow breaths that are felt mostly in our lungs and deep breaths that fill our tummy. Ideally, when doing breathwork, you want to make sure you are using a stomach-breathing style rather than a chest-breathing style. You can check this by placing your hand on your stomach and feeling it rise while you breathe in.

In order for your body to run efficiently, there needs to be a balance between oxygen and carbon dioxide. Depending on our level of activity, sometimes we need more and sometimes we need less of each. For example, when we are relaxed, we need less of each to remain balanced. When we become anxious, the balance can become easily disrupted. Often, we end up over-breathing, or even hyperventilating, which can lead to breathing too much oxygen. When your body notices this imbalance, it can respond with chemical changes that produce physical symptoms such as dizziness, breathlessness, blurred vision and muscle stiffness. The good news is you have everything you need to restore the balance, decrease your heart rate and create a sense of calm by using breathwork.

The breath is truly amazing. It brings us life and energy, it sustains us, and most of the time we don't even notice it. While we don't have to focus on our breathing to stay alive, paying attention to it while we meditate or sit can remind us of the miracle of life. It can be really powerful to sit and observe our breathing, counting the inhales and exhales.

But Chelsea, why would simply being aware of my breathing help restore my balance?

When we focus on our breathing and intentionally slow it down, achieving a more controlled rhythm, we activate the parasympathetic nervous system; this helps create a sense of calm that decreases heart rate, blood pressure and muscle tension. It also helps you reconnect to your body and shifts your awareness away from the continual chatter in your mind (or the panic attack that may be holding you hostage). Need one more selling point for breathwork? It can dampen your sympathetic nervous system, which is associated with your fight-or-flight response. It's your body's built-in chill pill!

From his lab at Stanford University, respected American neuroscientist Dr Andrew Huberman is constantly releasing compelling research on the benefits of using breathwork to destress, focus, sleep better, heighten or lower your arousal, and enhance your cognitive performance. You only have to listen to 20 seconds of his podcast, *Huberman Lab*, or watch him on YouTube to discover that there are *a lot* of different ways we can breathe. However, if you're looking to dial in to a calm and focused state, you're going to want to work on box breathing first.

Here's How You Can Do Box Breathing:
1. Take a deep inhale through your nose for four seconds.
2. Hold your breath for four seconds.
3. Exhale through your mouth for four seconds.
4. Hold your breath for four seconds.
5. Rinse and repeat!

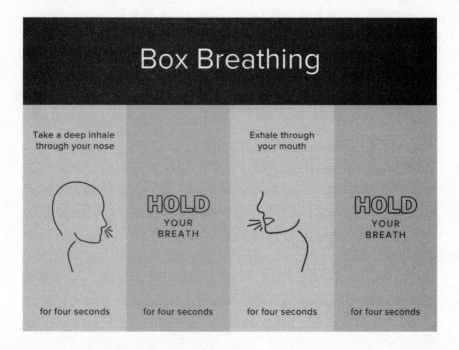

Box Breathing

| Take a deep inhale through your nose | HOLD YOUR BREATH | Exhale through your mouth | HOLD YOUR BREATH |
| for four seconds | for four seconds | for four seconds | for four seconds |

Now let's try a breathing exercise designed to help reduce anxiety and stress called physiological sigh breathing. Dr Huberman often talks about our need to be able to self-regulate and destress in real time because it's not always possible to disengage from every stress-inducing activity. He also talks about how our brains typically do a good job of knowing when our CO_2 levels get too high and triggering adjustments to our breathing, even when we sleep! Have you ever noticed someone take two inhales before a big exhale while they're sleeping? Or have you ever found yourself doing it when you're feeling claustrophobic? This double inhale, single exhale style of breathing does a few things. The first inhale dilates the air sacs of your lungs and pulls out carbon dioxide, while the second inhale dilates them a little more, removing even more carbon dioxide from your lungs. It engages the neurons in the brain stem, improves your nervous system, calms the phrenic nerve, balances the ratio of carbon dioxide and oxygen in your body and causes a direct calming response.

Let's try physiological sigh breathing:

1 Take a deep and extended inhale through your nose.
2 Before exhaling, take another inhale through your nose. (This one won't be quite as deep but try to make it count!)
3 Now do an extended and audible exhale through your mouth (like a loud sigh).
4 Repeat as many times as needed.

We've been told from a young age to *be quiet* and *calm down* and are literally shushed. At school and in the workplace, we are told both explicitly and implicitly not to make waves and to work quietly. Needless to say, there is something inside of us that is craving some unbridled release, and physiological sigh breathing is one way to do this. For example, let's say you hit your finger with a hammer (*hard*) ... are you going to be quiet about it? Chances are you're going to scream *OUCH* (or another four-letter word that starts with F). That's because making loud noises can help us to cope with pain and it can even have

⌐ SIXTY SECONDS TO BREATHE ⌐

1. Find a comfortable spot to sit, stand or lie down.
2. Gently close your eyes or gaze softly in front of you.
3. Take a deep breath in for four seconds* (through the nose if possible).
4. Hold your breath for two seconds.
5. Release the breath for six seconds (through the nose if possible), then pause and repeat steps three through five.
6. Say to yourself: *I am calm and I am relaxed.*
7. Do this for one minute (or more!).

If you find it difficult to slow your breath to this rate, you can breathe in for three seconds, hold for one and then breathe out for four seconds.

an analgesic effect. It's incredible that the sound, air and vibration of your own voice can convert into electrical properties within your inner ear, acting like energy to your brain, nourishing your nervous system and having a profound effect on your mood. Of course, you probably can't do this at 9 am in the open-plan office, but whenever you're feeling stressed or triggered, find a space and put some sound to your breath. This is – to date – the fastest way we know of to disengage with stress.

While breathwork is something that can help you calm down when you're feeling stressed or panicked, it's also something that can help you remain mindful about your body and energy levels regularly. I suggest trying to practise slow breathwork once or twice a day. By simply taking a minute to consciously breathe, you will develop a more relaxed breathing habit across the board. Remember, the key to progress is practice, so try to set some time aside each day. You can do this by having an alert on your phone or make it part of your morning or evening routine.

MINDFUL MOVEMENTS

Practising mindfulness doesn't just mean sitting cross-legged under a tree and meditating before starting your day. In fact, being mindful can be applied to all of your daily actions, including when you move. In Chapter 7: Your Movement and Energy, I talked about how your movement impacts circulation, digestion, metabolism, immunity and brain function. When moving for mindfulness, you simply require action and awareness. The difference between mindful movement and other sport-based or goal-driven exercise is the intent behind the practice. For example, when we go about mindful movement, we aren't aiming to win, beat a certain running time, or lift a heavier weight, and so the competitive aspect is eliminated. Instead, mindful movement focuses on the present moment and is an opportunity for us to non-judgementally celebrate what our body can actually do. As well as the physical benefits, mindful movement helps boost mental and emotional health. When we become more connected and show greater self-awareness, we also develop empathy, compassion, focus and curiosity.

You only get one body and, when used, moved and treated correctly, it can be our greatest weapon against depression. Mindful movement should be a celebration of what your amazing body can do. Every day, fall in love with taking care of your body.

MINDFUL MOVEMENT WALKING EXERCISE

One of the best ways to start mindfully moving is putting one foot in front of the other. That's right! Take a walk. You can do this before you start your day, on your coffee run, during a lunch break, with the kids on the way home from school or in the evening after dinner.

1. As you begin walking, become aware of your posture. What are your shoulders doing? Is your weight evenly distributed on your feet? Can you feel the soles of your feet pressing the ground?
2. Walk slowly and notice the gentle rhythm you're creating as each foot touches the ground.
3. Notice how your feet feel in your shoes and acknowledge the sensation of creating a comfortable stride, then bring your attention to your breath. Take a big inhale and then slowly exhale.
4. Return to a comfortable breath and now start looking at everything around you. What do you see, hear, smell and feel? Can you reach out and run your hand through leaves? Can you feel moisture in the air? Do you smell a bakery making fresh loaves of bread?
5. Now, take a moment to notice your thoughts. What is your general mood? Are you feeling any emotions? As you take note of what they are, simply breathe, relax and smile.
6. Bring your awareness back to the sensation of your feet on the ground. Listen to your breath. Thank your body for taking the time to move.
7. Continue this for five to 15 minutes, or for however long you feel comfortable and present.

TACKLING ANXIOUS THOUGHTS

One minute you're captivated by the lilies you just planted and then, all of a sudden, you're hit with a wave of anxiety and one of the following thoughts:

My dog is going to die one day.

My colleagues must hate me for not supporting their pitch.

The pain in my stomach must be cancer.

Anxious thoughts love creeping in, which is why I like to look at them head-on and mindfully ask:

1. Is it realistic?
2. Is it happening now?
3. Is it within my control?
4. Will it matter in 10 years?

Nine out of 10 times, only one of these questions (if any) gets a 'Yes'. When that happens, it's time to turn to a friend, family member, GP or therapist.

MINDFUL HOBBIES

Have you ever noticed how much easier it is to sit with your thoughts if you can keep your hands busy? By adding in an activity such as knitting, gardening or doing a puzzle, you can simultaneously make something pretty cool while observing your thoughts in a calm and controlled manner.

Hobbies That Promote Mindfulness:
- knitting, crocheting, sewing, cross-stitching
- crossword puzzles
- jigsaw puzzles
- chess and other board games

- painting
- colouring in
- gardening
- pottery
- beading.

MINDFUL EATING

The cool thing about mindfulness is that it teaches us the power of being fully aware. While it definitely helps us become less reactive to the world around us, it also teaches us to *enjoy* the world around us. All too often, we drift through life not really taking notice of the sensory experiences we are having at any given moment. One of my favourite activities to encourage this is mindfully eating ... chocolate. If you have chocolate nearby, go and grab a piece. If not, dog-ear this page and come back later because I'm going to tell you how to have the ultimate chocolate-eating sensory experience!

Mindful Chocolate-eating Activity:
- Touch: Take one piece of chocolate and hold it in the palm of your hand. What is the weight like? Is it heavy or light? Is it cold, warm or room temperature? Is it slightly melted?
- Sight: Take the time to really look at the chocolate. Does it have any grooves or ridges? Are there any bits of nuts or candy sticking out? Turn it over in between your finger and thumb. What does it look like on the other side?
- Scent: Hold the chocolate beneath your nose. What do you notice as you breathe in? Does it have a smell? Are there any other flavours you can smell in the chocolate? Mint? Citrus? Caramel?
- Taste: Put the chocolate on your tongue and gently close your mouth. What does the chocolate taste like? Explore the sensations with your tongue. What is your mouth doing? Are you salivating? Is the chocolate melting?
- Hear: As you're chewing the chocolate, do you need to crunch any nuts? Can you hear a snap in the block?

- Feel: How is your body responding to the chocolate? What is your tongue doing? Is it cleaning your teeth? Exploring the roof of your mouth?
- Visualise: Notice the urgency to swallow the chocolate. See if you can visualise it going down the back of your throat, down your oesophagus and into your stomach. Notice a second or third swallow. Notice what your tongue does after you have finished swallowing. Is it cleaning your teeth again?
- Reflect: Spend a few moments noticing what your mind is doing. Is there an aftertaste? Have you ever experienced eating chocolate like this before? How often have we eaten chocolate while watching a movie and the entire packet has vanished before we even remember tasting one bite? Did you notice your experience of eating the chocolate was transformed by the simple act of focusing on it?

When people are experiencing stress in their lives, they often reach for food for comfort. (Can you even say you've studied for exams if you haven't panic-binged a pack of Tim Tams?) By trying to eat mindfully at every snack and meal, you're less likely to overeat because your body and brain will get the message that you're nourishing it thanks to the focus you're giving your senses!

On the flip side, sometimes stress can take away our appetite, which leaves our bodies and brains seeking nourishment. When we're hungry (even if we aren't aware of it), we can find it difficult to focus, we lack energy and it can feel like we have brain fog. A great way to ensure you're eating mindfully is by blocking out your mealtimes for each day, taking away distractions and actively noticing the sensory experience.

MINDFUL EATING TIPS

☐ Schedule in your mealtimes.

☐ Prep your meals if necessary.

☐ Eat without distractions (e.g. don't check your email or scroll through social media).

☐ Take notice of the colours and textures of your food.

☐ Inhale the aromas.

☐ Thank your body and brain by giving it the food it needs to feel nourished.

GRATITUDE AND MINDFULNESS (AS GOOD TOGETHER AS VEGEMITE AND TOAST!)

Mindfulness and gratitude go hand in hand, which is why I want to bring up the importance of gratitude again. I know we talked a lot about this in Chapter 6: Your Morning Routine, but I want to reiterate that when we are grateful in a given moment, we are less likely to be swept up in the past, caught up in reactivity or hyper-focused on the future. While just 30 seconds of expressing gratitude a day physically makes the insula part of your brain stronger, the real power of gratitude is that it makes you focus on what is working in your life in the present moment.

You can express your gratitude anytime and anywhere, but I suggest setting a few reminders on your phone each day to take a moment to either think, say or write the following:

- someone whom you're grateful for
- an opportunity you're grateful for
- an aspect of your health that you're grateful for.

BE GRATEFUL FOR ALL OF YOUR EMOTIONS (EVEN ANXIETY)

As someone who experiences anxiety from time to time, I find it really helpful to consider the anxious feelings in my stomach or thoughts racing through my mind with gratitude. Sounds a little counterintuitive, but by saying, 'I'm grateful that I'm feeling like this because it shows I really care about what I'm doing,' I help welcome the somewhat-unwelcomed feelings and channel them into my drive for whatever I'm working on or trying to overcome.

SHOWING LOVING-KINDNESS TO YOURSELF AND OTHERS

I love to surf, but I admit I have no technique and I am not trained. I just love the feeling when my board hits the water and, as the mist cools down my face, how I think about nothing else except the sensory experience I'm having.

While surfing allows me to be free and to simply play, it also does something else: it shows me how I judge myself and how, if I let myself, I can get in my own way. When I'm mindfully surfing, I'm taking notice of how the wax on my board feels against my feet. I'm feeling my hair on my face, the seawater in my eyes, the burn in my muscles and the sensation of water catching me when I fall. I'm also highly aware of my inner monologue:

You should be standing up on all waves. Why haven't you mastered this yet?

You can't surf just for the sheer joy of it – you need to be doing more productive things with your time.

When people see you on a surfboard, they think you are an amateur.

When we engage in a new hobby, a new job, a new relationship, a new project, our inner critic loves to get involved. It likes to tell us we are not good enough. So how do we silence our inner critic and put it in its place? The answer is self-compassion.

Embracing Self-Compassion and Compassion for Others

By cultivating self-compassion, we can fundamentally shift how we relate to ourselves and other people. Instead of meeting our imperfections with self-blame and our inner critic, we can mindfully bring a sense of kindness and love to our experiences, thoughts and emotions. As you develop your ability to show self-compassion and compassion for others, you'll not only improve your emotional wellbeing, but also increase your happiness as well as that of those around you. Living a life of compassion is easier than you think. Consider a few of these ways to do things differently, silence your inner critic and ego and, as a result, live a life of fulfilment.

1. Practise Independent or Guided Loving-kindness and Compassion Meditations

These types of meditation practices allow you to send loving-kindness to yourself, someone whom you love, a stranger, someone whom you have a difficult relationship with or the whole globe. Many guided meditation apps, such as Headspace, Calm and Smiling Mind, have loving-kindness and compassion meditations to get you started. If you'd like to do a meditation without assistance, I recommend repeating the following phrases with your eyes shut:

May I be happy.   *May I live with ease.*

May I be safe.   *May I live with peace.*

2. Do a Random Act of Kindness

A random act of kindness is doing a selfless act for someone without expecting to be repaid. Paying it forward like this is contagious and has a positive effect through social networks far and wide. Here are some ideas for random acts of kindness:

- Hold the door open for someone.
- Bring a bag to pick up rubbish on your walk.
- Pay for a stranger's coffee.
- Give a compliment.
- Volunteer your time to a charity.

LOVING-KINDNESS MEDITATIONS

Did you know that when we meditate and practise loving-kindness and compassion, studies have show there is an increase of grey matter concentration in multiple areas of the brain, including the temporoparietal function? One of the happiest humans on this planet to be measured by science is Matthieu Ricard. When his brain was scanned in an MRI machine during a state of happiness, researchers noticed his temporoparietal junction activation was off the charts. When asked what he was thinking about, he said he was practising a loving-kindness and compassion meditation.

3. Reframe Your Thoughts.

As discussed in Chapter 3: Your Mind, reframing your thoughts is a powerful tool to help build resilience and shift from negative to positive thinking. If you hear your inner critic or ego chiming in to say you can't do something, feel free to acknowledge the thought and then actively turn it around into something helpful. This can also be used when someone gives you criticism that's hard to hear. Instead of thinking, *James must think I'm failing in my role,* reframe your thought to, *James must really believe in me, which is why he's delivering such open and honest feedback.*

MAKING SPACE FOR CLARITY

We touched on this in Chapter 8: Your Sleep, but a cluttered space can often mean a cluttered mind. Your home, office, car and backyard are a reflection of who you are. Is it a mindful oasis or is it cluttered with knick-knacks, unpacked boxes and an overflowing wardrobe?

Ever since declutter expert and author of *The Life-Changing Magic of Tidying Up* Marie Kondo came on the scene, there has been a lot of research on the positive side effects a spring-clean can have on our psychological health. According to neuroscientists, 'multiple stimuli' from a disorganised space increases the brain's cortisol and limits the ability to focus and process information properly.

While decluttering has the obvious benefits of an organised home, it also has the benefits of an improved mood and decrease in stress. That's a big enough motivator for me to initiate action! It's recommended to pick one room and start by removing unnecessary clutter in order to make the space aesthetically appealing and provide clarity. If this sounds like something you think you're ready to take on, I suggest starting small. For example, let's do your wardrobe. Why the wardrobe? People seem to have the greatest emotional attachment to their clothing. Does this internal chatter sound familiar:

Those are my goal jeans.

Jackie gave me that coat so I better keep it.

That T-shirt reminds me of my trip to Europe.

I've had that hat forever. I might as well keep it.

My daughter may want that purse one day.

People also tend to let their wardrobes trickle into other spaces, like the chair in the corner of your room, your dining room table and the passenger seat of your car. By tackling your closet, you'll see your wardrobe and mind get clearer, then you can move on to the rest of the house!

DIGITAL DETOX FOR CLARITY AND MINDFULNESS

As I've already mentioned, we check our phones far too often. When you go out for a meal, do you notice couples, parents and kids paying more attention to their phones than each other? When I went to a Coldplay concert a few years ago, I couldn't help but notice just how many people watched the show through a smartphone rather than being immersed in the experience. We know that technology can have amazing benefits and will continue to enhance our lives, as long as it's not taking priority over real human experiences. If you feel you are losing your grip on the

real world, meaningful conversations and just being in the moment –
perhaps it's time to use some strategies to unplug for a while and nurture
a healthier relationship with technology.

Tips for Doing a Digital Detox

Disable notifications

This one is crucial for productivity as notifications are a constant source
of distraction. We check into our social-media accounts more than we
should, so do we really need another trigger when someone likes a photo
or makes a comment?

Leave your phone at home

Next time you're going out for dinner or for a lunch date with friends,
leave your phone at home or in the car. This may sound difficult or
challenging at first, but the reality is, once you arrive at your destination,
you will be truly engaged with your friends. At a minimum, don't allow
phones on the table.

Don't check your phone first thing in the morning

You already know how I feel about this, but remember that when you
look at your phone before setting your intention for the day or expressing your gratitude, you're handing your power to your phone.

Go off the grid

Can you switch your phone off for the whole day? I do this on Sundays.
It feels like the 24 hours lasts for two weeks. If this is too drastic, try
powering down for two hours on a chosen day. Baby steps first, if you
feel like an off-grid day would make you anxious.

Remember, nobody goes through life unscathed. It's inevitable that
each one of us will go through trials and tribulations. Some of them will
be our own fault and some of them not. Mindfulness is a key part of
building and maintaining resilience. It's our mind's way of overcoming
stress, burnout and anxiety.

IN YOUR JOURNAL

Take a moment to reflect by answering the following questions:

- Has practising a daily meditation helped your mood, connection with yourself/others and performance? If yes, how? If no, why do you think that is?

- Was there a stressful situation over the last week when you could have used breathwork to help calm down?

- Are there any digital habits you wish you could dial back on or break altogether?

10
YOUR GUT HEALTH

IN CHAPTER 6: Your Morning Routine, I briefly touched on the fact that we produce 90 per cent of our serotonin and 50 per cent of our dopamine in our gut, which is why making a probiotic or prebiotic part of your morning routine can be so beneficial. Often referred to as our 'second brain', our gut directly impacts our mood, ability to focus, memory, energy levels and overall health. When our gut is inflamed or filled with the wrong types of bacteria (or parasites), we are at risk of developing an autoimmune disorder, diseases, anxiety, depression, weight loss or weight gain, brain fog and the type of pheromones that will make you swipe left on your would-be love.

Up until about 2006, we only knew of around 200 species that inhabited the human gut. In the last decade, scientists have discovered more than 15,000 species! Take a moment and put your hand on your gut. In there is a little ecosystem, not too dissimilar to the Amazon Rainforest, that's full of bacteria essential for keeping you healthy and strong. However, there also may be a few (million) incompatible bacteria making life a little hard for you. While you may be thinking, *But Chelsea, I don't need a chapter on gut health, I need a bottle of Gaviscon,* I promise that the information I'm about to share will be a game-changer for both your physical and mental health.

In this chapter, I'm going to go over what your microbiome is and how it affects your mental and physical health. I'm also going to talk about how to know if your gut is out, what you can do to help heal inflammation and restore a healthy balance, as well as why you should think about *how* you're sitting on the toilet. That's right, we will be chatting about all things poo, toilets and what we can learn from what comes out of what we put in!

WHAT IS THE MICROBIOME?

The human microbiome is the community of genomes of microbiota inhabiting the human body. Basically, we have protozoa, archaea, eukaryotes, viruses and lots of bacteria living symbiotically on and within various parts of our bodies. When we have a healthy, diverse microbiome and, in particular, gut microbiome, our bodies are able not only to digest the food we eat well, but also to suppress harmful bacteria, synthesise vitamins, process drugs and increase our chances of maintaining a healthy mindset. Our gut, often referred to as our gastrointestinal (GI) tract, runs from our mouth to the anus and has about 9 metres of tubing (including our stomach) that is lined with a single layer of cells with tight junctions. If irritating food, liquids, drugs or inanimate objects (I don't know what you're into) get in, the cell junctions can get super pissed off and widen or split, allowing toxins into your body, which cause an inflammatory response.

While I'd love to say that our bodies are operating as a democratic state, meaning that our brains and bodies get equal say in how we think, act and feel, the truth is, the bacteria in our guts are the real pilots and we're just passengers. The only reason people still exist is because bacteria need stomachs, skin and bloodstreams to ride around in. If you're feeling like I'm telling you that you're essentially an avatar, you're right. The bacteria in your body are making all the decisions. (Unfortunately, though, that defence will likely not stand up in a court of law.)

MICROBIOME 101

☐ It regulates mood, cognitive abilities, immunity, inflammation, vitamins and appetite.
☐ It is composed of roughly 100 trillion gut bugs.
☐ Gut bugs outnumber the cells in our bodies 10:1.
☐ On a cellular level, the human body is 90 per cent bacteria.

Microbiome and Your Physical and Mental Health

A healthy microbiome is essential for our development and survival. From birth, it plays an integral role in helping our bodies and brains develop, our immune system grow strong and ensures our organs receive the nutrition they need to function properly. With so many antibacterial soaps and hand sanitisers on the market (especially since the global pandemic), it's no wonder the word 'bacteria' has a negative connotation. I know I said earlier that we are basically their host to control, *but* I need to point out that we get a whole lot of good from them, too! The majority of bugs in our bodies are there to knock the pathogenic ones out and help us ward off autoimmune diseases such as diabetes and multiple sclerosis, among numerous other diseases and cancers. As a result, 70 per cent of our immune systems are housed in our guts.

On top of being a key player in our body's physical health, gut bacteria can dramatically impact our mental health. Because the gut acts as a home base for neurotransmitters, there is a tremendous overlap between irritable bowel syndrome (IBS) and depression or anxiety. For a long time, doctors didn't understand that, for some people, the root of their mood swings could be a gastrointestinal issue. It's now much clearer that a change or damage to your gut bacteria can also alter your body's serotonin levels, which will definitely affect your mood. A 2011 study found that when mice consumed a certain type of good bacteria, some areas of the subjects' brains were altered. They became less anxious and had reduced psychological distress.

Remember: when you feel sick to your *stomach* or like you've been punched in the *gut*, it's because a large portion of your happiness and reward hormones are manufactured there. If they're not able to travel through your vagus nerve to your brain to remind you that you are a total legend and that everything is going to be okay, it's no wonder you're feeling 50 shades of blue. Your vagus nerve is the most important route from the gut to the brain. It runs through the diaphragm, between the lungs, up along the oesophagus, through the neck to the brain. Studies done on humans show that stimulating the vagus nerve by different frequencies can make a person feel comfortable or extremely anxious. Since 2010, people with severe depression have been treated with stimulation of the vagus nerve. This nerve works as a telephone cord between your gut and your brain. The gut tells the brain how your body is going. On the flip side, your mood can also impact your gut. Yes, it's a two-way street. In times of emotional stress or fatigue, your gut can become inflamed, irritable and unable to function optimally. This is why it's important that you look after both your mind and your gut!

Are YOU the Chocolate Addict or Is It the Ferrero-Rocher–loving Bacteria Inside You?

Two points if you guessed it's the bacteria! There are two types of people in this world: chocolate-neutral and chocolate-craving. (I'm the latter.) When scientists studied samples under a microscope, they learned that a person's love for chocolate is dictated by the specific types of bacteria in their gut. Ever found yourself craving grapes? (And by grapes, I totally mean *wine.*) That's because we also have some booze-loving bacteria in our bodies that seem to really value a sneaky pinot. While we often might feel like we're at the mercy of our cravings or simply have a sweet tooth, it's possible for you to outsmart your gut. Through diet and lifestyle changes, you can absolutely change your body's microbiome. Think about it like performing an exorcism and replacing the demonic misbehaving gut-bugs with guardian angels (or those with amazing self-care skills).

Weight and Microbiome

For as long as I can remember, the diet industry has been peppering my TV, radio, magazines and, more recently, social-media platforms with the message that weight gain is within our control and all we need to do is work harder! Arguably responsible for the success of fad diets that tell you to only eat grapefruit, tuna and milk, this message isn't exactly accurate. Marketers don't mention that, *Oh, hey – there actually might be bacteria in your gut making it very difficult for you to lose weight.*

This is what researchers set out to discover when a report emerged about a young woman who underwent a faecal transplant for a chronic infection. Just like it sounds, a faecal transplant is where they take a stool sample from a healthy person and transplant it into someone who needs help restoring the balance of their gut bacteria. Sixteen months after this woman had her faecal transplant, she had dramatic and unexplained weight gain. Her body mass index (BMI) increased from a normal, healthy weight up to obese. Remarkably, nothing else had changed in this woman's life. Not her diet, not her stress levels, not her physical activity. She simply had some new gut bacteria guiding the ship. For the first time we had evidence in a human of something that has been shown repeatedly in animals: our gut microbiota has near-total control over the way that we process our food. So much control, in fact, that the same food can yield totally different effects depending on the gut microbiota involved. When scientists (and the press) got wind of her story, everyone went into a tizzy and that's when some very compelling research began!

One study looked at sets of identical twins in which one twin was obese and the other thin. Researchers took stool samples from each of the twins and transferred them into healthy mice and get this: the mouse that got the lean twin's stool stayed lean and the one who got the obese twin's stool became obese. That's even despite the fact that both mice were fed exactly the same diet, with exactly the same calories. The moral of this story is: if I'm ever going to get a faecal transplant, it's coming from Jennifer Lopez. The other moral of this story is: our gut health has enormous control over our metabolism, so we need to be mindful about maintaining a healthy gut!

HOW DO YOU KNOW IF YOUR GUT IS OUT?

I feel like a lot of people are conditioned to feel like crap. From dragging their bodies to the office on a Monday (and making a beeline for the coffee machine to see if they've managed a way to inject it intravenously) to finishing a meal and needing to lie down because they feel so bloated and tired, we've just accepted feeling like less-than-optimal versions of ourselves.

There are a number of conditions that can lead to these outcomes. Food intolerances, allergies, inflammation, too much of a good thing (yes, you can overload on fibre and healthy fats), too much of a bad thing (I'm talking about you, refined sugar), and, of course, the effects that medications, alcohol, caffeine and nicotine can have on the gut. Have you ever noticed how some medications say, 'Take with food'? That's because drugs like NSAIDs (non-steroidal anti-inflammatory drugs including Nurofen) can be quite harsh on the gut. Same goes for antibiotics. In fact, while antibiotics are busy killing all the bad bugs, there's a good chance they're wiping out the good ones, too. Most pharmacists will tell you how to correctly couple a probiotic with an antibiotic to help with this. Antibiotics are extra tricky because they're often prescribed prematurely. As a mother, I know how frustrating it is when you or your child is unwell but, more often than not, the illness is a virus, not a bacterial infection and the truth is: viruses can take two weeks or more to get over. By the time you've begged your GP for antibiotics (and you think they've magically cured you), your body was probably kicking that virus's butt anyway! The result: an upset gut, possibly thrush and contribution to the global problem of creating antibiotic-resistant bugs due to overprescription.

What if I told you that doing a quick audit and then making a few simple changes to your diet and lifestyle could have you skipping into work? Take a moment to consider the list below. How many of the following symptoms would you put a 'Yes' next to? They don't have to happen all day every day, but on a weekly basis, do you feel or have:

- brain fog
- anxiety
- depressed mood
- fatigue
- grumpiness
- abdominal pain
- smelly farts
- bloating
- skin breakouts
- inability to lose or gain weight
- repeated cases of thrush.

If you answered 'Yes' to one or more of the above, it's worth taking a look at your diet, alcohol consumption and lifestyle. If your symptoms are chronic or severe, you may want to speak to your GP or integrative doctor about having further testing done to look for an allergy, intolerance or more severe disease such as Crohn's disease, coeliac disease, gastroesophageal reflux disease (GERD) or peptic ulcer disease. You can also ask them to test your blood for micronutrient deficiencies. Don't worry, the majority of the time, you can heal your gut and restore balance with a few simple diet and lifestyle changes (which I'll share soon!).

Another Sign Your Gut Is Out: Pheromones Aren't Doing Their Job

You're probably thinking, *What does my gut have to do with my pheromones?* Have you ever been on a date and found yourself either *super* attracted to the person opposite you or *really* turned off? Sometimes it's confusing because on paper (or on their Bumble profile) they look *exactly* like the type of person you'd usually go for, but there's no way you want to make out with that person in the here and now. Same goes for someone you probably wouldn't have looked twice at but, for whatever reason, you want them in your bed (twice and then once again in the morning). Either way, you've had an extreme reaction and it has a lot to do with your pheromones, otherwise known as your odour profile. On top of examining values and table manners, a person's pheromones are one of the ways we decide if we like them or not. Note: sometimes it's hard to get a good whiff and analysis of a person's odour profile because we tend to overuse synthetic fragrances. (But I'm going to argue that if all you can smell is LYNX Africa, it probably wasn't going to work out anyway.)

Swiss biological researcher Claus Wedekind did a fascinating study in the mid-1990s around major histocompatibility complex (MHC) genes and pheromones. MHC genes are a significant component in the immune system. Because different MHC genes are better suited to fight different infections, a healthy person would typically have a wide range of MHC genes. When it comes to our biological drive to procreate, we instinctively look for a partner who has different MHC genes to our own so our children can have an even stronger immunity. In Claus Wedekind's study, he had the participating men wear T-shirts for two nights and then a group of women identify which scent they were most attracted to. The result: the women were all attracted to the scent of men who had different MHC genes to their own. Next comes baby (with a super-healthy immune system) in a baby carriage.

When it comes to the production of your pheromones, the magic happens (surprise, surprise) in the gut! That means if you're single and ready to mingle, the smartest thing you can do before performing a hey-look-at-me dive into the dating pool is to work on your gut health. I don't want to make you feel overwhelmed, but you're also going to want to be aware that not only are we smelling the person to determine if we're sexually attracted to them or not, but we're also *tasting*. When we kiss a person, we are exchanging roughly 80 million microbes with our mouths, meaning we're literally sampling the other person to see if we're a match. I'm sorry if I've turned you off kissing forever, but there's more to finding real love than just swiping right. A healthy microbiome produces a beautiful fragrance and flavour worthy of Aphrodite. An unhealthy microbiome does the opposite, which is why the best dating advice I could ever give is: not every microbe makes a great wingman.

WHAT TO EAT FOR OPTIMAL GUT (AND BRAIN) HEALTH

If you think a toddler is a fussy eater, just wait until you try to please all 15,000 species of bacteria in your gut! With so many mouths to feed, it's nearly impossible to satisfy all of them, which, in the case of restoring your gut health, is actually a good thing. For example, if you opt for the types of food the good microbes love and deny the bad microbes their usual morning feed of soft drink, cigarettes and French fries, the baddies will likely be starved into extinction. Each dietary choice you make will empower a specific group of microbes, while others die off. The key is making sure the *right* groups die off.

The American Gut Project founder Dr Rob Knight is world-renowned for being the guru of gut health. Credited with pioneering the largest and most diverse study of microbiomes of the industrialised world, Dr Knight has helped spread the knowledge that the single greatest predictor of a healthy gut microbiome is the diversity of plants in one's diet. According to Dr Knight, the best way to achieve and maintain gut health and microbiome diversity is to consume 30 different plants in a given week. While 30 different plants may sound like a lot, there are approximately 400,000 varieties of plants on Earth. Even though only 300,000 are edible, that should still give you a great range of choice.

How to Fit 30 Plants into Your Diet in a Week:
- Make a vegie juice for breakfast.
- Swap pasta for zoodles (spiralised zucchini).
- Throw another squash on the barbie.
- Munch on carrots and hummus.
- Snack on capsicum and guacamole.
- Munch on celery and nut butter.
- Add new vegetables to your roasting tray.
- Add greens to your sides: asparagus, beans, snap peas.
- My personal favourite: BRAGG Organic Sprinkles (24 plants in one hit!).

Top Ten Brain foods

There is a direct correlation between what we put in our mouth and brain health. Plenty of foods benefit our thinking and feeling. Many studies have shown that increasing your intake of antioxidant-rich foods helps reduce anxiety and depression. Here is a list of my favourite brain foods:

- Avocados: Provide monounsaturated fat that helps maintain blood flow.
- Blueberries: Great antioxidant and anti-inflammatory properties. Protect your brain from oxidative stress and improve cognition.
- Broccoli: Powerful antioxidant and packed with vitamin K that improves cognitive function and memory.
- Dark chocolate: Stimulates endorphins and has flavonoids that may enhance memory and help slow down the effects of brain ageing. The darker the better; I go for at least 70 per cent.
- Eggs: Contain brain-energising choline, vitamins B6 and B12 and folate (B9), which are all good for mood and memory.

- Green leafy vegetables: Good source of vitamin E and folate (B9).
- Nuts: Contain healthy fats, antioxidants and vitamin E to protect cells against free-radical damage and help slow mental decline.
- Pumpkin seeds: Have powerful antioxidants that protect the brain from free-radical damage. They also contain zinc, which is important for nerve signalling.
- Salmon: About 60 per cent of your brain is made of fat and half of that is omega-3. Rich in omega-3, salmon helps reduce the effects of brain ageing.
- Turmeric: A potent antioxidant and anti-inflammatory that boosts serotonin and helps new brain cells to grow.
- Water: Although it's not a food (and comes in at number 11 on this list) it's just as important! Your brain is approximately 75 per cent water. Dehydration can cause brain fog, fatigue and slower reaction times.

I know that adjusting your diet can feel overwhelming, which is why I engaged one of my very good friends and qualified nutritionist, Michele Chevalley Hedge, to make you a weekly meal plan specifically designed to restore, balance and maintain optimal gut health.

⌐ RAW VERSUS COOKED VEGIES ⌐

You actually get different nutrients depending on how a vegetable is cooked. Because both raw and cooked vegetables offer important nutrients, try to make sure you're having both! This will help increase the diversity of your microbiome.

Weekly Meal Plan

BY MICHELE CHEVALLEY HEDGE

DAY 01	BREAKFAST	Zoodles with herb sprinkles
	LUNCH	Tahini chicken salad
	DINNER	Carrot cashew spread, lentil chili and green salad
DAY 02	BREAKFAST	Berry coconut yoghurt bowl with blueberries, nuts and seeds
	LUNCH	Roasted and raw salad bowl
	DINNER	Miso-glazed salmon with broccolini
DAY 03	BREAKFAST	Pancetta frittata
	LUNCH	Fishcake salad
	DINNER	Nutty chicken schnitzel
DAY 04	BREAKFAST	Cashew and quinoa stir-fry
	LUNCH	Lemon-roast veg and chickpea salad
	DINNER	Thai tofu bowl
DAY 05	BREAKFAST	Cashew and quinoa stir-fry
	LUNCH	Creamy vegetable soup
	DINNER	Mexican fish bowl
DAY 06	BREAKFAST	Berry coconut yoghurt bowl with blueberries, nuts and seeds
	LUNCH	Simple curried fish with bok choy
	DINNER	Meatballs with ragu and zoodles
DAY 07	BREAKFAST	Zesty lentil soup
	LUNCH	Mexican chicken burgers
	DINNER	Tacos with zucchini tortillas

Do I HAVE to Buy Organic?

You don't *have* to do anything, but in my opinion, yes, you should absolutely be buying organic vegetables and fruits. When something says it's organic and, more importantly, certified organic by a reputable third party, it means that it's been farmed from healthy soil without the use of pesticides, herbicides and other potentially toxic chemicals. If you're not able to commit to living a fully organic lifestyle due to finances or availability, my rule of thumb is: if the skin is thin, buy organic! This is because the thinner the skin of a fruit or vegetable, the more likely it is going to have chemicals such as pesticides all the way through. Don't forget that you can always buy the organic frozen version of things. I do this for all of my berries, bananas and spinach. I also opt for tinned versions of organic tomatoes, chickpeas and coconut milk. Honestly, the long-life versions of organic foods are every bit as good so don't think you always have to go fresh.

Referred to as 'The Dirty Dozen' by the Environmental Working Group (EWG), thin-skinned fruits and vegetables you should buy organic if possible include:

- strawberries
- spinach
- kale
- nectarines
- apples

- grapes
- cherries
- peaches
- pears

- capsicums and other peppers
- tomatoes
- celery.

The good news is the EWG also has a list of less penetrable fruits and vegetables that are less important to buy organic, including:

- avocados
- sweet corn
- pineapples
- onions
- papayas
- honeydew melons

- sweet peas (frozen)
- eggplants
- asparagus
- broccoli

- cabbages
- kiwis
- cauliflower
- mushrooms
- rockmelon.

WASHING FRUITS AND VEGIES

If you're unable to buy the organic version of a fruit or vegetable, running it under water for three-and-a-half seconds isn't going to suffice if you *really* want to get the pesticides off. Be sure to give it a proper wash and scrub.

Healthy Fats

Low-fat … fat-free … When did fats get such a bad reputation? You've heard of different fat types: trans, saturated, monounsaturated, polyunsaturated. Omega-3 and -6 fats are polyunsaturated fats, and they're considered essential because our body is not capable of making them, which is why we need to get them from our diets. If you don't consume them, you develop a deficiency, which can lead to sickness. Polyunsaturated fats are important for many functions in the body. Here's the issue: you've probably heard about omega-3s more than omega-6s. Part of the reason why is because the modern Western diet provides an excessive amount of omega-6s and an inadequate amount of omega-3s. The ratio of omega-6s to omega-3s is a marker of health. Humans evolved with a nearly even mix between omega-6s and omega-3s, while most Westerners are now functioning with a ratio of about 16:1 of omega-6s to omega-3s. It's a ratio that can promote cardiovascular disease, cancer, osteoporosis and autoimmune diseases. Our goal is to balance this ratio, which means that we need an influx of omega-3s in our diet.

Where to Find Omega-3s:
- fish such as salmon, mackerel, herring, sardines
- seafood such as oysters and caviar
- walnuts
- chia and flax seeds
- soybeans.

Sugar Really Isn't So Sweet (Neither Are Artificial Sweeteners)

From an inflammation point of view, sugar is really bad for our health and can lead to numerous chronic illnesses. It's also notorious for giving us a quick hit of energy and then zapping us into a sugar coma! The hormone insulin regulates blood-sugar levels in the body. Your cells need sugar (glucose) for energy; however, the cells find it tough to get it from your bloodstream. This is when we say hello to their trusty friend: insulin. When you eat carbs, your pancreas releases insulin, which acts like a key that unlocks the cells' front door to get the glucose from your food. Be wary though: not all carbs are on a level playing field.

Complex carbs like vegetables, brown rice and whole fruits help insulin work in the right way and stabilise your blood sugar to help you stay focused, make great decisions and have good energy for the day. But, simple sugars like soft drinks, bags of lollies and biscuits can cause blood-sugar levels to go berserk. Why is this a problem? If there's too much sugar in your bloodstream, your body will tell the insulin to head to the liver for storage, which can eventually lead to weight gain and fatty liver disease. One of the main problems with consistently eating a high-sugar diet and being obese is a decrease in insulin's ability to regulate blood sugar, leading to pre-diabetes and diabetes.

How Does Sugar Affect Your Mental Health?

Eating sugar has a roller-coaster effect, where the blood-sugar levels will spike and then crash. This roller-coaster effect can impact your mood and mental health. Research shows that high-sugar diets and blood-sugar levels are associated with:

- anxiety
- depression
- irritability
- anger
- trouble concentrating.

If you want to get your mental health right, it is so important to start removing sugar and other refined carbs from your diet to regulate your insulin and stabilise your blood-sugar levels.

But Chelsea, I'm not eating sugar. I use Stevia!

Hold my (non-sweetened) drink …

When zero-calorie drinks came on the market, we all rejoiced. They are tasty and better than sugar, right? Wrong! Artificial sweeteners change the microbiome and promote inflammation and insulin resistance. The result: you will be less likely to tolerate sugar when you use artificial sweeteners.

Okay, so I can't eat lollies or have Coke No Sugar. Does this mean I have to steer clear of natural sugar, too?

There is a huge amount of fear about fruit and sugar! Please don't associate fruit with sugar. You absolutely should be eating fruit. The good news is the sugar in fruit is by no means the same as processed sugar. Not to mention, fruit is packed with vitamins, minerals and fibre.

Apples, for example, have prebiotic fibre, healthy microbes and numerous beneficial phytochemicals that contribute to reduced risk of heart diseases, stroke, lung cancer and weight gain. Oranges contain loads of vitamin C and antioxidant flavonoids that protect against hypertension and iron deficiency.

My all-time favourite, though, is berries. The colour comes from a phytochemical (phyto means 'plant-based') called anthocyanins. Without anthocyanins, blueberries would be green! That's why under-developed blueberries aren't blue, because the anthocyanins haven't come in yet. Anthocyanins are pretty phenomenal. They help protect against cancer and they also boost cognition. In one recent study, women who ate just two servings of strawberries or one serving of blueberries per week postponed cognitive decline and made their brain behave like it was 30 months younger. When wild blueberries were given to kids, researchers saw almost immediate improvements in cognitive performance that increased based upon the number of blueberries they ate.

Juice Cleanse? Yay or Nay?

Is juiced fruit the same as sinking your teeth into whole fruit? No, unfortunately, it's not. When you process food, the rules change. By juicing your fruit, you are removing most of the fibre and artificially concentrating the sugar. For example, one small orange has 45 calories, 2.3 grams of fibre and 9 grams of sugars. One cup of OJ packs in 134 calories, just 0.5 gram of fibre and 23.3 grams of sugars. Fruit juice is a sugary beverage, created by the manipulation of a whole food.

┌ **HOW TO REDUCE YOUR SUGAR INTAKE** ┐

- Switch from soft drinks to still or sparkling water or spa water (water with fresh lemon, lime or a mint leaf in it).
- Toss the table sugar in the bin.
- Compare food labels and choose products with the lowest amounts of added sugar.
- When baking, cut back on the amount of sugar or try using extracts (like vanilla extract) as a substitute.
- Go the unsweetened route: e.g. unsweetened apple sauce.
- Have a vegetable juice instead of fruit juice.

Probiotics and Prebiotics: What's the Difference and Do I Need Them?

While the probiotics you might be thinking of come in capsule or liquid form and have a catchy TV-ad jingle or animated brand mascot, probiotics are simply helpful bacteria found in select foods and are vital for our life and to defend our gut. The thing that makes probiotics so amazing is that they produce small fatty acids like butyrate. These acids support the villi in the gut (the tiny finger-shaped structures in your small intestine), and the bigger the villi grow, the better they are at absorbing nutrients, minerals and vitamins. The more stable they are, the less rubbish they let through. This means the body receives more nutrients and less damaging substances. Examples of probiotic foods that contain live bacteria include kefir, kombucha, yoghurt (unsweetened), kimchi, pickled fruits and vegetables, and sauerkraut. I recently discovered that you can also buy Natural Wine (which is wine only made with grapes and yeast) that contains probiotics as a result of the fermentation process.

Prebiotics, on the other hand, are foods that contain dietary fibre that can only be eaten by the friendly bacteria in the gut. Bad bacteria can't process prebiotics at all, so it helps in starving out the bad guys. Examples of foods containing prebiotics are asparagus, Jerusalem artichokes, onions, garlic, leeks, endives and digestion-resistant starches like potatoes and brown rice that are boiled and then left to cool. (This process allows the starch to crystallise, making it more resistant to digestion.) While it's common to get prebiotics in supplement form, I like to get mine from my diet. With that being said, when you're going through major gut revival, supplementing can be extremely beneficial. Just be careful: some blends of bacteria may work well and others could make things even worse! It just depends on what your gut needs.

Alcohol and Gut Health

I am the first to admit that, on a Friday, I love to kick back with a glass of shiraz and silently quote Will Ferrell in *Old School*. *(It's so good when it hits your lips.)* BUT I am highly aware of what science says about alcohol. First, let's talk about binge drinking. No matter how hard I begged him to tell me my college drinking left me unscathed, my good friend Dr Will Bulsiewicz explains that consuming excessive amounts of alcohol in a short period of time causes damage to the gut microbiota, which then increases intestinal permeability and signals the release of bacterial endotoxins. This causes dysbiosis, which is ultimately how alcohol causes cirrhosis of the liver. Sadly, this doesn't just apply to weekend ragers. Will hit me with the hard truth: just a single crazy Friday night can damage your gut.

But Chelsea, surely I can still enjoy one glass of wine a night, right?

Again, Will is the Debbie Downer here. He says that just one drink per day increases your risk of high blood pressure and stroke. Even just a half drink per day has been associated with an increased risk of cancer. One of the main issues is that alcohol kills bacteria: both the good and the bad, which isn't great for our gut! If you were to have one glass, experts say that red is best. I avoid alcohol from Monday to Thursday, but on Friday evening, I crack open a nice bottle of shiraz with my husband. We each have a maximum of only two wines so it doesn't impact our sleep and also has less impact on our guts.

FASTING 101

Look, fasting is not for everyone, but it's something that has dramatically improved my mental and physical health, so I want to share my experience with you. I started intermittent fasting (not eating for 16 hours) a couple of times a week after reading a few studies that said not eating for 16 hours can have an anti-ageing effect on the brain. Studies show that when you fast for this amount of time, the telomeres on the ends of your chromosomes not only repair but also lengthen. You'll remember from Chapter 7: Your Movement and Energy, the reason it's so crucial to look after and nourish your telomeres is because, as you age, your chromosomes unravel, which puts you at risk for things such as Alzheimer's and cardiovascular illness. Some people worry they're going to become 'hangry' or have stomach cramps, but if you go from 7 pm the night before to 11 am the next day, that's your 16-hour block and you've most likely slept for around half of it!

Potential Benefits of Intermittent Fasting for 16 Hours:
- has an anti-inflammatory effect on the body
- heals your gut lining
- repairs and encourages telomere growth
- decreases your caloric intake, which can assist with weight loss
- helps clear out mitochondrial cells.

    Disclaimer: always speak to your doctor before fasting. Do not fast if you're pregnant, under 20 years old or have diabetes.

WHAT GOES IN, MUST COME OUT

Let's talk about smart toilets. No, I'm not talking about the ones in Japan that are designed with more buttons than a remote control. I'm also not talking about the ones that wash, dry, warm you and play relaxing music so you can (cough) finish the job. I'm talking about a toilet that Stanford University designed to detect possible diseases, certain types of cancers and digestive disorders in urine and faeces ... with butthole recognition. You may be asking yourself, why butthole recognition? I asked the same thing. Because the scientists wanted to be able to send the 'user' detailed information about their health, they needed a way to identify who was sitting on the toilet. Since some people may not be able to flush on their own, those clever minds at Stanford quickly figured out a solution: they'd use a technology that captures a person's anal print. (Welcome to a world where 'anal print' is a thing and it's actually in someone's job description to create the tool that captures it!) Anal prints aside, as someone who's sent a faecal sample by Australia Post on a number of occasions to have my stool tested, the idea of an in-home laboratory-lavatory is something I'd love to see hit the mainstream. And it's actually not too far away. A company called Toto has a 'wellness toilet' in the works that is designed to send a message to your phone shortly after your 'business meeting' to let you know how your poo is looking. It has very similar technology to the toilet designed by Stanford. From there, it offers suggestions on how you can improve your wellbeing through your diet. (If you're thinking, *I'm not taking advice from my toilet, it's full of crap!*, you can go sit with all the other dads cracking jokes.)

Jokes aside, there's a lot we can learn from spending time on the toilet. Take a moment and think about how long it takes you to poo. Are you someone who waits until it's fully primed before you take aim, or do you like to let things work themselves out when you get there? How frequently do you have a bowel movement? What's the consistency? I'm sorry that I'm getting all up in your shit, but this shit matters!

The Poop Spectrum

Runny, Loose and Diarrhoea

This can be from something you ate, caused by stress or a sign of inflammation or infection. While it should typically resolve itself within a few days, chronic loose stools is something you should speak to your doctor about, especially if you notice dark blood. (Bright red blood is typically from the anus and can be from dryness or stretching.) Dark blood is from the bowels and is concerning.

Pellet, Dry or Not-at-All

If you're passing pellets and feel like you'd rather birth a baby than spend another hour on the toilet trying to poop, there's a good chance you're constipated. When you're backed up, not only does that waste block other waste from making its way out, but it also prevents your body from cycling out hormones like oestrogen and testosterone, which is why constipation is linked to mood swings, dark thoughts, poorer mental health, haemorrhoids and abdominal pain.

⌐ CONSTIPATION AND PMS ⌐

Do you suffer from constipation the week before your period? Do you also suffer from raging PMS? The two might be linked. If you're unable to poo, your oestrogen builds up, which makes you: A. super emotional; B. feel like you want to murder someone and yourself, and; C. unable to give testosterone the moment it wants to have. It's no wonder you don't want to do anything other than cry while watching a rom-com (and cradling a salty snack in your lap). The solution: tackle your constipation, and your hormones will balance out!

Struggling to Poo?

While it could very much be your diet and stress levels that are preventing you from 'dropping the kids off at the pool', I'm going to argue it's
partly the Western toilet's fault. (Here I go again with toilets!) Hear me
out: when it comes to the biomechanics of our gut, we are not designed
to sit on a Western toilet. The 90-degree angle of our legs and back
when we sit causes a kink in the bowel, making it difficult for us to get a
full release. Think about washing your car with a hose. If the hose gets
kinked (which it can and WILL), the water can't get out. Same thing for
our sigmoid colon – if your body is at a 90-degree angle, you're kinking
your colon and won't get a full evacuation. The solution: we need to
raise our knees and lean slightly forward!

Tell me you've heard of the Squatty Potty. While this brand is
arguably the pioneer of the game-changing stool that's designed to raise
your knees 22 cm (9 inches) in order to unkink the bowel, there are
plenty of options on the market. We have one at every toilet in our home
and if I'm travelling, you best believe that I'm kicking over the hotel
room bin to use as a prop for my feet. #anythingtopoo. While raising
your knees is a major part of assuming the correct position, it also helps
to lean your upper body forward, so why not do both?

FAECAL TESTING AND TRANSPLANTS

When you were looking at the list of symptoms of an unhealthy gut,
did you say 'Yes' to having general feelings of fatigue, brain fog, grumpiness, bloating and constipation? A consistent presence of one or more
of these is usually a good indicator that something is not quite right with
your microbiome. If you've tried adjusting your diet and are still not
feeling better (or if you just love data and biohacking), you can get your
microbiome tested with a poo sample. There are quite a few companies
that do it, but I go through Microba. In fact, I do it every year. They're
based in Queensland and their doctors and scientists analyse and make
recommendations to you on how to starve out the baddies in your belly
and feed up the goodies.

Want to hear something even more wild? Evidence suggests that our gut microbiomes may predict or even cause immune conditions such as asthma. As a mother, I spent the first two years of my daughter's life up to my armpits in poo. Parents are constantly cleaning poo, encouraging poo and checking it to make sure it looks the way it's supposed to look. Recently, researchers did a study that analysed the dirty nappies of 300 babies. The kids were only three months old, but even at such an early age, scientists discovered that specific changes in the gut bacteria predicted which kids would develop asthma years later. Fascinating, right! Want to know how they proved it?

They transferred the poo samples from the nappies of babies they suspected would develop asthma into special germ-free mice via a faecal transplant. Remarkably, the mice all developed inflamed lungs, a key marker of asthma. The conclusion: the gut influences your immune response and sets you up for a life of either chronic challenges or wellness.

TEN THINGS YOU CAN DO TO IMPROVE YOUR GUT-BRAIN CONNECTION AND OVERALL HEALTH

1. Cut out processed foods from your diet – this includes deli meats, juices and most pre-packaged snacks.
2. Scale back on your sugar consumption.
3. Eat a range of plants, the magic number is 30 per week.
4. Ensure you're consuming both probiotics and prebiotics.
5. Eat a mix of healthy fats and complex carbs.
6. Swap to organic fruits and vegetables (even if frozen or tinned).
7. Invest in a toilet aid that helps you assume the correct position.
8. Cut back your alcohol consumption or quit altogether.
9. Speak to your doctor about intermittent fasting.
10. Get your gut health checked by sending a stool sample to a company like Microba.

For further reading on gut health, check out *GUT: The Inside Story of Our Body's Most Underrated Organ* by Dr Giulia Enders.

IN YOUR JOURNAL

- Over the next week, start keeping a journal of what you're eating and how you're feeling. Try to be as detailed as possible to begin making links between food and beverages that may be disrupting your microbiome.
- Note your bowel movements over a week and see if you can trace a pattern.
- List some recipes with lots of vegies so you have a resource when you're feeling stuck.

11
YOUR
CONNECTIONS

YOU'VE HEARD THE SAYING, 'You are what you eat,' but what about everything else you consume? From the true-crime podcast that keeps you entertained on your commute to the weekly life chat with a friend over a glass of wine, the words, stories and energies you absorb are impacting who you are as a person, which is why I'm going to argue that you are what you eat *as well as* what you read and watch, listen to and whom you connect to.

The need to connect to the world around us is deeply human. We gravitate towards romantic relationships, friendships, careers, cultures, communities and elements in nature because we feel a *connection*. But what happens when some of these connections are actually doing us more harm than good? Or what if you're missing a particular connection altogether? The COVID-19 pandemic is the perfect example of how being forced to physically distance can fuel mental-health issues such as anxiety and depression. We make jokes about coming out of lockdown in desperate need of hair dye, but let's be real here: we were actually in desperate need of a hug.

In a 2012 study, researchers found that subjects who were experiencing chronic loneliness or social isolation tended to take more warm baths and showers because they craved the warmth that was missing from other people's touch. Humans aren't designed to live a life of solitude. Solitary confinement is a form of torture. On the other end of the spectrum, many people went into lockdown with people who were not good for their mental or physical health. In this chapter, I'm going to talk about how mindfulness can play a role in helping you connect (and disconnect) from others, connect with nature and, most importantly, connect with yourself.

CONNECTING WITH YOURSELF

In Chapter 3: Your Mind, I spoke about self-efficacy. Now I want to add self-respect into the mix. While your self-efficacy is built on personal attainment, social modelling, verbal persuasion and your emotional state, your self-respect is built on the loving-kindness you're able to show yourself.

Think of a friend in your life whom you truly respect. When they succeed at something, you feel happy and proud, right? When they fail at something, you might feel sad for them, but you're also fully confident that they'll either: A. get back up and try again, or; B. find a different, even better path. When they put up a boundary, either at work or in a social situation, you feel inspired by how fiercely they are protecting their mental and physical health. Do you have that person in mind? Great! Now, think about yourself. Take a moment to acknowledge a success (or three) in your life that makes you feel happy and proud. Now think about a time (or two) that you've failed. Even though it was sad, did you flex your resilience muscle and persevere with confidence? Finally, when was the last time you put a boundary in place to preserve your mental health or values? Hopefully, you are about to fist-pump the air because you're loving and respecting the experiences you've had in life. If you're not, don't worry – we're going to work on it. Self-efficacy and self-respect go hand in hand to form your self-esteem. This is what's going to ultimately help prevent you from feeling insecure, experiencing impostor syndrome, people-pleasing or letting people overstep your boundaries.

SIGNS OF LOW SELF-ESTEEM

☐ You apologise a lot (even for situations that are out of your control).

☐ You downplay your achievements.

☐ You're highly critical of yourself.

☐ You're afraid that people won't accept you for who you are.

☐ You have trouble saying 'No' to things you don't want to do.

☐ You tend to react emotionally rather than rationally.

If you just read that list and thought, *#thatsme*, we need to talk. Life is too short to walk around feeling insecure and not every bit as amazing as you are. As someone who grew up in a lower socio-economic family and was extremely tall, I spent a few years of my life wishing I could shrink away. However, that was something my parents would never allow and for that I'm incredibly grateful. I'm 5'11" and my dad would always tell me to stand tall with my chin high. The way we hold our bodies can directly impact our confidence so, before you even get dressed for the day, take a moment to roll your shoulders back and consciously stand tall. My dad also used to tell me to slow down when I was talking. People who feel they aren't worthy of being listened to tend to talk quickly. I know it's not always easy to stroll into a room, strike a power pose and confidently deliver your views, but the more you practise, the more natural it will become. One of the ways I gained the confidence to own my body and my voice was by empowering myself with knowledge. Read, listen, learn and experience as much as you can.

But Chelsea, I feel like such an impostor!

Ah, yes, the infamous impostor syndrome. This often goes hand in hand with perfectionism. When we are constantly comparing ourselves to others or setting unrealistic expectations for ourselves (at work, at home or with a group of friends), we run the risk of feeling like we're falling short. This is where you need to dial back the negative self-talk and revisit your ability to show yourself love and respect.

Believe me, when I first started stepping onto stages to deliver keynote speeches on mental health, I had jarring moments of self-doubt. Why would anyone want to listen to what I had to say? What if I completely bombed it? Am I really an expert? Negative self-talk loves to creep in and whisper sweet nothings about being an impostor or falling short. By becoming aware of the harmful narrative in your head, you can begin to consciously talk back. For example:

People want to listen to what I have to say because humans need connection, hope and guidance.

I won't bomb my speech because I've practised for months and am fully prepared.

While 'expert' is a big word, I am qualified because I've lived through a severe mental-health crisis, educated myself and am completely immersed in the space on a daily basis.

When in doubt, call bullshit on the voice inside your head telling you that you're not enough. Being able to switch your negative thoughts to focus on the good is a powerful and proven strategy you can maintain for the rest of your life.

One of the other ways to feel better about yourself is to show loving-kindness to others. I know that it sounds a bit counterintuitive to shift the focus from yourself, but every time you give of yourself to others, your brain will create an algorithm that actively looks out for things to appreciate. When you make a consistent effort to tune in to what is good in your world, you'll find that you'll be tuning in to yourself before you know it.

Signs You Are a Good Person:
- You truly care about the welfare of others.
- You consistently lend a helping hand.
- You try to go the extra mile.
- You are kind to others and aim not to judge.
- You are honest in relationships.

- You give out genuine compliments.
- You smile a lot and say, 'thank you'.

┌ **SHOW SOME LOVE** ┐

Take a moment to think of a living person whom you care about. Write them a quick email or text saying hi and telling them how much they mean to you and why. Next, take a moment to write a similar note to yourself in your journal.

Do You Take Things Personally?

I know it doesn't feel great to experience rejection, criticism, a lost opportunity or a backhanded compliment but, before you take something personally, remember this: the way people treat you is more about them and how they view the world than it is about you. You are not the main character in other people's stories. (Sorry, Leos.) While you don't have control over the things that are said to you, you do have control over whether or not you let them impact your life. Sometimes people say or do things out of habit or because they don't know any better. It's not because they want to consciously hurt you.

When COVID-19 forced us to limit the number of visitors we were able to have at our homes, I noticed that a lot of people (myself included) were feeling left out. Now referred to as 'making the COVID cut', the reality of living in a global pandemic meant that we had to make tough choices about whom we could and could not spend time with. As much as it sucked not getting included in something, it felt equally horrible to not be able to include everyone that I wanted to. Pandemic or not, you just can't invite everyone to everything. Before you get yourself worked up, have a good hard think: *Did you actually want to go or did you just want to be wanted?* (I'm going to argue you probably would have preferred to binge some Netflix, braless.)

When You Start Feeling Overwhelmed, Remember:
- Criticism can help you grow as a person.
- People are allowed to disagree with you.
- Your values and beliefs are not objective truths.
- Just because you're not invited to everything doesn't mean you're not loved and adored.

⌐ ARE YOU EXPERIENCING FOMO, JOMO OR FOKU? ¬

FOMO: Fear of Missing Out
JOMO: Joy of Missing Out
FOKU: Fear of Keeping Up

Are You a People Pleaser?

One of the outcomes of taking things personally is inadvertently becoming a people pleaser. When you're worried about how your thoughts and opinions will be received, it's easy to chameleon your personality depending on who is around you.

Do Any of the Below Sound Like You?
- You pretend to agree with everyone.
- You feel sad or disappointed when you discover someone doesn't like you.
- You don't admit when your feelings are hurt.
- You go to great lengths to avoid conflict.
- You have a hard time saying 'No'.
- You downplay your achievements.
- You are worried that people won't accept you for who you are.

If you answered 'Yes' to some of those, you need to take a moment to realise that you always have a choice and a voice. Putting yourself first doesn't mean you don't care about others. It means you're smart enough to know you can't help others if you don't help or honour yourself first. Here's the other thing to consider: do you truly like everyone? It's natural to be drawn to certain personality types and feel repelled by others. More often than not, the people we're trying to please aren't even people we really like, care about or respect. While you should always be kind, civil and fair, you do not need to do or say anything that compromises your values, beliefs and confidence just to win someone's approval.

Food for Thought:
- Some chapters in our lives have to close without closure.
- Don't lose yourself trying to fix something that will always remain broken.
- Your value is not determined by the people you don't match with.
- There is much more to you than the part that was rejected by someone else.

⌐ DEALING WITH REJECTION ⌐

Rejection can feel pretty painful but remember that the pain isn't really coming from the other person telling you 'No'. The pain you're feeling comes from the conversation that you're having with yourself afterwards. Rejection isn't a confirmation that you're lacking something. Rejection comes from an opinion and you should never allow someone else's opinion to become your reality.

I'm So Sorry That I Keep Saying Sorry!

Are you someone who apologises chronically? Over the next few days, I want you to start noticing how much you're saying 'sorry'. Next, I want you to think about why you feel the need to apologise. Did you truly do something wrong? For example, let's say you just worked a massive day and rushed home to cook and serve dinner for your family. To be fair, it's not your best work and it's cold. Instead of saying, 'I'm so sorry it's cold!' try 'Thank you for waiting to eat.' It doesn't matter that your meal isn't being served at an optimal temperature, what matters is that you made time to create nourishing food for the people you care about. When you stop over-apologising, you can get better at recognising and celebrating the parts of you doing amazing and kind things. This will boost your self-esteem and confidence. There are a few things you never have to say sorry for: doing what is best for you; saying 'No'; saying how you are feeling; being upset; wanting to have some alone time; your personal growth; and who you are.

Let's Go Back to Boundaries

In Chapter 4: Your Purpose, I spoke about the importance of having boundaries and saying 'No'. Making yourself a priority is the ultimate form of self-respect and self-care. When you take time to learn about and connect with yourself, you'll be able to identify what makes you feel overcommitted, overstimulated and under-cared for. By protecting your mental health, time and energy, you will find more happiness and less stress. Ultimately, you'll have the boundaries in place that will allow you to recharge and protect you from burnout.

Empathy Fatigue

I seem to come across *a lot* of empaths. (Takes one to know one, right!) Essentially, empaths are the type of people who feel more than others. Often described as passionate, deep, creative and in touch with their emotions, they may experience compassion fatigue from constantly trying to help others, can be drained from people drawing on their positive energy or simply exhausted from carrying the weight of the world on their shoulders.

As you consciously begin to connect with yourself, I want you to be mindful of the toll that empathy is having on you. (This can be something to watch for whether or not you're an empath.) So much of how we feel about ourselves is dictated by others, which is why it's wise to be aware of what's going on with our brains when we are consumed by empathy, compassion or someone else's energy. Interestingly, researchers discovered that compassion is the result of a group of specialised brain cells that allow people to mirror emotions and to share another person's pain, fear or joy. Empaths are said to have hyper-responsive mirror neurons, meaning they feel deeply and reflect upon other people's feelings. This happens because mirror neurons are triggered by external events and situations. For example, when your child cries you feel sad as well. Research has also shown that many people pick up the emotions of those around them. For instance, one person loudly expressing anxiety in the workplace can influence other workers. This ability to synchronise moods with others is crucial for good relationships. It's important for people to surround themselves with other positive people to ensure they aren't brought down by negativity.

Empath or not, it's easy to feel overstimulated from compassion overload. This can happen from scrolling through your Facebook feed and being hit with distressing news headlines, irritating comment threads, photos that trigger emotions or the whisper in your head that's telling you to *Stop procrastinating on social media and to reply to the 14 unread texts I have!* Compassion overload can even happen from going to dinner with friends, catching up for morning coffee with colleagues or having to make small talk on an airplane. Each of these experiences can leave you feeling anxious, depressed, sick or exhausted. By recognising the triggers, you will be able to quickly act to remedy the situation.

Some common factors that can contribute to compassion overload include fatigue, illness, rushing, traffic, crowds, loud environments, toxic people, low blood sugar, arguing, overwork, chemical sensitivities, too much socialising and feeling trapped in overstimulating situations such as parties and cruises. Keep in mind that stress mixed with low blood sugar can equal drama and exhaustion. Since it's not that easy to slip away to an idyllic cabin overlooking rolling hills every time you're spent, let's look at some ways you can relieve your symptoms in everyday life.

Overcoming Empathy Overload:
- Slow everything down and unplug from surrounding stimulations. If possible, find a quiet room without bright lights. Try doing breathwork or meditation to help recalibrate.
- Find a balance between relieving yourself from overstimulation and isolation. Try not to isolate yourself too much. Listen to your intuition about what is right for you.
- One of the best ways to minimise empathy overload is to turn inward and practise meditation to recharge yourself.

Dealing with an Emotional Hangover

Have you ever left someone's presence or an event and felt like you needed to sit on your couch and stare vacantly at a reality TV show about competitive baking? That, my friends, is what an emotional hangover can look like! This comes about when you experience leftover energy from an interaction, particularly a negative one. Toxic emotions can linger for a while after a bad interaction or situation, which is why I suggest the methods on the following page to get rid of negative energy.

'Empathic illness' is a term coined by American psychiatrist Dr Judith Orloff and is used to describe the experience of feeling someone's physical symptoms as if they were your own. For example, if a friend has a stomach-ache, so will you. You may sit next to a Negative Nancy, even in an otherwise positive environment, and leave the situation feeling sad. Empathic illness is not always negative; you can absorb positive feelings, too. After all, the saying 'laughter is contagious' exists for a reason! The nearer you are to a person with such feelings, the stronger you might be influenced. It's crucial to take time to protect yourself from negative people as well as too much stimulation.

Ridding Yourself and Your Space of Negative Energy:
- Ask yourself: *Is this symptom or emotion mine or someone else's?* Do you notice a sudden change of mood or physical state around another person?
- Breathe: When negativity strikes, focus on your breath for a few minutes. Slowly and deeply inhale and exhale to expel the uncomfortable energy. Breathing circulates negativity out of your body. Holding the breath and breathing shallowly keeps negativity in. Revisit the breathing exercises in Chapter 9: Your Mindfulness.
- Have a shower: Running water produces negative ions, which help increase oxygen flow to the brain. This will give you more mental ability to mindfully release negative energy. While the water is running down your body, repeat the following affirmation to cleanse off the energy: 'Let this shower wash away all the negative energy from my mind, body and spirit.'
- Use negative ion generators or salt lamps: These are great for clearing the air of dust, mould, pollen, odours and bacteria. They can also help remove leftover negativity in a house or office space.
- Try aromatherapy: Use a diffuser to disperse essential oils. Lavender and spearmint are calming scents, while spraying rosewater can be cleansing.

- Get out in nature: Breathing fresh air and spending time in nature are great cures for emotional hangovers. They can restore your mood and energy and allow you to calm down. (More on connecting with nature soon!)
- Meditate: Try a guided meditation to re-centre yourself.
- Seek emotional support: If you are feeling lingering negative effects, it can help to talk through your situation with a friend or therapist.

Most importantly, when you feel sad, just remember that you no longer look the way you did in Year 8.

CONNECTING WITH OTHERS

American entrepreneur Jim Rohn explains that we are the average of the five people we spend the most time with. While your first priority should be connecting with yourself, you also need to focus on your connections with others. How much do you think your social network, friends and partner influence areas of your life such as your mood, your weight, your chance of divorce and your happiness? According to Dr Nicholas Christakis, Professor of Medicine and Sociology at Harvard University, it is 45 per cent. This means that if your closest friend gets divorced, you are 45 per cent more likely to consider getting divorced. If your friend is experiencing a low mood, guess what – you're 45 per cent more likely to also have a low mood that day! The relationships we keep in our lives have a profound impact on our wellbeing. We are social animals and our experiences actually depend on the networks we spend our time in, which is why I'm all about carefully selecting, nourishing and sustaining them.

Social Network Audit

Take a moment to think about your current social network and mentally note how each person makes you feel.

Step 1

Make a list of the five people you are around the most (not including your kids if you're a parent or primary caregiver). Just to be clear, these aren't the five people you wish you could hang out with. These are the five adults you are exposed to the most in a week.

Step 2

Look at your list and ask yourself these questions:

- Do these relationships uplift or drain you?
- Are you able to be yourself in these relationships?
- What is the communication like in these relationships?

Circle the people who don't uplift you. Are there conversations you can have to change the relationship dynamic? If not, you may want to consider limiting interactions or removing them from your life.

Hopefully, all of these relationships are making you feel respected, happy and grateful. If they're not, that's okay. Later in the chapter, I will discuss why we may need to disconnect from some people and how to do it diplomatically. A little 'social spring-cleaning', if you will!

Building Your Social Network

When we truly connect with someone, it feels pretty great, right? We can enjoy an easy laugh, and a sense of confidence is shared. While your ability to build rapport with someone depends on having a bit of natural chemistry, research also points to several human factors that can increase the level of warmth and trust between two people.

Tips for Forming Connections with Someone

Ask Questions

Whenever we meet a new person, our brains do some fast work to decide how to react. Do we recognise their face? Are they a threat to us? Are they like us? In sociology, this is seeing someone as part of our in-group.

When you are meeting someone for the first time, I encourage you to ask enough questions to find things in common with them so you can get a better sense of who they actually are.

Mirror Body Language

Not only does mirroring someone's body language help you feel like you are on the same wavelength, but it also shows that you are engaged and listening. Make sure you use a subtle approach here.

Remember Their Name

Want to know what the sweetest sound is to anyone's ears? Their own name. A lot of people have trouble remembering other people's names. Here are my tips: repeat their name out loud after they introduce themselves and then mention their name twice in conversation. For example: 'Jane, it's nice to meet you'; 'Jane, this is Lisa'; 'Tell me more about that, Jane.'

You can also try connecting their name to something familiar. The more outrageous and left-field the connection, the more likely you are to remember it. (Confession, when I first met Jay, I connected it to 'vajayjay'.)

Check Your Posture

One of the first things people notice is how you carry and present yourself. Do you walk and stand with confidence? The most important thing you can do to ensure correct posture is probably similar to what my mother taught me: stand tall as if a string is being pulled from the centre of your head. You want to portray to people that you are confident and sure of yourself.

Shake Hands

To connect instantly with someone, shake hands, when possible. Touch is the most primitive and powerful non-verbal cue. Touching someone on the arm, hand or shoulder for as little as a fraction of a second creates a human bond. In the workplace, physical touch is established through the handshaking tradition, and this tactile feedback makes a lasting and positive impression. Fun fact: a study on handshakes by the Income Center for Trade showed that people are twice as likely to remember you if you shake hands with them. Another fun fact: the temperature of your hands impacts how people perceive your trust-worthiness. No one likes to shake a cold, clammy hand, so before you meet someone, make sure you warm those hands up!

What Makes Someone a Good Friend?

One of my favourite sayings is that friends are in your life for a reason, a season or a lifetime. While it's important to be mindful and realistic that sometimes life, space or other issues can drive us apart, it's also important to actively seek out the behaviours (in yourself and in others) that make a good friend. I know that I want to be friends with people who speak openly from the heart, are comfortable being vulnerable, do what they say they're going to do and are willing to stand up for me.

Signs of a Good Friendship:
- You always make time for each other.
- After spending time together, you both feel happy and content.
- You can be 100 per cent yourselves around each other.
- You encourage each other to follow your dreams.
- You're not afraid to show each other some tough love (but keep it respectful).
- You don't try to chip each other down or hold each other back.
- You let go of your ego in their presence.
- You make each other feel at ease.
- You support each other during the highs and lows.
- You make each other feel more confident.
- You're happy for each other's successes, not jealous.

Maintaining Friendships

Even though the world is becoming smaller and smaller, and we seem to have more ways to communicate than Beyoncé has costumes, finding time and energy to invest in friendships seems to be a significant challenge. I get it, we're all BUSY. Here are my tips for finding ways to invest in and maintain the friendships in your life that matter.

A Picture Is Worth a Thousand Words

If you're on Facebook or Instagram, have you ever noticed how they'll prompt you to look back on photo memories? The same feature exists on smartphones in your camera roll. I love being able to quickly forward the photo memory with a note to a friend reminding them of a special shared time.

Schedule the Catch-up into Your Week

As fun as it is to play phone tag, I promise it's much more effective if you find a time to book in your call or Zoom catch-up.

Share Your Gratitude

Commit to sending each other daily, weekly or monthly gratitude emails. While you don't need to express your gratitude about each other (however, you can), it's a fun way to spread positivity back and forth.

Send Memes

Humour is such a powerful tool when it comes to coping, bonding and connecting because when we laugh, we release the trifecta of feel-good hormones: oxytocin, serotonin and dopamine. I love a good meme because it's so easy to send and rarely warrants more than a laughing emoji in response. When we first went into lockdown, I don't think I would have made it out the other side without the copious COVID-19 memes my friends and I sent back and forth!

Celebrate the Wins

If your bestie just started a new business, got a promotion or sold their house, celebrate! Send a congratulatory card or bottle of champagne. These little gestures are powerful and can literally make their day. You can also send gifts during the tougher times. When one of my very good friends went through breast cancer, a few of us chipped in to send her an organic meal delivery service over the three months she was having chemotherapy. Not only did it help nourish her body and save her the hassle of shopping, but every time a box arrived, it was also a reminder that we were there for her.

> ## ⌐ THE SECRET TO LIVING TO 100 ⌐
>
> The Italian island of Sardinia has more than six times as many centenarians as the mainland and ten times as many as North America. Why? According to longevity researcher Susan Pinker, it's not a sunny disposition or a low-fat, gluten-free diet that keeps the islanders alive so long. It's their emphasis on close personal relationships and face-to-face interactions.

Connecting with Colleagues

It doesn't matter if you're an employee, freelancer or on a volunteer committee, getting along with others in a professional capacity is an incredibly important aspect of excelling in any field. When there is friction at work, we're liable to underperform or take the emotional frustrations home with us. Many of us are emotional sponges and tend to pick up on other people's energies. This can be amazing when the vibes are good, but when they're negative, it can be detrimental to our mental and physical health. Below are my tips for building solid workplace relationships (and identifying the ones that need work).

Build Rapport

When things are strictly business, the workday can drag on or even feel soul-destroying. While I'm not saying you should try to make Barbara from human resources your bestie, I am saying that it's important to build rapport. Small talk, when done right, can help people become more approachable, more engaged and more likely to work well together. Good ways to build rapport are to find common interests and goals, avoid heated political or religious debates and offer help without being asked.

Establish Boundaries

If you don't want to mix work with pleasure, it's best not to share too much of your personal life or engage in extracurricular activities such as happy-hour drinks. Since we're now living in the age of social media, you can also take time to decide if Patrick from accounting is someone who needs to see your Instagram posts showing off your latest IKEA win or #sodrunkrightnow selfie.

Acknowledge and Celebrate Your Colleagues' Wins

Give credit where credit is due; show your gratitude and offer praise. There's nothing worse than spending extra time on someone else's project only for them to bask in all your glory … It's also nice to hear your own hard work acknowledged.

Resolve Workplace Conflict Diplomatically

You're not always going to agree on how something should be done. In fact, Susan from customer care probably hates your new system because it's just *another* thing she needs to learn. But here's the thing: you have done the research and it is 100 per cent the best thing for the business. Instead of telling Susan to kindly F-off and stay in her own lane, try respectfully offering your reasoning for implementing the new system. Next, acknowledge her concerns and offer empathy. Last, explain how you'll support her through the change.

Don't Become the Workplace Therapist

There's always that one person who is having relationship issues and just loves to unload by the water cooler, right? Most of the time, they're not going to take your advice anyway, so nip your moonlight performance of Dr Fix-It in the bud!

CONNECTING WITH YOUR PARTNER

If you've chosen to be in a romantic relationship with someone, you'll know that after all that 'happily ever after' jazz comes a whole lot of 'your chewing makes me want to die' and 'why don't I want to have sex with you anymore?' Okay, so I may be exaggerating a bit, but let's be honest: romantic relationships are tough and can often leave emotional residue hanging in the air, which can limit your ability to reach your full potential. That is why I want to unpack what makes a healthy union as well as some of the ways you can improve the connection you have with your partner. That way, you can deepen intimacy and avoid conflict in the long term.

In an ideal relationship, you participate in each other's personal growth, you value each other's independence, you don't have to walk on eggshells and you always feel like you can say what's on your mind. You trust each other without question, you share similar values, you respect each other and you're able to move forward together through change. Most importantly, you give true apologies. (For the record, a true apology does not include the word 'but' and doesn't try to shine a light on who started it.) You take action to fix a situation. You're also aware that your partner can't be your everything. As nice as it would be to have a person be your lover, best friend, guiding light, financial guru, career coach, mindfulness mentor and personal chef, it's just not realistic. You need to recognise that you're never going to get everything from one person. You also need to recognise that you can't be everything to one person.

Take a moment and think about you and your partner. How quick are you to agree that the words loyalty, respect, trust, love and emotional stability ring true for you? Would you describe each other as reliable, practical, proactive, organised and kind? Would you say that you both acknowledge that relationships take work and compromise? If you're thinking, *Yes, we are all of these things!* then you're on a great path. If you're thinking, *Ughhhh, we could be better with a lot of these* then let's talk about signs of an unhealthy relationship and habits to avoid.

Signs of an Unhealthy Relationship:
- feeling insecure in the relationship
- feeling empty
- fear of upsetting a partner or causing conflict
- lack of personal growth
- feelings of inadequacy
- feeling like you can't make your own decisions.

In many circumstances, these feelings are a direct result of both conscious and subconscious habits. Below, I've outlined some of the things we do that can make a relationship unhealthy.

Bottling Up Your Feelings

As fun as it would be to read each other's minds, it's just not (always) possible. If you're feeling frustrated, unheard, annoyed or afraid, speak up. This doesn't need to be in an accusatory manner. Try using language such as, 'I would have liked to be part of making such a big decision.' If you don't speak up, I guarantee you will inadvertently, or knowingly, become extremely passive aggressive.

Being Overly Critical

Too much criticism, constant complaints, nagging and expressions of dissatisfaction can really be a relationship killer. While some things definitely need to be addressed, I promise it's worth letting the little things go.

Ignoring Your Partner's Concerns

A person is only going to voice concerns to someone who doesn't respond so many times before they start to feel rejected, unheard or ignored.

We need to be listened to and heard in order to receive empathy and compassion.

Losing Your Shit

I admit that it's way easier to blow up and yell, 'What the f#*$ were you thinking?!' than take a moment to pause and calmly express your dismay. One of the tools I use is asking for 10 minutes to digest what was said before responding to a discussion we're not seeing eye to eye on. This always helps me work through how I'm actually feeling and brings me down a few levels so we can rationally discuss the issue.

Engaging in Technoference

Technoference is when it feels like a partner is paying more attention to their phone or computer than you. Instead of spending the weekend parallel liking the same memes on social media, try putting the phones down and having a conversation.

⌐ COMPLIMENTS THAT HAVE NOTHING TO DO WITH APPEARANCE ⌐

While it's nice to hear, 'You look smokin' hot in those pants!', it's also nice not to feel like your self-worth is purely based on your appearance all the time. Below are things you can say to your partner to strengthen their self-efficacy (without making it sound like you're always objectifying them).

- ☐ You inspire me to be a better person.
- ☐ I am proud of you.
- ☐ You're great at telling stories.
- ☐ I learn so much from being around you.
- ☐ You're a good listener.
- ☐ I admire your confidence.

Not Giving Each Other Enough Space

I'm going to dive deeper into this shortly, but one of the biggest issues couples face is spending too much time together. Like I said before, you can't be each other's everything.

Making Up After an Argument

I know it's easier said than done, but after an argument, it's a good idea to take time to cool off. If you talk too soon, you're likely going to fire up again and trigger each other. Get some headspace by doing a meditation and then come back to the discussion when you have a calm and rational mind. Don't pretend it didn't happen, don't do the ostrich approach. Don't keep pushing the person's buttons, just pause and listen. Apologising is not saying the other person wins. It acknowledges hurt feelings and makes space for a solution. The repair is what matters so try to learn something from the argument or the underlying cause.

Space Is a Really Good Thing

One of the best things I ever did for my relationship was acknowledge and honour the need for personal space. When you're living, parenting and working with a romantic partner, it's easy to feel smothered. This particularly rings true for those who are easily overstimulated. By defining what feels good for you, you're keeping negative energy out and making time for self-care, which is one of the best forms of self-preservation.

Questions to Ask Yourself:
- Would I prefer more alone time?
- Would I like to sleep by myself sometimes?
- Do I want to talk/have sex/hang out more or less?

For a healthy relationship, there are a few things you can do to help create space in your day-to-day life.

Clarify Your Preferred Sleep Style

Traditionally, partners sleep in the same bed. However, some people find it hard as they like their own sleep space. The constant overstimulation of noises, movements and sounds can make sleeping in bed with your partner torture. Perhaps this means sleeping in separate beds, rooms or even houses. You may need to make a compromise with your partner if they would prefer to sleep together. This could be sleeping separately during the work week and then sharing a bed on the weekends. Whatever you choose, try to make it as mutually beneficial as possible.

Establish Privacy or Space in Your Household

Have you ever come home from work and just needed to chill out? This can be hard to do if your partner is everywhere you go or already flicking on the TV that you couldn't wait to lounge in front of. Here are some ideas for establishing personal space in your own household:

- Make a rule that you don't debrief on your day for the first 30 minutes of being home.
- Set up a section of your home that is a sacred zen space for you. I use our guestroom as a space to meditate.
- Take a mini-break by going for a walk around the block.
- Before bed, have your wind-down time separate from each other. For example, you could go read in the bedroom while your partner does a puzzle in the kitchen.
- If you're parents, be sure to give each other breaks from the kids.

Travel Wisely

Travelling is one of the trickiest things to do as a couple because both of your routines may be thrown off kilter. If it's viable, try to book two rooms or find accommodation that has plenty of space for you to disconnect and do your own thing. Also, try going away separately. Twice a year, Jay and I go on our own holidays with our own friends. We both find these trips to be really recharging.

Conversations to Have with Your Partner About Space and Boundaries

You must learn to communicate authentically and set clear boundaries with your partner in order for the relationship to grow and flourish. Depending on your partner, there are different ways to communicate effectively.

If your partner is a deep thinker, logical and analytical, consider asking for help, mentioning one issue at a time and regularly communicating. For example, 'I would like some time alone to recharge, it is not personal, all I need you to do for now is allow me to spend the afternoon alone.' If your partner is more sensitive, it is important to communicate about your triggers and create a plan for handling them together. Try saying, 'Let's take separate cars to the event tonight so neither of us feels obliged to stay if one of us wants to leave.' If your partner struggles to open up and express their emotions, consider regularly expressing gratitude for them, asking them to express verbally at least one emotion a day and spending quality time together.

If you're really struggling to create an open channel of communication, it might be time to consider seeing a couples counsellor or therapist. (I'll talk more about this in Chapter 13: Your Support.)

The Difference Between Connection and Attachment

We've all seen the movie *Swimfan*, right? (If you haven't, definitely add it to your list so you can keep up with the clever pop-culture references people throw your way.) Stalking might make for a fantastic movie, but in the real world relationships need to be built on a connection, not one-sided obsession, attachment or infatuation. While one version of this could be straight-up stalking, another could simply be someone falling in love with someone else's potential. Another could be you staying in a relationship because you're emotionally and financially dependent.

People often become attached to the wrong people because they develop unrealistic expectations surrounding the relationship. A healthy connection is when partners are mutually committed to the relationship and both want to open their hearts and minds to each other. In contrast, attachment is when we cling to someone with a death grip, hoping the person will change or that they can change us. Attachments are dangerous because they can keep us linked to unavailable people or toxic relationships.

DISCONNECTING FROM A RELATIONSHIP OR FRIENDSHIP

Our bodies are like sponges. However, instead of absorbing 'good vibes only' we're more likely to take on the good, the bad and the extremely negative energy of others. When you're surrounded by positive energies, the ability to absorb others' feelings can be great! However, when you're hanging out with an energy vampire, you can have the mental and physical strength sucked out of your very being.

One sign that you're spending time with an energy vampire is noticing that you leave their presence feeling emotionally exhausted. You could also feel as though you are always walking on eggshells and taking the blame for the negative circumstances in their life. Energy vampires tend to comment on flaws and imperfections, are never happy for your achievements and constantly make you feel responsible for their contentment and happiness. Energy vampires don't have to be outright baddies, they can also be people who identify as the victim or simply can't stop focusing on themselves.

What's hard about energy-vampires is that they are always attracted to people who are open, compassionate, empathetic and positive. (If that sounds like you, you better watch yourself!)

Let's talk about five common energy-vampire archetypes: the Narcissist, the Victim, the Nonstop Talker, the Gossiper and the Gaslighter.

The Narcissist

Arguably one of the most destructive types of people to spend time with, the Narcissist acts as if the world revolves around them. They need to be the centre of attention and require endless praise, which is why you feel like the only way to win their approval is by complimenting them.

The Victim

The Victim means well but, honestly, they're nearly as bad as the Narcissist. They never take responsibility for their own problems, walk around thinking 'the world is against me' and love to download all of their woes onto you *even though* they will never actually take your advice or ownership of their own destiny.

The Nonstop Talker

The Nonstop Talker might be a totally decent and great friend; however, they can drive the life-force out of you with their endless verbal assault (aka storytelling). Long story short, they're bad at picking up on social cues and never give you an opening. While you would be sad not to have them in your life, you know that you can only handle them in small doses.

The Gossiper

The Gossiper cannot be trusted. If they're saying something horrible about someone to you, I guarantee they're saying something not-so-nice about you behind your back. The Gossiper makes you feel unsure of yourself or like everything is a competition. They're jealous of your other friends, tend to be negative and overstep boundaries.

The Gaslighter

The Gaslighter makes you feel like you've done something wrong even though you haven't. Highly manipulative, they are experts in shifting the blame and reordering the story so that they look like the victim and you the culprit. If you feel like you're being gaslighted, it could be a sign of an abusive relationship.

Protection Strategies for Energy Vampires

When dealing with the Narcissist:

- Lower expectations of the Narcissist's emotional capabilities.
- Don't let yourself be manipulated.
- Don't expect them to respect your sensitivities.
- Don't get in a relationship with them.
- Try to avoid working with a narcissistic boss.

When dealing with the Victim:

- Set compassionate and clear boundaries.
- Set up a time limit for your phone call. For example, 'Hi <insert name>, I only have five minutes before my next meeting to chat.'
- Use breathing strategies to remain calm.
- Use a shield visualisation technique so you don't absorb their energy. (I will share one soon!)
- Offer tough love and then close the door on a particular point of discussion.

When dealing with the Nonstop Talker:

- Schedule in times to talk if you know it's a conversation that needs to be had.
- Set a time-limit rule if you bump into them. 'Hi <insert name>, it's great to see you. I'm just on my way to the shop.'
- Try saying, 'Excuse me for interrupting, but I need to go to the bathroom/to my next meeting.'

When dealing with the Gossiper:

- Don't fuel the fire by agreeing with the negative gossip they might be sharing.
- Try saying things like, 'There are two sides to every story and somewhere in the middle lies the truth,' before changing the subject.
- Do not make yourself vulnerable by sharing personal information that they could later use against you.

When dealing with the Gaslighter:

- Run, don't walk away!
- After an encounter, take a moment to decompress, then speak to a friend or psychologist to work out what just happened! (Sometimes you need a third party to remind you that no, you're not insane and yes, the person sucks.)
- If you have to see them again, keep records of conversations.
- Consider engaging a mediator to resolve any major disagreements.

The 'Shield Yourself' Technique

Shielding is a deliberately defensive technique aimed at guarding your feelings without repressing them. It works by visualising an enveloping white light (or any colour you feel imparts power) around your entire body. Think of it as a shield that blocks out negativity and physical discomfort but allows what's positive to filter in. Let's take an example:

imagine your sister is on a rampage. She's about to blow up; you don't want her anger to shatter you. Now, take a deep breath, centre yourself and engage your shield. Picture it forming a fail-safe barrier around you that protects against anger. It simply can't get to you.

Try the 'Shield Yourself' Meditation:

1. After finding a quiet place to sit with a tall spine, take a moment to shut your eyes and let your breath wash through your body.
2. Next, bring your breath to your heart space. Breathe naturally and adjust to becoming still.
3. Now imagine that you're sitting by a waterfall and feeling the sunlight touching your skin – think of the softness of it.
4. As you're breathing, visualise a warm light surrounding your body and extending a few inches beyond your skin. This shield of light will protect you from anything draining, stressful, toxic or overwhelming. Within this shield of light, you feel protected, grounded and energised.
5. Silently say, 'Thank you for this protection.'
6. Take an inhale and deep exhale, and feel yourself become anchored deep into the ground.
7. Feel an unwavering connection to the shield of this light and observe as the light begins to calm you.
8. Stay until you feel grounded and calm.

Signs You've Outgrown a Friendship

You don't have to be friends with an energy vampire to feel like a particular relationship has run its course. If you're finding a friendship or romantic relationship is depleting rather than energising, or if you feel like an outdated version of yourself when you are with them, it could be time to either work on or leave the relationship. Take notice if one person stops putting in the effort to maintain the relationship, if you have nothing in common with them anymore or if you're finding it hard to have a conversation. Remember what I said earlier: people can be in your life for a reason, a season or a lifetime, and that's okay.

Establishing Boundaries and Letting People Go

While some relationships can be salvaged, sometimes they simply need to go. One of the reasons that people do not get rid of negative friends or partners is because they don't know how to do it. As you'll recall from earlier in the chapter, there are plenty of ways of saying 'No' or removing people from your life without straight ghosting.

If it's a family member:

- Can you limit how often you speak each week?
- In a stern but fair way, let them know you are not open to receiving unsolicited advice.
- Can you attend a therapy session to help resolve your differences?

If it's someone at work:

- Can you consider a move within the company?
- Are you able to relocate your desk?
- Can you attend mediation to create a neutral (and less abrasive) relationship?

If it's someone in your social circle:

- Let them know you're not available for events – you can cite personal or professional reasons.
- Explain to mutual friends that you need a break from the person and that it's okay if they don't invite you to the same events.
- Invite them to have a coffee to let them know how they make you feel.

Spring-cleaning or minimising your social network doesn't have to be tactless. Go through your list and if there is someone pulling you down, try using one or more of the tips above to decrease the amount of time you spend with them.

Tips for Communicating Kindly:
- Be present and direct.
- Listen to their point of view without interrupting.
- Be mindful of trigger topics.
- If an argument is clearly becoming a game of just needing to 'win', end it.
- Don't use accusatory language. Opt for, 'When you did X, it made me feel Y.'

⌐ HOW TO DEAL WITH DIFFICULT FAMILY MEMBERS ⌐

Having conflict with a family member can hurt on multiple levels. So many of us have ideals of how our relationships should be with parents and siblings. Unfortunately, family can be a high-friction point for a lot of people, which is why it's important to be mindful of difficult family members. Many times, arguments can quickly evolve into personal attacks. Remember that your wellbeing needs to come first and you do not need to allow anyone to occupy your mental space.

DECIDING TO LEAVE A PARTNER

You could be three months, three years or three decades into a relationship and finding yourself wondering: Is it time to leave? The answer to that is extremely difficult and something that should not be taken lightly. While everyone's personal situation will be exactly that – personal – you may find this list of questions helpful when it comes to gaining clarity about the viability of a relationship.

- Do we treat each other lovingly and respectfully?
- Are we both open to change and evolving as a couple?
- Do we care about other people and have close friends of our own?
- Do we respect each other's boundaries?
- Are love and friendship priorities in our lives?
- Do we both feel independent and free to speak our minds?
- Are we both giving and unselfish most of the time?
- Are we both truly capable of love?
- And the real litmus test – do we both treat hospitality staff well? (This is super telling!)

If you find that you're saying 'No' to a number of these questions, it's probably a good idea to start thinking about taking action. Sometimes, it can be really difficult to find clarity around your relationship when you're immersed in it, which is why I recommend speaking to a therapist either individually or together. One of the main reasons why people stay in relationships longer than they should is because societal pressures weigh us down. We worry what people will think if we leave. We worry what will happen to our financial stability. We worry that we won't ever find love again. Trust that you have the capacity to rebuild your life. You are enough for you. Remember, if you can truly connect with yourself first, you'll be much more likely to connect with the right person at the right time.

CONNECTING WITH NATURE

Just like building and maintaining meaningful relationships, connecting with nature is critical for our mental health. Not only does it help keep our immune systems strong and our circadian rhythms in check, but being immersed in nature has been scientifically proven to lower our stress, increase empathy and improve our moods. A series of studies at the University of California looked at the impact of nature on people's behaviour. It showed that people who spent more time in nature made more ethical decisions, had greater generosity and more prosocial values.

Due to work pressures and our increasing tendency to socialise online, we're spending less time than ever outdoors. Intentionally or not, even when we are outside, most of us seem to have our eyes glued to a phone. If only we could look up, soak up some sunlight and let Mother Earth work her magic on us! Just like drinking enough water and eating nourishing food that promotes a healthy gut microbiome, time in nature is one of our body's best forms of medicine. First, the sun triggers our production of vitamin D, a hormone that's not only critical for a wide variety of biological processes but also directly tied to the brain's ability to synthesise serotonin (your happy chemical). Vitamin-D deficiency has been linked to depression and it's no wonder we're getting more depressed. Many of us are working in artificially lit office buildings in concrete jungles. Without getting enough natural elements onto our skin and eyes, we're inadvertently causing our bodies to operate in a way they're simply not designed to.

We've all heard the saying, 'Stop and smell the flowers,' right? Well, there's a bit more to that than just pausing to enjoy the present moment. In 2016, a study concluded that the olfactory stimulation of fragrances produces immediate changes in our physiology including to blood pressure, muscle tension and heart rate. Even more compelling, it showed that fragrances released in nature have a direct effect on different parts of our brain, including the area that helps us calm down. This is probably why we are drawn to the smells of freshly cut lawn, fresh flowers and fresh air!

But let's go back to taking time to stop and smell the flowers … Have you ever gone for a hike and at the very end found a majestic waterfall? How about seeing a rainbow after a big rainstorm? Did it make you feel calm instead of anxious and stressed? When we see something that is impressive, it has a positive effect on the way we deal with ourselves and others. Nature reminds us that we are really just like ants on the planet. When you take a step back, you'll realise we hold a relatively insignificant place in the universe. This realisation allows us to focus on others without disproportionately valuing our self-worth or our problems.

BENEFITS OF BEING IN NATURE

☐ boosts immune system

☐ lowers blood pressure and stress

☐ improves mood

☐ increases focus and energy

☐ improves empathy

☐ improves sleep.

People Who Connect with Nature Are Happier at Work

A 2016 study looked at what would happen if nature was introduced into an indoor workspace. It found that even the smallest changes, like putting a plant on the participants' desks, or hanging a photo of nature, lowered depression and anxiety and increased job satisfaction.

People Who Connect with Nature Recover Faster

In 2011, a study of 278 patients in a cardiac and pulmonary rehab centre in Norway compared the outcomes of patients with a view of nature to the outcomes of patients with a view blocked by buildings. The study found that patients whose windows were blocked by buildings experienced a worsening of physical and mental health compared with patients who had an unobstructed view. In 2012, researchers in Amsterdam placed plants and posters of plants in a hospital waiting room and observed that it led to lower levels of stress compared with patients waiting in the plantless waiting room. In another study conducted by the Mayo Clinic, just a mix of natural sounds and music was able to lower anxiety and pain scores in patients.

People Who Connect with Nature Have Less Stress

In a study analysing the blood and urine of female nurses during a typical work day and again after they spent three days and two nights in a forest, researchers found a significant increase in the nurses' blood levels of natural killer cells (a type of white blood cell that can fight tumours and viruses!) and a significant decrease of adrenaline and noradrenaline (the major chemicals involved in our stress response). Basically, being in nature, not to mention a well-earned break, boosted their immune systems and lowered their sympathetic nervous system's response to stress!

People Who Connect with Nature Are More Productive and Better Problem-solvers

A 2012 study tested 56 men and women in creative problem-solving before and after a four-day nature hike. The research found that their four days of immersion in nature, and the corresponding disconnection from technology, increased performance on problem-solving tasks by a huge 50 per cent.

What the research is showing us is that nature has a powerful effect on our bodies and minds. It heals us and restores our energy. It ultimately nourishes the brain for greater mental wellbeing and supports our body's systems. I recognise that it's not always possible to go for long leisurely nature walks or make ocean swims part of your morning routine. But it's still beneficial to carve out 30 minutes a week, bring plants into your home and workspace or even just look out a window or at a picture of the natural world. One of the best gifts I've ever given my daughter Clara was a chrysalis kit from Butterfly Adventures. Together as a family, we watched a cocoon hatch and got to spend a day with a gorgeous butterfly before releasing it into the wild. The joy and excitement of the natural world had us on a high for the whole day.

Add Nature to Your Life by:
- having your coffee and breakfast by a window, or on a patio or balcony
- taking a walk outside
- eating lunch in a park
- walking instead of taking the bus or train (even just once a week)
- going for a swim
- opting to camp instead of booking a hotel
- going for a horseback ride
- buying plants for your home and office.

Grounding Technique

Depending on whether you keep up with Gwyneth Paltrow's latest obsession, you may or may not have heard of 'grounding' or 'earthing'. Essentially, it's a way of connecting to the earth in an effort to feel calm and centred, and this practice can be really helpful when it comes to relieving anxiety and stress. Some people say putting your bare feet on the ground at your new destination can also minimise jet lag. (As someone who has fallen asleep at 4 pm and risen at 3 am more times than I'd like, I'm fully prepared to test this theory.) While the most common practice of grounding is to be outside touching the earth, you can also do it indoors and consciously connect (because sometimes it's just too cold to go outside, right?).

Grounding 101:

1. Find a quiet place outside on soft grass. (If you can't be outside, try sitting near a plant or somewhere you can see a picture of nature.)
2. Sit in a comfortable position and take a few deep breaths to relax your body. Just breathe and relax.
3. When thoughts come in, let them drift by like clouds in the sky. Do not attach to them. Focus on inhaling and exhaling, letting the stress leave your body as you connect to a sense of serenity.

4 In this tranquil inner space, visualise a large tree with a wide, strong trunk that extends down the centre of your body, from head to toe. Take a few moments to feel its power and vibrant energy, and then visualise the tree's roots growing from the bottom of your spine down into the ground, making their way deeper and deeper, creating a sense of stability.

5 Focus on these roots when you are anxious or afraid. Let the roots anchor you into Mother Earth, stabilising you.

Rooting yourself in this way provides an inner strength that will keep you centred and protected when life gets overwhelming.

IN YOUR JOURNAL

■ Using the framework provided in this chapter, do an audit of your social network. Is there an energy vampire (or two) that you may need to distance yourself from?

■ In your professional life, are there any relationships you'd like to improve? If yes, what are some actions you could take?

■ How would you describe your romantic relationship? If you have a partner, do you feel you're both satisfied and happy? If you're single, what would you look for in a partner?

■ How often have you been connecting with nature? How do you feel when you're outside? Are there more opportunities for you to get out and immerse yourself in nature?

12
YOUR PRODUCTIVITY

I'VE SPENT A lot of this book sharing strategies to improve your mental health for a high-performance mindset, but now I want to focus on your productivity. Have you heard the phrase 'Work smarter, not harder'? A common default for high performers is to go into beast mode (if you will) to power through mountains of work, hit sales targets, or train to climb Mount Everest. While there is a time and place for beast mode, I want to point out a few key areas in your work life where you can implement new practices and adopt habits that will make you not only more productive but also more effective.

Productivity impacts your quality of life and overall mental health in a number of ways. For starters, it's going to influence the speed with which you accomplish your short- and long-term goals. Depending on your circumstances, it can improve the profitability of your business. It's also going to allow you to have more time for your personal life. Whether that's going on holiday with family, taking time for self-care or volunteering in the community, being able to produce your life's work in a timely and effective way is going to help you achieve the goals in all seven areas of your life as we talked about in Chapter 5: Your Goals.

In this chapter, you'll learn how to boost your creativity and motivation, beat procrastination, prioritise and schedule tasks, minimise multi-tasking, uncover your circadian clock to find your optimal state of flow and improve your meetings and email efficiency.

BOOSTING CREATIVITY AND MOTIVATION

Can you think of the last time you had a 'totally genius' idea? Was it when you were running? In the shower? Were you swimming in the ocean? I'm going to guess it wasn't when you were sitting at your desk typing up a report while intermittently doomscrolling through your Facebook newsfeed ... I don't know if this is an actual scientific law or not, but ideas don't usually come when our minds are busy. In a world where people are paid to literally find ways to keep us engaged, it's becoming quite the challenge to consciously disengage in an effort to not only create new ideas but also solve problems. One of my favourite authors, Simon Sinek, often speaks about how the conscious mind can access around 4 feet of information while the unconscious mind can access 11 acres! So, while a brainstorming session is great for asking the question or posing the problem, you're more likely to find the solution when you disengage from actively trying to solve it.

While this will vary depending on the type of job you have or industry that you're in (or just how addicted to your phone you are), the most common creativity-blocking culprit is technology. From the moment we wake up in the morning, we are at risk of obsessive email checking, social-media sessioning and news-reading. I spoke about the negative impacts this type of behaviour can have on your mental health in Chapter 6: Your Morning Routine, but now I want to focus on how you can consciously disconnect from technology to boost your creativity and productivity. Instead of coming home from work only to cycle through phone notifications while watching TV, I encourage people to spend their evenings doing an activity that allows their brain to wander and process information from the day. For example, if you spend half an hour doing a mindfulness activity like piecing together a puzzle, knitting or painting, you're much more likely to properly decompress from your day and start fresh the next.

How to Detox from Technology:
- Have a phone-free commute.
- Turn off your desktop notifications.
- Turn off email notifications on your phone.
- Delete non-essential apps during work hours.
- Have off-grid days.
- When scheduling your day, book in times to go for a walk, look out the window or meditate.
- Schedule designated times to check your phone throughout the day.
- Swap meme-sharing for mindfulness activities.

Sometimes when we are so immersed in our own business or projects, we lose the ability to see things from a different perspective or simply lose steam due to mental fatigue. One of the ways I like to bring new ideas and motivation into my professional space is by reading, watching and listening to content about industries outside of my sector. Even though my domain is psychology and mental health, you'd be shocked by how many ideas I've had for EQ Minds based on what I learned someone was doing with lawnmowers in Sweden or takeaway salads in Sausalito. Even if I'm not picking up any marketing or business ideas, it's really inspiring to listen to how other entrepreneurs overcame hurdles, created unique partnerships or pivoted as the world changed. Being exposed to diversity of thought is a powerful thing and a great way to breathe fresh air into your own business. In fact, I love it so much that sometimes when I'm out to dinner, I ask the waiter to bring me whatever their favourite dish is instead of choosing for myself.

Over the next few weeks, keep an eye out for ways you can try something new. While it could be signing up for a dance class, it could also be as simple as flipping open a cookbook and choosing a recipe at random.

Another way to boost creativity and motivation, as well as gain guidance, is by working with a mentor or joining a business networking group. While you can find mentors through paid programs, I've personally never paid for one and recommend seeing whom you can connect with on your own before shelling out big money (especially if this is your first time and you're getting familiar with how the relationship can work).

The best way to begin looking for a mentor is to think about your objective. Are you a café owner thinking about franchising? Look for someone who has done just that! Are you an entrepreneur who needs help in the negotiation ring? Perhaps you want someone from the corporate world with a decade of deals under their belt. When I was looking for my current mentor, I knew I wanted someone who could help me scale EQ Minds. I also knew I wanted a female's perspective, as well as someone who'd started from the ground up. I mentally began going through my network and realised I had met someone at a women's networking event who'd recently sold her business for just over $800 million. This was totally my woman. After teeing up a call via email, I called her and asked if she could give me one hour of her time once a month. Thankfully she said 'Yes'. Look, I know it can be scary to ask someone for something, but it's already 'No' if you don't ask them. Might as well give it a go!

Mentors don't always have to be just for business strategy. For example, I mentor two kids (who are actually almost 30) and a lot of the wisdom they're searching for is around mindset and personal development. We discuss books, podcasts and local events they can attend to expand their knowledge and self-efficacy. At the end of the day, you want someone who is going to challenge your thinking in order to tap into an even better idea! You also want someone who isn't going to tell you what to do, but show you examples and case studies of how things can work so you can make your own decisions.

As for business-networking groups, these can also take many shapes. While some are elbow-knocking and drink-clinking soirees, others can offer more of a problem-solving workshop feel. I know it can make people really vulnerable to share their company's financials or weaknesses, but if you're able to find a group of individuals you trust, it can act as a mini advisory board.

RESTRUCTURING YOUR DAY FOR PRODUCTIVITY

Even though I'm about to talk about restructuring your day, I actually want you to start by restructuring your week. Every Sunday, I sit down with my diary to determine my top priority for the week and then break down what I can do each day to achieve it. Not only does this help alleviate the dreaded case of the Mondays, but it also helps me stay clear on what my goals are. In fact, it gets me pumped up! I'll be completely honest – my week doesn't always go to plan. Meetings get cancelled, speaking engagements that may have involved travel get diverted to a Zoom presentation (thanks, COVID), or a new opportunity presents itself that warrants my attention and energy. While you need to plan strategically, you also need to remain fluid. This is why I do my Sunday planning session as well as a daily morning plan.

At the start of my workday, the first thing I like to do (this is way before I even think about checking my email!) is identify my Most Important Task (MIT). Next, I look at the other tasks and prioritise them. Even though I'm an advocate for a to-do list, studies have shown that only 41 per cent of items on these lists actually get done. So, while I have my list, I also consciously pick a date and time to action each task. I also aim to do my MIT within the first two hours of my workday.

But Chelsea, the first two hours of my day are for drinking coffee and chatting about crap with Emily from the design department.

As necessary as workplace friendships are (and caffeine!), the first two hours of the morning are hugely important for overall productivity. The last thing you want to do is waste any of that magical brainpower on a conversation you could have another time. You also don't want to expend your energy on emails, phone calls or meetings … *yet.* This is the perfect time to find your flow and dive deep into projects that require intense concentration and focus. Brian Tracy, author of *Eat that Frog!*, is a huge advocate of doing your MIT first because it's often the thing you've been avoiding. If it's something really big and important, there's a good chance you feel like it's looming over you and creating unnecessary stress. By creating the habit of doing your MIT first up, you can give yourself a huge boost of confidence and sense of accomplishment that you can carry into the rest of your day.

After you have identified your MIT, you need to be ruthless with your prioritisation. As a rule of thumb, your hippocampus (memory centre) can keep three tasks clear in your mind simultaneously. For that reason, you should limit yourself to three tasks for the day. But which three? When I was at Johnson & Johnson, one of the best tips I ever received was, 'Chase the antelope, not the field mice.' What this means is focus on the business or client that is going to give you the biggest return on your time. We have such limited time and resources, so if you land a big client (antelope) it will make up for eight small ones (mice).

DON'T FORGET TO CELEBRATE

We are all so busy and our minds are so task-focused that we tend to rush from one thing to the next and miss taking time to celebrate what we are achieving. Your brain is motivated by rewards. It will intrinsically drive you to achieve more if you reward yourself regularly. Try celebrating the progress you have made on your goals weekly or monthly.

FLOW STATE AND YOUR ULTRADIAN RHYTHM

Sometimes referred to as being 'in the zone', your flow state is the time when you feel like you're in the groove. You could be writing a novel, practising a presentation or mapping out projected sales for the next quarter. Whatever it is, flow state is when your mind and body are fully connected, time has ceased to exist, and when you do finally wrap it up, you're left feeling satisfied, proud and on-track. Just like night-time circadian rhythms that cycle in 90 minutes of light and deep REM sleep, the body also has ultradian rhythms during the day of peak- and low-focus points. If you push through your workload for five hours without taking a scheduled break, your brain will become fatigued. Science recommends taking a scheduled brain break every 90 minutes for five minutes. When I'm working, I set a 90-minute timer to remind me to take a five-minute brain break. Note: this break should be technology free. This isn't you eating a bowl of cereal while checking work emails. It's you truly letting your brain rest. It could be a quick walk outside, making a snack in the kitchen, doing a meditation or listening to a song. Of course, if you're stopping for lunch or need to disengage to solve a problem, you can absolutely take longer than five minutes.

Tips for Finding Your Flow:
- Set a clear objective.
- Map out your steps.
- Eliminate distractions (put your phone on airplane mode and 'out of office' or 'unavailable' on your calendar).
- Choose an instrumental soundtrack.
- Set a timer and work in 90-minute intervals.

PROCRASTINATION

Rarely do I come across someone who doesn't procrastinate in some way. It could be to avoid making a work call, finally sitting down to write the novel they've been imagining, or a conversation they need to have with a family member. For whatever reason, they're experiencing

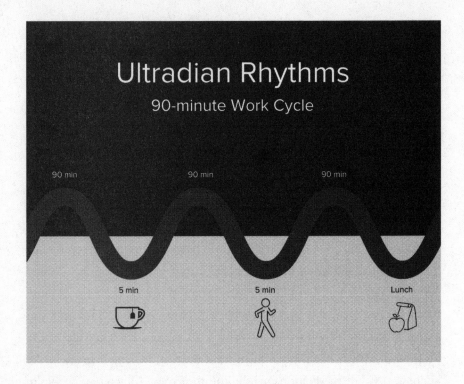

Ultradian Rhythms

90-minute Work Cycle

90 min   90 min   90 min

5 min   5 min   Lunch

a mental hang-up and that item is either moved from to-do list to to-do list or simply sitting in their brain and chiming in every day or so to say, 'Hello! I'm still here! I still need attention!'

According to Dr Alexander Rozental, a clinical psychologist and procrastination researcher, procrastination typically falls into one of four categories:

1. Expectancy: This is when you lack the self-belief that you will achieve the task or you assume you need to be in the 'right frame of mind' to complete the task.
2. Value: This is when you lack intrinsic motivation or don't truly understand why the goal is important.
3. Time: This is when the end point or reward is too far into the future and you struggle to view a project as a priority.
4. Impulsivity: This is when you like the rush of last-minute deadlines. You believe you work better under pressure.

Below are 10 techniques I use to overcome procrastination and avoid the stress, anxiety and poor performance that stems from completing things at the very last minute (or not at all).

1. Ask the One Key Question

What's the most important thing I can get done today? Every morning, return to your diary or journal to identify your most important task. As I mentioned before, it's usually the elephant on the list and the one people tend to avoid the most. Do it first no matter what.

2. Pre-commit

According to neuroscientist Dr Molly Crockett, research shows that pre-commitment works better than willpower alone when people are trying to resist temptation. If you want an effective way of making inaction look even less appealing: publicly declare that you're going to do it.

3. Have an Accountability Partner

Another highly effective way of staying committed to your task or goal is having an accountability partner. For example, let's say you want to go to the gym three times a week. You're much more likely to go if you know you're meeting someone there. Why not engage a friend or work colleague when trying to achieve a professional goal? Try asking someone who cares about you to do the task with you, or at least check in with you to keep you on track. Make sure the person is willing to have the difficult conversation if you are not moving in the right direction.

4. Get a Good 'Why'

If you are struggling to begin a task, spend a few minutes thinking more deeply about exactly why you need to do it. Research shows that when you find personal meaning behind something, it's easier to tap into your intrinsic motivation, which will give you a sense of purpose to achieve it.

5. Make a List and Break Down the Goal

This isn't just your to-do list! This is a list of every step you need to take to achieve your MIT. Many people get overwhelmed by the enormity of a project or anxious about the outcome. If this is the case, breaking down the overarching goal with smaller bite-sized tasks will help. Next, put a date and time next to each item so there is a deadline and accountability to help achieve the goal. Estimate how long you think it will take you to complete the task and then double the time so you don't fall into the cognitive trap of time bias, which can make you give up more easily. Once you start ticking off these smaller, more manageable tasks, it will increase your self-belief that you can achieve the larger goal!

6. Reward Yourself Along the Way

As you'll recall from Chapter 5: Your Goals, your brain is motivated by rewards. It's constantly striving for more pleasure and less pain. Therefore, finding ways to reward yourself along the way will greatly help you achieve your goals. For example, whenever I would submit an assignment at university, I rewarded myself with a takeaway dinner.

7. Minimise Distractions

Turn off your emails, shut down your phone and stay laser-focused on the task at hand. Distractions will constantly pop up during the day. Try to honour the 90-minute flow state of work and stay committed to your MIT.

8. Minimise Multi-tasking

I'm going to talk more about the multi-tasking fallacy soon, but many of us fall into the trap of 'busyness' and therefore multi-task ourselves into inefficiency. This is when we also make more mistakes. Take the time to land one plane first and get the job done.

9. Take a Break

Sometimes we feel burnt out, stressed or anxious. If you can't progress with your to-do list and find it hard to stay on point with your goal, it's time to take either a short or long break if possible. Focus on self-care, nutrition, sleep, exercise, meditation, rest and enjoyable leisure activities. These self-care breaks will actually refuel your productivity and help you make up for lost time.

10. Practise Mindfulness

Recognise when procrastination starts to creep in. If you notice thought patterns like *I don't feel like doing this now*, or *I'll get to this later*, then you need to recognise that you are about to procrastinate. Try to resist the urge and instead acknowledge it as just a thought and return your attention back to the task for at least a few more minutes.

It's inevitable that the urge to procrastinate will pop up from time to time. By becoming cognisant of the reasons why you procrastinate, and consciously overcoming these tendencies with the tools above, you may find it easier to keep your eyes on the prize and get started on those important (or stressful) tasks.

MULTI-TASKING

I don't care what some pipe-smoking, plate-spinning, phone call-making people say, multi-tasking is clinically proven to increase your stress and anxiety. From a productivity point of view, we lose focus, rush ourselves into inefficiency and make mistakes. One of the reasons why we think we are skilled at multi-tasking is because the speed at which the brain switches between two activities leads us to believe we are doing two tasks simultaneously. This isn't the case. Your brain is fully turning off and turning on different systems to help you type something, eat a snack, make a call, text a friend or put on a new playlist. Every transition costs the brain energy and is fatiguing your prefrontal cortex.

It could be that since movies portray top executives running on a treadmill while simultaneously emailing, executing trades through their wireless headphones and taking their bio-hacking miracle multivitamin, a lot of people tend to believe that by doing several things at once, we can fit more into the day. Let's take a closer look at our prefrontal cortex, also known as the 'thinking brain'. As I mentioned before, every time we switch tasks, it costs our brain a little time and energy. Instead of climbing into fifth gear and driving there for a solid hour, it's like shifting between second, third and fourth constantly. Trying to do more than one thing at once not only slows us down, but it also causes us to make mistakes and do things less efficiently. One study found that while people naturally get a little anxious when asked to handle a new task, they report twice the increase in anxiety if they're interrupted while trying to complete it. It's no wonder you often hear statements like, 'I can't hear myself think.' We make it harder for our brain's prefrontal cortex to do its job when we ask it to juggle.

But Chelsea, I can't help it when things pop up or I feel 'over' whatever I'm already working on.

I get it. Distractions creep in or we feel fatigued so we switch our brain over to something else, but I promise that gaining control of the urge to stray from the task at hand will make you not only more efficient but also more effective. Below are some of my tried and trusted tips for combating multi-tasking.

Take a Break Every 90 Minutes

Earlier, I talked about ultradian rhythms. If you're going nonstop, you're more likely to fatigue from your task and start something else. Set your alarm and honour the rest! Some of my favourite brain-break activities include walking outside, popping to the café for a coffee, chatting with a peer, doing a quick workout or meditating.

Implement a Traffic-light System

Another big distraction is people. How often are you working and someone comes and interrupts with, 'Hey, do you have a minute?' EQ Minds' polling of thousands of employees is proving that this is one of the biggest distractions. Some companies put in a traffic-light system above employee desks.

The Myth of Multi-tasking

Are you focused and productive? Or is switching between tasks
having a detrimental effect on your brain?

This activity will help you quickly understand the negative
impact multi-tasking has on your brain.

MULTI-TASKING IS A MYTH

A	
1	
A1	

FIRST ROUND

1. Get the stopwatch on your
phone ready.

2. In row A, write the alphabet. A to Z.
Write down how long it took you to
complete it.

3. In row 1, write the numbers 1 to 26.
Write down how long it took you to
complete it.

SECOND ROUND

1. Cover up the first two rows.

2. In row A1, combine both
the letters and numbers together.
Every time you write a letter, it
needs to be followed by a number.

Example: a1, b2, c3, d4
Write down how long it took you
to complete it.

Compare your results between the first and second rounds.

Typically, a person who is switching between tasks will:
- take much longer to complete the activity
- tend to make mistakes in the second round
- experience more personal stress and anxiety.

This is how the system works:

- Traffic light is green: Come over and talk to me.
- Traffic light is amber: I'm busy, however, if it's urgent, then come over.
- Traffic light is red: I'm right in the middle of something business critical, please don't interrupt me.

There are three rules with this traffic-light system:

1 You can't keep your light on red all day! We have to be available in the workplace and hopefully you are taking brain breaks every 90 minutes.

2 Everyone has to honour the system.

3 If the building is on fire, you must ignore all red lights!

The majority of the time, people who see the red light 'on' go back to their desk and solve the problem themselves! If your company can't afford this traffic-light system, here are some more cost-effective options:

- a card on your desk that says: 'I'm in the flow for 90 minutes'
- a sign on the back of your chair
- noise-cancelling headphones or phone earpieces.

If you are going to wear headsets, make sure you are listening to non-lyrical music so your brain can stay focused – unless you have ADHD or a related condition and find lyrics aid your ability to focus.

Turn Off Email, Desktop and Phone Notifications

According to a study done by the University of California Irvine, it takes an average of 23 minutes and 15 seconds to get back into the flow of work every time we are interrupted by a distraction. Take a moment to think about what happens when an email notification flashes on your screen. Whether you clicked on it or not, it still pulls your focus, doesn't it? Turn off your email and desktop notifications. (I'm actually going to talk a whole lot more about emails soon, so stay tuned!) You can also put your phone on airplane mode or even delete apps that you know pose a distraction.

Make a List

Many of us are tempted to multi-task because a thought enters our mind and we don't want to forget it. If you write it down immediately, you won't be as tempted to do two things at once.

Minimise the Number of Tabs and Programs You Have Open on Your Computer

Having multiple browser tabs open on your computer can cause cortisol levels to spike and can steer you off course. At EQ Minds, we have introduced a two-tab rule. Try it! It reduces the chance of you being tempted to swap to another item on your list. If you are a 10-tab person, try scaling back to six tabs the first week to make small adjustments, but have the end goal of two tabs.

Party of One

Schedule meetings in your diary with YOURSELF. If people can see you have some free time in your calendar, they are likely to book you in for a meeting. Therefore, by booking in for a Party of One with yourself, you can get through your own work.

EMAIL EFFICIENCY

There are two types of people in this world: Inbox zero and Inbox 476. While emails have made communicating with colleagues, business leads, customer-care teams, friends and family infinitely easier, it has certainly come at a cost. For starters (and I don't know who spread this rumour), emails make people think you're accessible at all hours. Second, tone can often be difficult to read, and it only takes the assumption that, 'As per my last email ...' is basically Todd saying, 'Bitch, can you read?' to completely change your mood for the day. Third, many of us simply become side-tracked and distracted by admin instead of focusing on our MIT.

After reading that Tim Ferriss, the author of *The 4-Hour Workweek*, schedules email-checking twice per day to make him more productive, I realised how much time I spent checking my inbox. Feeling like I needed to be more realistic about the speed at which my colleagues need responses from me, I decided to check and action my emails at 10 am, 12 pm, 2 pm and 4 pm. This has been part of my day's structure for years now, and my efficiency and productivity has gone through the roof.

On top of minimising the amount of time you spend on email, you can also adopt the following tips and tools to help save you time, improve productivity and break the chain of emails ruling your work life.

Turn Notifications Off – Immediately!

Without a doubt, the most important thing you can do to decrease your dependency on email is turn your notifications off! Every time the email notification pings or a number appears in your browser's tab, it causes a physical response in your body. Many people jump straight to the email, completely losing track of the task at hand. Remember, multi-tasking does NOT work.

Schedule Email Time

Like I said before, don't let emails rule *or* ruin your day. And remember, first thing in the morning is arguably the worst time to do your emails because they will derail your MIT and other priorities. An email is actually just another person's to-do-list item that has been assigned to you. It's NOT your to-do list. If possible, you can also use an auto-response message to notify senders that you only check your emails at certain times during the day to set their response expectations. You will be amazed how many issues have been resolved by the time you actually reply to the email.

Follow the 'One Touch' Rule

When it's the designated time to check your emails, I want you to avoid leaving an open email in your inbox for later. Instead, choose an action from the 3Ds: Do it, Delete it, Delegate it. When an email hits your inbox, revisiting the same email is not an efficient use of time. Create a system to ensure you only touch an email once, or twice if it's really necessary, such as emails that can be read at a later date. Emails that need actioning but can't be dealt with immediately become tasks.

Short Is Sweet

Short emails respect people's time and create an environment where they are expected. It's important to develop the habit of communicating ideas in the least amount of space possible. I like to use bullet points to ensure the message is communicated clearly and then bold or highlight what I want the reader's call-to-action to be.

Your Time (and Tone) Is Important

When responding to a lengthy message, ask yourself: *Is this email really worth my time?* Sometimes a face-to-face discussion or picking up the phone can resolve an issue that might take days over an email chain. Also, emails are often misinterpreted by the reader. Don't let a poorly written or misread email unravel your day, or worse, a relationship.

Consider Implementing a Company-Wide Title System in the Subject Line

Clarity around the action points of an email is essential for efficiency, which is why we at EQ Minds often advise businesses to implement a system that will make desired actions crystal clear.

Here are a few examples that have worked in practice:

- ACTION REQUIRED (AR): When a response or action is necessary

- URGENT ACTION REQUIRED (UAR): As above but of high importance – do not use this unless it's necessary
- FYI ONLY (FYI): Information for review but no response is required
- POLICY and PROCEDURE UPDATE (PPU): Needs to be read (and possibly actioned depending on the matter).

Ensure your emails have a relevant subject line so recipients can act accordingly. Consider using bold and underlines to highlight important aspects and action items. A concise email with clear action items is essential to working efficiently.

Use the Correct 'To' and 'CC' Fields and Leave People Off

In many office environments, employees choose to CC half the office when many people don't need to be part of the email chain. This causes frustration and also slows down the operation of the office. Ensure you correctly use 'To' and 'CC' as this will aid the receivers' requirement to respond and remove the common occurrence of too many people becoming involved in an email chain. Use 'To' for people who need to action something and 'CC' when it is just for their information.

Set Up Different Email Accounts

Your work account is for work. This means you shouldn't be buying stuff online with it, signing up for news subscriptions, or having any email chains with friends, family or your child's school. Not only will these eat up your time, but they can also lead to frustration. I like having a work email, a social email for friends and family and then a third purely for subscriptions and bill payments. Not only does this help keep me focused, but it also reduces the amount of spam each inbox is liable to receive.

Answer Your Emails in Batches, Not Individually

If you receive multiple emails from a co-worker or team each day, answer with just one reply. The one message covers your replies to all recent correspondence. Once you begin this practice, don't be surprised if some of your colleagues follow your example, leading to overall reduced email traffic. Just remember to clearly articulate the matters you are addressing so points do not become confused.

Remember Emails Are NOT Private

Ever had a private email forwarded? Nearly everyone has. It can lead to anger, frustration and even distress. Emails create a record and the messages you send and receive via company email are the property of your employer. They can be monitored, flagged and, in some cases, used as evidence to support punitive measures or legal action. Avoid writing messages on your company email that have an angry tone or that attack, gossip about or could potentially offend others. If you think an email you are about to send could get you into trouble, it may be wise to click 'delete' instead.

'Inbox 0' Is a Daily Requirement, Not a Daily Goal

I'm not going to lie, the first day of your new email life will be time-consuming. Schedule the time and set up a system that works for you. That means no emails in your inbox. Every email must be actioned, filed, unsubscribed, spam-filtered or deleted. Emails that can't be actioned immediately become tasks on your to-do list. There are a few third-party sites like Unroll Me that enable you to instantly see a list of all your subscription emails and then hit unsubscribe in one go.

Unsubscribe and Mark as Spam

Unfortunately, marketing emails have a way of sneaking in, so be sure to regularly unsubscribe from emails you do not read and don't be afraid of the spam or junk button. Do this on a regular basis to quickly and permanently get rid of these messages that aren't useful. Develop rules that suit your needs. For example, if you haven't read an email you receive daily in five days, hit unsubscribe.

At the end of the day, you can either control emails or let them control you. The most productive people manage emails wisely and, as a result, increase both the quality and quantity of their job performance. Most importantly, managing emails will make you a much happier person.

P.S. Don't you dare open that email app on holiday!

MEETINGS

Just like emails, meetings have their pros and cons. According to research done by Oracle and Workplace Intelligence, throughout the first 12 months of the COVID-19 pandemic, people were spending more time and energy in meetings than ever before. As much as I love a good meeting to clarify an action plan and next steps, they can be a huge time waster due to people having side conversations, not coming prepared or not having clear objectives. In our corporate workshops and surveys, the number-one trend we see that causes workplace stress is meetings and the amount of time they can take away from the workday. One of the biggest things I've noticed is that meetings tend to expand to fill the time that was scheduled. I also keep questioning why the default for meetings has become one hour.

At EQ Minds, we tend to do 15-minute meetings, even with our major clients. Time is one of the things we give away the most (and usually for little return), which is why we've started fiercely protecting ours and our clients'. It doesn't matter if it's a face-to-face meeting, video meeting or phone call, we're up-front about the fact that we have only allotted 15 minutes for the discussion, which keeps everyone laser-focused on achieving the desired outcome. We've also found colour-coding to be a helpful timing tool for enabling employees to get in the right mindset for a meeting. Even though I'd love to do 15 minutes for everything, sometimes you need a bit more time if you're brainstorming or working on strategy. In our office calendar, green indicates a meeting will be 15 minutes while blue indicates 60 minutes. By visually establishing the length of time allocated for the meeting, you're more likely to prepare adequately and stick to the agenda, and (in a perfect world) get out of there with time to spare! I hope I'm not sounding anti-meetings. We need meetings because we need to stay connected and we need to keep the communication lines open. However, I know they can be done more efficiently and effectively. Let's go over some ways you can get more time back in your diary.

Before planning or agreeing to attend a meeting, spend a few minutes answering the following questions:

- Are the right people in the meeting to make the decision?
- Is there anyone on the list that doesn't really need to be there?
- Where do we want to be by the end of this meeting?
- Which questions can we send to the team in advance, which we want them to come prepared to answer?
- Does everyone have a clear understanding of the etiquette expected at the meeting?

In a study looking at meeting inefficiencies, the Yale School of Management found meetings aren't the best use of people's time when it comes to *creative* ideas. This is because 80 per cent of the time, we go with the highest paid person's opinion. However, this doesn't necessarily mean we're getting the best solution. When it comes to creativity, you need to have diversity of thought. You can work to achieve this is by: 1. Making sure you have the right people attending the meeting, and; 2. Sending them a prompt or problem to start working on prior to the meeting. If everyone is able to bring a solution to the table (or Zoom call), then even the introverts will get a voice.

By asking where you want to be at the end of the meeting, you're essentially asking: What is the desired outcome and plan of action? Your agenda is the map that will get you and your team to your final destination. Of course, we've all been in a meeting where someone brings something up that's in the neighbourhood of relevant but totally not on the agenda. If you feel like you *must* give them the floor, try introducing an eggtimer system. At EQ Minds, if someone brings something up that's not on the agenda, we use an eggtimer to give them five minutes on the topic. If there is no resolution by the end, we either tell them to take the conversation offline or add it to another meeting's agenda.

Now let's talk about note-taking and minutes. Keeping track of what was said, who said it and why it was said matters big time. Realistically, everyone should be taking notes, but it's a good idea to designate a note-taker who is also responsible for delivering the minutes. Speaking of minutes – does anyone actually read them? I'm going to argue that if they're sent as a Word attachment, no one is opening them. I suggest sending minutes in the body of an email with clear, colour-coded and highlighted key points, priorities and next steps.

Tips for Keeping Meetings Short and Sharp:
- Circulate a clear agenda in advance.
- Send attendees questions they should be prepared to answer.
- Change default meeting lengths from one hour to 15 minutes.
- Prepare the room and any required tech 15 minutes before the meeting is due to start.
- Use an eggtimer to keep off-topic discussions in control.
- Make it a walking meeting (even better – do it outside to soak up some vitamin D!).
- Don't allow personal tech in the room (or have a hands-off phones rule). It shows mutual respect for your colleagues and removes the temptation to be distracted.
- If it is a longer meeting, schedule in five-minute breaks for bathroom/phone checking.
- If the meeting is getting off-track, end it and reschedule.

YOU'RE LATE!

When Jay was working in finance, nothing frustrated him more than having someone stroll into a meeting five minutes late. (Don't even get him started if they didn't think to bring a pen and paper ...) To resolve this issue, he started closing the door and taping up a sign saying, 'If you're not on time, you can't come in.' While this may seem harsh, it's a waste of company time to have to wait around for someone to show up. Think about the multiplier effect. If 20 people are in the room, and one person is five minutes late, you've just wasted 105 minutes of company time. Don't. Be. Late. (Fun idea: if someone is late, you can make them scribe the minutes the next time!)

MINDFULNESS TOOLS FOR STRESS MANAGEMENT AND NEGATIVE-FEEDBACK LOOPS

When you're going after big goals, it's inevitable that you're going to be jumping through hoops, putting out tiny little fires and scaling mountains. (Clichés come with the job, right?) There's no doubt that some days are going to feel incredibly stressful and that's okay. I find it useful to remember that stress promotes growth. When you're lifting weights in the gym or pounding the pavement on a run, your muscles and cardiovascular system are under stress. However, when you stop to recover, they rebuild *stronger* than before. If you're never stressed, you're probably not stepping out of your comfort zone enough. If you're constantly stressed, you're probably stepping out too far or simply not giving yourself the self-care needed to sustain such a high level of stress.

WHAT DOES CHRONIC STRESS IMPACT?

☐ memory
☐ cognitive function
☐ immune system
☐ gastrointestinal function
☐ cardiovascular health
☐ ability to fight disease.

Typical work-related stress can stem from tight deadlines, conflict with a colleague or mismanagement. Added to that, when you're constantly replaying negative-feedback loops, there are often consequences like depression, anxiety, post-traumatic stress disorder, binge-eating and binge-drinking. I'm not sure if you get road rage, but I understand why people do. When I lived in Sydney and commuted to work every day, I used to become extremely agitated by people cutting me off on the road. However, I wouldn't have called it road rage. (I'd just hunt down the car, beep the horn and sometimes give them the finger.) Next, I'd talk about it with peers, girlfriends or Jay. While I thought that venting about the douche in the Audi was helping me rid myself of my work-commute stress, neuroscience taught me otherwise!

If you're someone who constantly replays stressful work conversations and interactions, you could be doing yourself more harm than good. Neuroscientist Dr Jill Bolte Taylor has proven that every emotion has a chemically induced life cycle of 90 seconds. If left alone, the chemical the emotion triggers will arise, peak and be flushed out of your mind and body within that time period. However, if you feed the emotion by talking about the situation or thinking about it again, you're physiologically re-enacting it, and it will stay around much longer than 90 seconds. When worry or a negative-feedback loop arises, if you can simply observe it without running away from it and deep breathe with the emotion, the worry will dissipate within 90 seconds. However, if you fuel it with your stories, you are, in effect, forcing the emotion to outlast its natural 90-second life cycle.

It takes a lot of practice to remember to stop and step back from your thoughts before these worry tapes start playing their stories. However, it's well worth the effort and, with time and consistency, you will be able to break the feedback loop. Below are a few other tips and tools for calming stress and stopping negative-feedback loops.

Label Your Response

Recent studies have shown that when we label our emotions, it makes us learn to be emotionally responsible and can even make anger, sadness and pain less intense. Try regulating your immediate response by acknowledging it, accepting it and allowing it to be digested. If you are angry, try saying, 'I feel angry right now after you told me that.' Then feel it for 90 seconds, let the emotion go and move forward.

Practise Deep Breathing

I spoke about this in Chapter 9: Your Mindfulness, but deep breathing for as little as one minute can decrease your cortisol levels and calm down your emotional brain. It can also connect you to your body and get you out of your head.

Journal

Journalling brings perspective and peace. When you are stuck repeating a story inside your head, actively think about the situation looking through your eyes, their eyes and then a fly-on-the-wall perspective. No one needs to read it. It will better equip you with clarity on the situation.

Practise Gratitude

Studies have shown that those who practise gratitude on a regular basis are more likely to curb rumination as they are living in the moment and appreciate the good they have in their lives. It is impossible to be grateful and worried at the same time. It is impossible to be grateful and angry at the same time. Try it.

Take a Walk in Nature

A study from Stanford University found that a 60-minute walk in nature decreased both ruminative thinking and neural activity in the subgenual prefrontal cortex (responsible for obsessive thought patterns), whereas a 60-minute walk in an urban setting had no such effects on rumination or worry. In other words, go for a hike in nature after work or on the weekends as it can lessen the impacts of fear, worry, paranoia and obsessive thinking.

Focus on Your Senses Over Your Morning Hot Drink

Deliberately focusing your attention on what you are seeing, hearing, feeling, sensing or smelling in the moment can help your brain deactivate the default mode network (DMN), which is an automatic mind-wandering state. Focus mindfully on your latte or tea and experience being in the present moment. This activates the on-task network, which will make you feel more alert and present.

Practise Meditation

Mindfulness meditation is a practice that can teach you to gain control of the focus of your attention and help you to let go of the obsessive stories. In one study, researchers scanned the brains of beginner and advanced meditators. The results were fascinating as the experienced meditators showed less DMN activation and reported less mind-wandering and worry compared with the beginner group.

Where Possible, Change or Remove the Cues that Trigger Rumination

Once you identify the contextual cues that trigger rumination and worry, altering or removing them will reduce the likelihood of the habit and thus reduce the amount of worry and rumination overall. Sometimes specific features of the environment may act as triggers. For example, listening to sad music or looking at reminders of a past relationship. Removing or replacing these cues (such as playing different music and replacing triggering imagery) could be beneficial.

Treat Worry as a Visitor Who Is Just Passing Through

Instead of reacting and trying to run away from your negative thoughts, treat them as a visitor who's made an uninvited appearance. If you are worried about getting anxious before public speaking or a meeting, try saying, 'Hello, Anxiety, thanks for turning up today. You must be here to get my body prepared for this talk.' This can help take the power out of the anxiety.

Don't Identify with Worry

When you have a thought such as *I'm so worried about what will happen if something goes wrong*, reframe it to: *Worry is present.* By removing yourself from the thought, you're removing 'worry' as a feature of your personality.

Adopt a Helicopter Perspective

If you can adopt a self-distanced perspective while discussing a difficult situation, it allows you to make better sense of your reactions and you will experience less emotional distress. You are also less vulnerable to recurring thoughts or feedback loops, will experience less emotional distress and display fewer physiological signs of stress. Other research indicates that self-distancing practices help reduce aggressive thoughts, angry feelings and aggressive behaviour, and increase the ability to better manage relationship conflicts.

Picture Your Best Self

If you are really caught up in negative-feedback loops, try imagining your life five years from now. Journal where you will be in five years as if you are already there, describing your ideal life. Where are you living? What are you doing? Who is in your life? What holidays are you going on? Who are you sharing the experience with? Identify small actions that you can take to bring yourself closer to this vision. When you bring awareness and intention to who you want to be, you can shift your focus from negative-feedback loops and instead focus on your dream life and take small steps to achieve it.

Try Cognitive Behavioural Therapy

Sometimes, through no fault of our own, we get stuck in vicious cycles. I'll go deeper into this in the next chapter, but cognitive behaviour therapy is about finding out what is keeping us stuck and making changes in our thinking to positively improve the way we feel.

⌐ TOOLS TO LOWER STRESS ⌐

- ☐ deep breathing
- ☐ meditation
- ☐ take a break to go for a walk
- ☐ consciously transition between meetings or projects
- ☐ practise gratitude.

BURNOUT

If I had to pinpoint the main reasons why people I work with burn out, I'd say they're lack of boundaries, lack of focus on the self and the constant need to tick every single item off the list. The most glaring issue is lack of boundaries. It's easy to let energy vampires talk us into taking on something that they should be doing, it's easy to let the need to prove yourself override your need to rest and it's certainly easy to believe that you'll feel so much better once your to-do list is done.

All high performers need rest and self-care. Make sure you schedule in downtime and activities that nourish you and give you energy. Schedule in exercise, meditation and a coffee with a friend. Don't look at your phone first thing in the morning and have regular breaks. When you feel like you're slipping down the exhaustion funnel, schedule a relaxing weekend away. (This is not the time to go on a bender.) Research shows that if you are able to take care of your health, you are more creative, productive and happier. Boundaries are crucial for your success.

Look, you need to accept that your list will never be fully ticked off because every day that you're alive and working towards your purpose, new opportunities are going to flow your way. There is no point in trying to work through the night and weekend to just action those last few items so you can start fresh on a Monday.

Pre-COVID, it was easier to keep work at work and home at home, but with so many of us now working remotely, the lines are becoming increasingly blurred, which makes boundaries very difficult to define. More than ever, people are quitting their jobs and walking away from career paths they've been following for years citing burnout.

If you feel like you're entering the neighbourhood of burnout, here's my advice: take the weekend to completely log off from work. This may not be an option, but if possible, take the Friday off and then spend three days doing nothing but sleeping well, eating well, not engaging in technology and not binge drinking. Truly rest and only do things that nourish you. You might like to journal, move, walk and talk with family and friends. If you're still absolutely exhausted by Monday and can't see the forest for the trees, consider seeing if you have any annual or sick leave you can use for an extended break. Remember, this isn't for #winetime with your besties or to get on the cans in Mykonos … this is time to book a retreat or escape to a cabin. After that week, if you come back and you're still struggling, it is probably time to go back and look at your purpose, your values, your goals, your habits and your daily routines.

I want to flag that burnout isn't just feeling over it. Burnout can make you feel brain-foggy, depressed, anxious and even irrational. I also want to flag that managing burnout may warrant speaking to your boss about adjusting your workload or changing your work environment. Note: if you're experiencing burnout due to harassment from a boss or colleague, that's an even more pressing issue and one I suggest speaking to a therapist or HR department about. This is a crucial time to make careful decisions and even seek professional help to find guidance, which brings us to the final chapter of this book: Chapter 13: Your Support.

Protection Strategies to Avoid Burnout:
- Set clear boundaries at work (and at home).
- Don't overbook yourself. Limit clients and colleagues to what feels right.
- Eat well – don't skip meals, and ensure you're getting enough protein.
- Practise deep breathing regularly.
- Plan regular breaks to walk, eat, meditate and rest.
- Create a serene work environment.
- Surround your workspace with plants and photos of nature.
- Wear noise-cancelling headphones when possible.
- Walk outside to get fresh air.
- Create an emotional rescue playlist.
- When meditating, focus on things you're grateful for.
- Visualise a protective light around you.
- Detoxify in water by having a bath with Epsom salts at the end of the day.
- Try a grounding technique.

IN YOUR JOURNAL

Take a moment to reflect by answering the following questions:

- How do you feel about your current workload?
- How do you feel about your current performance?
- What's one major task you've been procrastinating on?
- What are three habits you can adopt this week to enhance your performance?
- How will you feel when you've improved your performance habits?

13
YOUR SUPPORT

AS MUCH AS I would love to say that hunkering down to reflect on your values, build your self-efficacy, set your goals, establish a morning routine, commit to daily movement, prioritise your sleep, begin meditating, heal your gut, audit your connections and adopt more productive habits is a one-and-done thing, your mental health and ability to perform well isn't something you can set and forget. It doesn't matter who you are, where you live, how much money you have or how #blessed you feel by the stunning world you live in, adversity does not and will not discriminate. This could come in the form of a cancer diagnosis, global pandemic, relationship breakdown, loss of a loved one, or pure mental fatigue. What matters most is your ability to recognise when things aren't okay and knowing which tools you have to fix things.

At the end of 2020, I had a mental-illness relapse. From the outside my life looked really good. I had just signed the deal for this very book, EQ Minds had trained 90,000 people in the corporate world in the span of 12 months and my family was thriving. But here's the thing: we all have our special brand of breakdown and looks can be very deceiving.

For me, it was overcommitting so I had to be hyper-productive, which bordered on manic.

Of course, I can paint the house while doing my taxes at the same time! You need 70,000 words by May? No sweat! Oh, you'd like me to create a keynote speech by 10 am tomorrow? No worries, but can we make it 11 am? I'm running a marathon at 6 am and will need time to grab breakfast.

Okay, so I wasn't running marathons, but I was running amok! In hindsight, I was burning out, but in the moment, I was so deeply invested in achieving these goals that I missed every single sign I knew to look for. It wasn't until I woke up one day, and before I could even put my feet on the floor, I was bawling my eyes out. Jay, who is arguably the most supportive, genuine and caring man on the planet (yes, I know I'm biased), saw my distress and said these very wise words: 'Honey, it's going to be okay. We've been through this before and we know what to do.'

The relief I felt was almost immediate. Sometimes you just need someone to see where you are and to help you find your way out. Was I suicidal again? No, but I knew if I didn't address my mental health immediately, it could have very well led me to a place where my mind is utterly irrational. I recognise how lucky I am to have had Jay in my home recognising the signs of my relapse. Currently, there are 264 million people worldwide with an anxiety disorder and many of them live alone. The WHO says that by 2030 depression will be our biggest cause of ill health, which is why I want to take the time to talk about the signs to look for when you or someone you know is having a mental-health crisis as well as the tools you have to help repair your mind, body and soul.

RECOGNISING THE SIGNS OF MENTAL ILLNESS

People tend to think that mental-health crises happen when you're in a crisis but, as you've seen with me, the opposite can be true. Just because everything may appear to be in order on the outside, doesn't mean you're coping on the inside. Have you ever made plans with your friends when you're pumped and truly excited to catch up, but when the actual day rolls around, you are completely dreading the idea of it and silently hoping that there is a road closure or some sort of non-life-threatening emergency? This is totally normal, but when it becomes a pattern, it's a problem. While developing social anxiety is one sign to look for, there's actually quite a bit more to be aware of. When it comes to identifying someone who may be silently suffering (yourself included), there are three key areas to observe: words, actions and situations.

Words – What are you saying and how are you saying it?
- Are you moody or confused?
- Are you unable to switch off?
- Are you saying you are a burden to people?
- Are you expressing that you're lonely?
- Are you lacking self-esteem?

Actions – What are you doing and why are you behaving like that?
- Are you withdrawing from social situations?
- Are you starting confrontations with people?
- Are you isolating yourself from friends and family?
- Do you seem less interested in your appearance than usual?
- Are there changes in your sleep patterns?
- Are you becoming increasingly sedentary?
- Are you becoming manic about exercise?

Situations – What's going on that could be contributing to the change?
- Are you having relationship issues?
- Are you experiencing major health issues?
- Are you under constant stress at work?
- Have you lost someone or something?
- Are you having financial problems?

We are all vulnerable to mental illness. While it is often easier to show compassion to others when you pick up on these signs and symptoms of a mental-health breakdown, it's important to be mindful of your own words, actions and situations and to treat yourself the same way you'd treat a family member, friend or colleague. After overcoming postnatal depression and immersing myself in the mental-health space, I truly believed I was immune. In my mind, I was tough, high-achieving, happy, driven and mindful. This was all true until it wasn't. To be completely honest, I wasn't as gentle with myself as I should have been once Jay helped me realise I needed help. I was frustrated that I had let myself get to the point of a breakdown. Shouldn't I have known better? And that's when my many years of studying psychological well-being from the greats around the world came into play. I knew it wasn't going to be helpful to play the victim. I also knew that the main thing I needed to tap into was my resilience. Once I flexed that muscle, I'd be able to reach for the tools in my toolbox to help get me back on track.

WHAT TO SAY WHEN SOMEONE ELSE NEEDS HELP

In 1995, Barry Larkin took his own life and left a huge circle of family and friends overwhelmed by grief and wondering what they could have done. Determined to help prevent others from experiencing this level of tragedy, his son, Gavin Larkin, launched the much-needed and hugely successful mental-health campaign R U OK? in 2009. If you're wondering how to approach someone (or yourself) regarding their mental health, it can be as simple as asking, 'Are you okay?'

Of course, there will be those who are avoiding facing their feelings, don't want to be a burden or aren't even aware they're not okay. The best thing to do is try to empathise with them, give them permission to be vulnerable and show them that they have support options. Below are a few ideas for things you can say when you feel like someone may need help.

- 'You've been carrying a lot on your plate lately. Is there anything I could do to help lighten your load?'

- 'Are you okay? I know if I were in your shoes, I'd be feeling pretty overwhelmed at the moment.'
- 'How are you sleeping lately? Do you find your mind is difficult to shut down at night?'
- 'When was the last time you took a day or two to truly rest?'
- 'I love how driven you are, but don't forget that you also need to recharge, too.'
- 'Have you had a chance to speak to anyone about what happened at work?'

⌐ HOT TIP ⌐

The number-one thing you shouldn't say is, 'You look really tired.' I promise that this person will not only feel crappy on the inside, but also feel overly conscious of how they look on the outside.

It can be really scary to admit when things aren't okay. Sometimes it helps if you share something about yourself first. For example, if you volunteer that things aren't all rainbows and sunshine in your mind, it can empower someone to share what they're going through, too.

WHERE TO TURN WHEN YOU NEED HELP

In Chapter 2: About You, I shared a huge checklist of things you can do immediately to start taking control of your mental health. Whenever you need to, go back to that list and make the changes you know you can make on your own. This could be cutting out caffeine and alcohol, going for a walk with a friend or going off-grid for a weekend to truly rest and recharge. You will also find strategies throughout the book on how to look after your mental health. However, if you know you're slipping somewhere that feels too deep to climb out of on your own, remember that there are some mental-health power tools at your disposal.

Medical Professionals

First, make an appointment with your general practitioner or integrative doctor to let them know how you're feeling. While they can do a comprehensive check-up to ensure there isn't anything going on physically that would impact your mental health, they can also refer you to see a psychiatrist or therapist. In many countries, the government offers a mental-health care plan. Therapy of any kind can be quite expensive, so be sure to ask if there are any subsidies that you qualify for. The reason I say get a referral to see a therapist or psychiatrist is because they're specialised in the field of mental health and will be able to get a full picture of your current lifestyle choices, diagnose any mental-health conditions and prescribe medication if needed.

Therapy 101

While you're probably envisioning lying back on a leather daybed while a Sean Connery-type gnaws on a pipe and asks you about your mummy issues, therapy actually comes in many shapes and forms. It can be done in person or on a video call and done solo or with a partner, family member or in a group setting.

One common type of therapy people refer to is cognitive behavioural therapy. This is when a therapist helps you identify and actively change your thought patterns, habits and behaviours. They offer a non-biased point of view and can also give you breathing and visualisation techniques to help cope with anxiety or depression. If you're not in the right mindset, making major decisions about your career, relationship and finances can be really dangerous. A therapist can help make sure you're making choices with a clear mind. One thing I want to flag is that you may not click with the first therapist you work with. You might also outgrow your therapist. One size does not fit all, and sometimes you simply need a fresh perspective. When it comes to choosing a therapist, there is no need to settle and you definitely don't need to be monogamous!

For those who've experienced major trauma or have debilitating anxiety and depression, it's worth exploring other types of therapy such as the ones listed below.

- Psychiatry: Psychiatrists are trained to diagnose mental illnesses such as severe depression, obsessive compulsive disorder and bipolar disorder, and prescribe medications to treat them.
- Eye Movement Desensitisation and Reprocessing (EMDR): In Chapter 8: Your Sleep, I talked about how your brain processes memories from the day during the REM stages of sleep. When something traumatic happens, it can be difficult for this type of information to be properly filed in the brain. Instead, it sits unfiled and nudges you to revisit and experience the trauma way more than you'd like to. EMDR is essentially a manual version of your REM sleep stage. By having your eyes move right and left while being guided through a memory, your brain is able to reprocess what happened and then hopefully store the memory away where it can be used in a healthy way.
- Hypnosis: (No, they won't be waving a pocket watch in front of your face and saying, 'You're getting very, very sleeeeepy …') Some therapists and hypnotists use hypnosis to get you into a state of consciousness that makes you more likely to modify your behaviour. This is because they are communicating without your usual cognitive roadblocks or biases in the way.
- Music therapy: Just like it sounds, music therapy uses music to help improve breathing, lower blood pressure, decrease muscle tension, reduce mental stress and manage behavioural problems.
- Art therapy: Remember how I said painting can be a great mindfulness activity to unwind from the day? Well art therapy is that on steroids! Through the use of art, you can not only lower your stress levels, but also increase your self-esteem, explore emotions and resolve other psychological issues.

Medication

When I was at the height of my postnatal depression (suicidal), someone suggested that I 'do some deep breathing and have a mindful shower'. No offence, but I was a day away from being admitted to a mental hospital and was so far gone from a 'mindful shower' being the solution, it's not even funny. My brain literally didn't have the capacity to make the changes I needed in order to heal. I needed major help. I needed medication. While I do believe that antidepressants are prescribed too frequently, if you're suicidal or have exhausted all of the tools in your toolbox, they are 100 per cent necessary. After my most recent relapse, a woman I had coffee with expressed her disapproval that I had made the decision to go back on Zoloft. 'Have you heard of St John's Wort?' she asked. There's no denying that there is a stigma surrounding antidepressants, but as someone who very much feels like they saved my life, I need to share what I know.

First of all, people like to ask me if antidepressants are a one-pill wonder. In my mind, they're just another tool in the toolbox. If you're eating well, getting enough vitamin D, moving your body, not abusing drugs and alcohol, have dialled back your workload where possible and are still struggling to sleep or feel extremely stressed, depressed or even manic, medication may be necessary to get your hormone levels where they need to be. Alternatively, they can also help if you're simply unable to manage your anxiety and depression to a point where you can take the behavioural advice of a psychologist and apply it to your life. Some people go on them for a couple of years at a time while others are on them for life. I've personally gone on and off antidepressants three times since my PND diagnosis and am currently staying on them for the foreseeable future.

Along with not being a one-pill-fix-it-all, antidepressants are also not one-size-fits-all. They come in many different formulations and are commonly referred to as old school and new school. The new-school ones (SSRIs), which are more popular, work by increasing serotonin in the brain. While it can feel a little bumpy weaning onto an antidepressant, the right one shouldn't numb you out. When I had my first mental-health relapse, a few years after having Clara, I knew I needed to take a month off work to double down on self-care, which included going back onto medication. I also knew to be extremely gentle on myself because my brain was trying to heal. Think about it: when you have an ankle injury, you wouldn't go running, right? You'd ice it, rest it and slowly rehab it. Whenever I needed to hit reset or begin taking an antidepressant, I knew that I couldn't really handle much more than playing LEGO, colouring or doing Play-Doh with Clara. I had to cancel all of my social plans and just do things that nourished me. I also had to have a major mindset shift because some of the side effects can be pretty intense. For example, I found myself more anxious at night and dizzy during the day. Instead of fearing the symptoms, I tried to reframe my thoughts.

Original thought: *This tingling makes me feel icky.*
Reframed thought: *Every time I'm feeling tingling, I know the medication is releasing serotonin into my cells. The drugs are working.*

When going on medication, it can feel like you're in the trenches, but it's worth trusting the process. You can also trust that the side effects are usually gone after four to six weeks. Even though you might not have the strength to do much in the moment, you can always make plans for the future as something to look forward to. As I mentioned previously, I have gone on and off medication. Unlike beginning a new treatment, going off can cause very few side effects if done slowly and under the guidance of a health professional. For example, it took me 18 months to wean off antidepressants completely last time. At the end of the day, what worked for me will not always work for you. We are all beautifully unique and different! This is why I recommend speaking to a psychiatrist about your options.

┌ **DIALOGUE FOR DEFENDING YOUR TREATMENT CHOICES** ┐

If you're considering going on antidepressants or attending therapy and plan on talking about it, brace yourself for some friction. It could be an eye-roll worth a thousand words from your mother-in-law or slightly offensive unsolicited advice from a man in the doctor's waiting room; there's always going to be someone who knows better. Below are a few things you can say to shut them down kindly.

☐ 'Thanks for sharing that suggestion, but I am going to follow the advice of my psychiatrist.'
☐ 'I appreciate your concern, but I'm feeling really confident with my current plan.'
☐ 'I've done a lot of research and work around this area and feel that this is what's best for me.'

WHERE TO GET HELP NOW

If you're reading this and feeling hopeless, distraught or scared, call someone right now. You are loved and you matter. Below is a list of helplines that can offer support 24 hours a day, seven days a week, 365 days a year.

Australia & New Zealand
Lifeline: 13 11 14

North America
National Suicide Prevention Lifeline: 1-800-273-8255

United Kingdom
SupportLine: 01708 765200

CONCLUSION

OVER THE LAST decade, I've learned that the human brain is much like a malfunctioning smartphone. Sometimes you simply need to POPO (power off, power on). No matter how tangled your life may feel or how ginormous your vision and goals are, you always have the option of taking stock of what habits are and aren't working and hitting refresh.

Remember, this might mean putting boundaries in place. Other times it could be doing a deep dive into your gut health to see if there's a pesky bug (or 2 million) making you feel sluggish. Every now and then, it might be going off-grid to re-examine your values and goals. Being a true high performer means being able to look at each area of your life and then mindfully observing how they are impacting one another. If your relationship is suffering, your work might suffer. If your work is suffering, chances are there's a bit of passive aggressiveness happening around the dining table. Everything is connected, which is why taking a holistic approach to your mental health is so impactful. Everything is also always changing, which is why you must remain fluid, proactive and aware.

Even though it may try to tell you otherwise, your mind is yours. Be bigger than your self-doubt, be better than your vices and be braver than you think you can be. Most importantly, trust that everything is going to be okay because not only do you have the information and tools to achieve a sustainable high-performance mindset, but you also have the support of me and the entire team at EQ Minds. If you ever feel lost, come back to these pages. While you may not need to revisit your movement, you might want to refresh what's happening with your sleep, for instance. This book is always here for you and so is your mind.

Mental Fitness Challenge

It's time to jump-start your journey. Our paths are rarely linear – your journey to wellness won't be either. Copy this mental fitness calendar, pin it to your wall and tick off one action each day for 30 days. You'll be surprised by the results.

☐ Set 3 goals you are going to tick off by the end of this month	☐ Journal a gratitude list for 5 minutes	☐ Read a book tonight to unwind instead of watching TV	☐ Pay it forward to a neighbour or friend	☐ Surprise date night with partner or friend
☐ Keep all meals tech-free today	☐ Try a guided meditation with me on Insight Timer	☐ Make 2 out of 3 meals today 'meatless'	☐ Buy a keep cup and use it for your coffee	☐ Take your workout outdoors and get an endorphin and nature high
☐ Don't check your mobile phone until 8 am	☐ Drink 500 mls of water when you wake up	☐ Try switching to decaf drinks in the afternoon	☐ Unfollow people on social media who don't inspire you	☐ Declutter your wardrobe
☐ Go through your phone and delete anyone who is toxic	☐ No complaint day	☐ Compliment a friend day	☐ Send a thank you card to someone you care about	☐ Delete apps you no longer use
☐ Set up a budget	☐ Eat a probiotic-rich food today	☐ Pursue a passion project	☐ Research into helping out a charity	☐ Start a new hobby
☐ Join a local Facebook group and engage with your community	☐ Organise your pantry to clean out foods that aren't good for you	☐ Spring-clean your beauty products and get rid of the toxic ones	☐ Treat yourself to some kind of self-care, like a massage	☐ Plan a 30-minute pre-sleep routine before bed

ACKNOWLEDGEMENTS

TO MY HUSBAND, JAY – I hit the jackpot with you. Thank you for being my rock. Thank you for knowing my signs and taking immediate action. Thank you for being an exceptional role model for Clara. Our life is better because you're in it.

To my daughter, Clara – you are a much-needed light in this world. Thank you for teaching me about love and evolving me into a better person. Thank you for giving me a reason to grow and refine who I am. Thank you for being my inspiration and motivation daily. I'm so honoured that you chose me to be your mum.

To my incredible parents, Geoff and Margaret Grant – you empowered me with independence, self-belief and determination, and they are such tremendous gifts. Thank you for believing in every single dream I've ever had and always pumping up my tyres. Thank you for your fierce love, for being confidants and for making my life always feel magical.

To my siblings, Brodie and Dean – thank you for your faith in me and for always having my back. You both always inspire me to be brave and to live a happy and fulfilling life. I love you both dearly.

To my cousin and incredible doctor, Dr Genevieve Curran – thank you for keeping me upright when I slipped and for getting me to safety. Because of you, I was able to heal in the right place and in the right way. Your reassurance and constant visits at the hospital meant the world to me. You and Wade amaze me.

To my beloved in-laws, Robyn, Tom, Tory, Andrew and Michelle – your unwavering generosity and love have always made me feel so supported, valued and respected. I love you all. To my nieces and nephews, Izaac, Lucas, Hannah, Thomas and Henry – thank you for teaching me how to laugh until I cry, love without boundaries and live life to the fullest.

To my co-writer, Summer Land – thank you for patiently reading, refining, tweaking and being such a champion for this book. Your keen eye for detail, writing expertise, warmth and hilarious nature have made me want to write a million more books. Let's do this again soon, hey?

To my mentors, Gary and Cathie – I have deep gratitude for both of you. Thank you for always holding space for me to be able to shine and making me a better person. I'll never stop thanking you.

To my tribe of girlfriends near and far – I f*cking love you. While there are too many names to list here, with my hand on my heart, I thank you for being my people. Thank you for celebrating with me in good times and acting as a light source for me in the darker times. I'm blessed to have you in my life.

To my agent, Jeanne Ryckmans – thank you for helping me navigate the wild and wonderful publishing world and ensuring that my book found the right home at the right time.

To the team at Murdoch Books, Julie, Kelly, Lou and Alice – thank you for enabling me to share the science, tools and practices that I believe in so deeply with the world. You've always had my back and I'm both humbled and forever grateful that you've given me the opportunity to bring my dreams to life.

Thank you to my EQ Minds team, Jay, Sam, Charli and Grace – you all show up in mind, body and spirit every single day, and for that, I thank you. Without your endless support, energy and expertise, I wouldn't be able to say proudly that I've seen so many of my big ideas come to fruition (like this book). You are all remarkable.

And to you, dear reader – thank you! Thank you for choosing this book and allowing me to share my story and tools with you. Together we can change this world, one deep breath at a time.

With love and gratitude, Chelsea.

Connect with Chelsea at eqminds.com and on Instagram at @eqminds.

NOTES

02 About You

Moore, W. et al., 'The Cultivation of Pure Altruism via Gratitude: A Functional MRI Study of Change with Gratitude Practice', *Frontiers in Human Neuroscience*, vol. 11, 599, 12 December 2017.

World Health Organization, 'Depression and Other Common Mental Disorders: Global Health Estimates', 2017, accessed 12 November 2021.

03 Your Mind

Hanson, R., 'Overcoming the Negativity Bias', accessed 6 January 2022.

Fuchs, E. & Flügge, G., 'Adult Neuroplasticity: More than 40 Years of Research', *Neural Plasticity*, 2014, no. 541870.

Hanson, R., 'Stephen Colbert: We Don't Need To "Keep Fear Alive"', *Huff Post*, 2010, accessed 12 November 2021.

Ackerman, C.E., 'What Is Neuroplasticity? A Psychologist Explains [+14 Exercises]', *Positive Psychology*, last modified 10 September 2019, accessed 12 November 2021.

Yaribeygi, H. et al., 'The Impact of Stress on Body Function: A Review', *EXCLI Journal*, vol. 16, 21 July 2017, pp. 1057–1072.

Center for Substance Abuse Treatment (US), 'Trauma-Informed Care in Behavioral Health Services', *Substance Abuse and Mental Health Services Administration (US)*, 2014, Chapter 3, Understanding the Impact of Trauma.

Bandura, A., 'Self-efficacy: Toward a Unifying Theory of Behavioral Change', *Psychological Review*, vol. 84, no. 2, 1977, pp. 191–215.

'How Many Thoughts Do We Have per Minute?', *Reference**, last modified 8 April 2020, accessed 8 March 2021.

Wansink, B. & Sobal, J., 'Mindless Eating: The 200 Daily Food Decisions We Overlook', *Environment and Behavior*, vol. 39, no. 1, January 2007, pp. 106–123.

'Decades of Scientific Research that Started a Growth Mindset Revolution', *Mindset Works*, accessed 12 November 2021.

Robbins, T., 'Life is happening for me', *Tony Robbins*, accessed 12 November 2021.

'The Dangers of Toxic Positivity Part 1 of 2', *Dare to Lead with Brené Brown* podcast, 1 March 2021.

'This Neuroscientist's Solution for Stress Will Surprise You: Andrew Huberman on Health Theory', *Impact Theory with Tom Bilyeu* podcast, 21 May 2022.

Hone, L., 'Sorrow and Tragedy Will Happen to Us All – Here are 3 Strategies to Help You Cope', *IDEAS.TED.COM*, 13 November 2019, accessed 12 November 2021.

04 Your Purpose

Filkowski, M. et al., 'Altruistic Behavior: Mapping Responses in the Brain', *Neuroscience and Neuroeconomics*, vol. 5, 2016, pp. 65–75.

'TED Talk of the Week: Your Life Purpose in 5 minutes', *Good Net*, 5 May 2015, accessed 12 November 2021.

05 Your Goals

Lyubomirsky, S., *The How of Happiness*, London: Piatkus, 2007.

Doran, G.T., 'There's a S.M.A.R.T. Way to Write Management's Goals and Objectives', *Management Review*, vol. 70, no. 11, November 1981.

'Nicholas Christakis: The Hidden Influence of Social Networks', *TED*, February 2010, accessed 12 November 2021.

'Coping with Financial Stress', *Help Guide*, accessed 12 November 2021.

Abdullah, G. et al., 'A Study of the Impact of the Expectation of a Holiday on an Individual's Sense of Well-Being', *Journal of Vacation Marketing*, vol. 8, no. 4, September 2002, pp. 352–361.

'The Importance of Taking Breaks', *The Wellbeing Thesis*, accessed 12 November 2021.

Lally, P. et al., 'How are Habits Formed: Modeling Habit Formation in the Real World', *European Journal of Social Psychology*, vol. 40, 1 October 2010.

Clark, L., 'Neuroscience is About Discovering Our Limits, Then Hacking to Get Around Them', *Wired*, 17 October 2013, accessed 12 November 2021.

Begley, S., 'The Brain: How The Brain Rewires Itself', *Time*, 19 January 2007, accessed 12 November 2021.

Page, S. et al., 'Mental Practice Combined With Physical Practice for Upper-Limb Motor Deficit in Subacute Stroke', *Physical Therapy*, vol. 81, no. 8, 1 August 2001, pp. 1455–1462.

06 Your Morning Routine

Roomer, J., '3 Reasons Why You Shouldn't Check Your Phone Within 1 Hour of Waking Up', 1 August 2019, accessed 12 November 2021.

'People Check Their Phone 85 Times a Day', *Nottingham Trent University*, 2015, accessed 12 November 2021.

Johnston, W. & Davey, G., 'The Psychological Impact of Negative TV News Bulletins: The Catastrophizing of Personal Worries', *British Journal of Psychology*, vol. 88 (Pt 1), 1997, pp. 85–91.

Emmons, R., *Thanks!: How the New Science of Gratitude Can Make You Happier*, Boston, MA: Houghton Mifflin Harcourt, 2000.

Seligman, M.E.P. et al., 'Positive Psychology Progress: Empirical Validation of Interventions', *American Psychologist*, vol. 60, no. 5, pp. 410–421.

Morin, A., '7 Scientifically Proven Benefits of Gratitude', *Psychology Today*, 3 April 2015, accessed 12 November 2021.

Redwine, L.S. et al., 'Pilot Randomized Study of a Gratitude Journaling Intervention on Heart Rate Variability and Inflammatory Biomarkers in Patients With Stage B Heart Failure', *Psychosomatic Medicine*, vol. 78, no. 6, 2016, pp. 667–676.

Korb, A., 'The Grateful Brain', *Psychology Today*, 20 November 2012, accessed 12 November 2021.

Amen, D., *The End of Mental Illness* (illustrated ed.), Carol Stream, IL: Tyndale House Publishers, 2020.

'Adm. McRaven Urges Graduates to Find Courage to Change the World', *UT News*, 16 May 2014, accessed 12 November 2021.

Duhigg, C., *The Power of Habit*, New York, NY: William Heinemann, 2012, Chapter 4.

Armstrong, L.E. et al., 'Mild Dehydration Affects Mood in Healthy Young Women,' *Journal of Nutrition*, vol. 142, no. 2, February 2012, pp. 382–388.

Rajkumar, H. et al., 'Effect of Probiotic Lactobacillus salivarius UBL S22 and Prebiotic Fructo-oligosaccaride on Serum Lipids, Inflammatory Markers, Insulin Sensitivity, and Gut Bacteria in Healthy Young Volunteers: A Randomized Controlled Single-Blind Pilot Study,' *Journal of Cardiovascular Pharmacology and Therapeutics*, vol. 20, no. 3, May 2015, pp. 289–298.

Buijze, G.A. et al., 'The Effect of Cold Showering on Health and Work: A Randomized Controlled Trial', *PLOS ONE*, vol. 11, no. 9, 15 September 2016, 30161749.

Taren, A. et al., 'Dispositional Mindfulness Co-varies with Smaller Amygdala and Caudate Volumes in Community Adults', *PLoS ONE*, vol. 8, no. 5, 2013, e64574.

Holzel, B.K. et al., 'Mindfulness Practice Leads to Increase in Regional Brain Gray Matter Density', *Psychiatry Research*, vol. 191, no. 1, 30 January 2011, pp. 36–43.

07 Your Movement and Energy

Lin, X. et al., 'Effect of Different Levels of Exercise on Telomere Length: A Systematic Review and Meta-analysis', *Journal of Rehabilitation Medicine*, vol. 51, no. 7, 8 July 2019, pp. 473–478.

Warburton, D., 'Health Benefits of Physical Activity: The Evidence', *Canadian Medical Association Journal*, vol. 174, no. 6, 2006, pp. 801–809.

Ruotsalainen, I. et al., 'Physical Activity, Aerobic Fitness, and Brain White Matter: Their Role for Executive Functions in Adolescence', *Developmental Cognitive Neuroscience*, vol. 42, 2020.

Guszkowska, M., 'Wpływ ćwiczeń fizycznych na poziom leku I depresji oraz stany Nastroju', [Effects of Exercise on Anxiety, Depression and Mood], *Psychiatria Polska*, vol. 38, no. 4, 2004, pp. 611–620.

Schwarb, H. et al., 'Aerobic Fitness, Hippocampal Viscoelasticity, and Relational Memory Performance', *NeuroImage*, vol. 153, 2017, pp. 179–188.

Mackenzie, R., 'Gray Matter vs White Matter', *Technology Networks*, 20 August 2019, accessed 12 November 2021.

Taubert, M. et al., 'Rapid and Specific Gray Matter Changes in M1 Induced by Balance Training', *NeuroImage*, vol. 133, 2016, pp. 399–407.

Fields, R., 'Neuroscience. Change in the Brain's White Matter', *Science*, vol. 330, no. 6005, 2010, pp. 768–769.

Driemeyer, J., 'Changes in Gray Matter Induced by Learning – Revisited', *PLoS ONE*, vol. 3, no. 7, 23 July 2008, e2669.

Sexton, C., 'Poor Sleep Quality is Associated with Increased Cortical Atrophy in Community-Dwelling Adults', *Neurology*, vol. 83, no. 11, 2014, pp. 967–973.

Bauman, A., 'The Descriptive Epidemiology of Sitting. A 20 Country Comparison Using the International Physical Activity Questionnaire (IPAQ)', *American Journal of Preventive Medicine*, vol. 41, no. 2, 2011, pp. 228–235.

World Health Organization (WHO), 'Physical Activity', 26 November 2020, accessed 12 November 2021.

Blair, S.N., 'How Much Physical Activity is Good for Health?', *Annual Review of Public Health*, vol. 13, 1992, pp. 99–126.

White, M.P. et al., 'Spending At Least 120 minutes a Week in Nature is Associated with Good Health and Wellbeing', *Scientific Reports*, vol. 9, no. 7730, 2019.

Crockett, M., 'Restricting Temptations: Neural Mechanisms of Precommitment', *Neuron*, vol. 79, no. 2, 2013, pp. 391–401.

08 Your Sleep

Suni, E., 'Sleep Foundation, Sleep Statistics', updated 12 November 2021, accessed 13 November 2021.

Walker, M., *Why We Sleep*, New York, NY: Scribner, 2017.

Colrain, I.M. et al., 'Alcohol and the Sleeping Brain', *Handbook of Clinical Neurology*, vol. 125, 2014, pp. 415–431.

'Exercising for Better Sleep', *Johns Hopkins Medicine*, accessed 12 November 2021.

'Sleep Restriction and CBTI', *Stanford Health Care*, accessed 12 November 2021.

09 Your Mindfulness

Holzel, B.K. et al., 'Mindfulness Practice Leads to Increases in Regional Brain Gray Matter Density,' *Psychiatry Research*, vol. 191, no. 1, 30 January 2011, pp. 36–43.

Taren, A. et al., 'Dispositional Mindfulness Co-varies with Smaller Amygdala and Caudate Volumes in Community Adults', *PLoS ONE*, vol. 8, no. 5, 2013, e64574.

Pagnoni, G., 'Dynamical Properties of BOLD Activity from the Ventral Posteromedial Cortex Associated with Meditation and Attentional Skills', *Journal of Neuroscience*, vol. 32, no. 15, 11 April 2012, pp. 5242–5249.

Harte, J. et al., 'The Effects of Running and Meditation on Beta-endorphin, Corticotropin-releasing Hormone and Cortisol in Plasma, and on Mood', *Biological Psychology*, vol. 40, no. 3, 1995, pp. 251–265.

Levine, G. et al., 'Meditation and Cardiovascular Risk Reduction: A Scientific Statement from the American Heart Association', *Journal of the American Heart Association*, vol. 6, no. 10, 2017, e002218.

Gard, T. et al., 'Pain Attenuation Through Mindfulness is Associated with Decreased Cognitive Control and Increased Sensory Processing in the Brain', *Cerebral Cortex*, vol. 22, no. 11, 2012, pp. 2692–2702.

Xu, M. et al., 'Mindfulness and Mind Wandering: The Protective Effects of Brief Meditation in Anxious Individuals', *Consciousness and Cognition*, vol. 51, 2017, pp. 157–165.

Busch, V. et al., 'The Effect of Deep and Slow Breathing on Pain Perception, Autonomic Activity, and Mood Processing – An Experimental Study,' *Pain Medicine*, vol. 13, no. 2, February 2012, pp. 215–228.

10 Your Gut Health

Bravo, J. et al., 'Ingestion of Lactobacillus Strain Regulates Emotional Behavior and Central GABA Receptor Expression in a Mouse via the Vagus Nerve', *Proceedings of the National Academy of Sciences*, vol. 108, no. 38, 20 September 2011, pp. 16050–16055.

O'Reardon, J. et al., 'Vagus Nerve Stimulation (VNS) and Treatment of Depression: To the Brainstem and Beyond', *Psychiatry*, vol. 3, no. 5, 2006, pp. 54–63.

Alcock, J. et al., 'Is Eating Behavior Manipulated by the Gastrointestinal Microbiota? Evolutionary Pressures and Potential Mechanisms', *BioEssays: News and Reviews in Molecular, Cellular and Developmental Biology*, vol. 36, no. 10, 2014, pp. 940–949.

Bulsiewicz, W., *Fibre Fuelled*, Sydney: Penguin, 2021, p. 16.

Wedekind, C. et al., 'MHC-dependent Mate Preferences in Humans', *Proceedings Biological Sciences*, vol. 260, no. 1359, 1995, pp. 245–249.

Sandoiu, A., '"Largest" Microbiome Study Weighs in on Our Gut Health', *Medical News Today*, 15 May 2018, accessed 12 November 2021.

Naidoo, U., 'Nutritional Strategies to Ease Anxiety', *Harvard Health Publishing*, 28 August 2019, accessed 12 November 2021.

Chang, C. et al., 'Essential Fatty Acids and Human Brain', *Acta Neurologica Taiwanica*, vol. 18, no. 4, 2009, pp. 231–241.

'EWG's 2021 Shopper's Guide to Pesticides in Produce™', *Environmental Working Group*, 17 March 2021, accessed 12 November 2021.

Simopoulos, A., 'Evolutionary Aspects of Diet: The Omega-6/Omega-3 Ratio and the Brain', *Molecular Neurobiology*, vol. 44, no. 2, 2011, pp. 203–215.

Amen, D., *The End of Mental Illness* (illustrated ed.), Carol Stream, IL: Tyndale House Publishers, 2020, p. 265.

Bulsiewicz, W., *Fibre Fuelled*, pp. 153–154.

Enders, G., *GUT*, Melbourne/London: Scribe Publications, 2015, p. 235.

González-Estévez, C. & Flores, I., 'Fasting for Stem Cell Rejuvenation', *Aging*, vol. 12, no. 5, 2020, pp. 4048–4049.

Kan, M., 'Toto's Wellness Toilet Will Analyze Your Poop', 12 January 2021, accessed 12 November 2021.

Fujimura, K. & Lynch, S., 'Microbiota in Allergy and Asthma and the Emerging Relationship with the Gut Microbiome', *Cell Host & Microbe*, vol. 17, no. 5, 2015, pp. 592–602.

11 Your Connections

Bargh, J.A. & Shalev, I., 'The Substitutability of Physical and Social Warmth in Daily Life', *Emotion*, vol. 12, no. 1, 2012, pp. 154–162.

'Redemption in Solitary Confinement', *Hi-Phi Nation* podcast, 30 May 2020.

Orloff, J., 'What Is Your Emotional Type?', *Psychology Today*, 28 February 2011, accessed 12 November 2021.

Winerman, L., 'The Mind's Mirror: How Mirror Neurons Explain Empathy', *American Psychological Association*, vol. 36, no. 9, October 2005, p. 48.

Goman, C., 'Why Women in Business Should Shake Hands,' *Forbes*, 22 May 2013, accessed 12 November 2021.

Williams, L. & Bargh, J., 'Experiencing Physical Warmth Promotes Interpersonal Warmth', *Science*, vol. 322, no. 5901, 2008, pp. 606–607.

Pinker, S., *The Village Effect*, London: Atlantic Books, 2015.

Petric, D., 'Psychological Archetypes: Vampires', *The Knot Theory of Mind*, December 2019.

Piff, P. et al., 'Awe, the Small Self, and Prosocial Behavior', *Journal of Personality and Social Psychology*, vol. 108, no. 6, 2015, pp. 883–899.

Sowndhararajan, K. & Kim, S., 'Influence of Fragrances on Human Psychophysiological Activity: With Special Reference to Human Electroencephalographic Response', *Scientia Pharmaceutica*, vol. 84, no. 4, 2016, pp. 724–752.

An, M. et al., 'Why We Need More Nature at Work: Effects of Natural Elements and Sunlight on Employee Mental Health and Work Attitudes', *PLoS ONE*, vol. 11, no. 5, 2016, 0155614.

Raanaas, R. et al., 'Health Benefits of a View of Nature Through the Window: A Quasi-experimental Study of Patients in a Residential Rehabilitation Center', *Clinical Rehabilitation*, vol. 26, no. 1, 2012, pp. 21–32.

Beukeboom, C. et al., 'Stress-reducing Effects of Real and Artificial Nature in a Hospital Waiting Room,' *Journal of Alternative and Complementary Medicine*, vol. 18, no. 4, 2012, pp. 329–33.

Baur, B. et al., 'Effect of the Combination of Music and Nature Sounds on Pain and Anxiety in Cardiac Surgical Patients: A Randomized Study', *Alternative Therapies in Health and Medicine*, vol. 17, no. 4, 2011, pp. 16–23.

Li, Q. et al., 'A Forest Bathing Trip Increases Human Natural Killer Activity and Expression of Anti-cancer Proteins in Female Subjects', *Journal of Biological Regulators and Homeostatic Agents*, vol. 22, no. 1, 2008, pp. 45–55.

Ryan, R. et al., 'Vitalizing Effects of Being Outdoors and in Nature', *Journal of Environmental Psychology*, vol. 30, no. 2, 2010, pp. 159–168.

12 Your Productivity

Mooney, M., 'The Beautiful Mind of Simon Sinek', *Success*, 11 July 2017, accessed 12 November 2021.

Choi, J., 'How to Master the Art of To-Do Lists by Understanding Why They Fail', *I Done This Blog*, 25 January 2021, accessed 12 November 2021.

Baer, D., 'Why You Need To Unplug Every 90 Minutes', *Fast Company*, 19 June 2013, accessed 12 November 2021.

Ducharme, J., 'Psychologists Explain Why You Procrastinate – And How to Stop', *Time*, 29 June 2018, accessed 12 November 2021.

Crockett, M., 'Restricting Temptations: Neural Mechanisms of Precommitment', *Neuron*, vol. 79, no. 2, 2013, pp. 391–401.

Amen, D., *Feel Better Fast and Make It Last*, Carol Stream, IL: Tyndale Momentum, 2018, p. 179.

Cherry, K., 'How Multitasking Affects Productivity and Brain Health', *Verywell Mind*, 30 July 2021, accessed 12 November 2021.

Mark, G. et al., 'The Cost of Interrupted Work: More Speed and Stress', *Conference on Human Factors in Computing Systems – Proceedings*, 2008, pp. 107–110.

Chang, J. et al., 'When the Tab Comes Due: Challenges in the Cost Structure of Browser Tab Usage', *Conference on Human Factors in Computing Systems*, 2021, pp. 1–15.

'As Uncertainty Remains, Anxiety and Stress Reach a Tipping Point at Work', *Workplace Intelligence & Oracle*, 2020.

'Leading Effective Decision Making', *Yale School of Management*, 2018.

Yaribeygi, H. et al., 'The Impact of Stress on Body Function: A Review', *EXCLI Journal*, vol. 16, 21 July 2017, pp. 1057–1072.

Robinson, B., 'The 90-Second Rule That Builds Self-Control', *Psychology Today*, 26 April 2020, accessed 12 November 2021.

University of California Los Angeles, 'Putting Feelings Into Words Produces Therapeutic Effects In The Brain', *Science Daily*, 22 June 2007, accessed 12 November 2021.

Chowdhury, M., 'The Neuroscience of Gratitude and How It Affects Anxiety & Grief', *Positive Psychology*, 9 October 2021, accessed 12 November 2021.

Bratman, G. et al., 'Nature Experience Reduces Rumination and Subgenual Prefrontal Cortex Activation', *Proceedings of the National Academy of Sciences of the United States of America*, vol. 112, no. 28, 2015, pp. 8567–8572.

Garrison, K. et al., 'Meditation Leads to Reduced Default Mode Network Activity Beyond an Active Task', *Cognitive, Affective & Behavioral Neuroscience*, vol. 15, no. 3, 2015, pp. 712–720.

Alena, M. et al., 'Self-Distancing as a Strategy to Regulate Affect and Aggressive Behavior in Athletes: An Experimental Approach to Explore Emotion Regulation in the Laboratory', *Frontiers in Psychology*, vol. 11, 2021, p. 3742.

Adams, J., 'The Value of Worker Well-Being', *Public Health Reports*, vol. 134, no. 6, 2019, pp. 583–586.

Pai, M., 'Burnout, A Silent Crisis in Global Health', *Forbes*, 20 July 2020, accessed 12 November 2021.

13 Your Support

Malhi, G. & Mann, J., 'Depression', *Lancet*, vol. 392, no. 10161, 2018, pp. 2299–2312.

INDEX

help, asking for 4, 15, 244, 249
help-lines 249
helping others 45–6, 49, 59–60
herbal teas 113
high performer, defined 1
hippocampus 83, 104, 123, 214
hobbies 138–9
holidays, setting goals for 61–2
Hone, Lucy 37, 38, 72
hormones, and meditation 123
Huberman, Andrew 34, 133, 134
The Huberman Lab (podcast) 133
hunger 112, 116
hydration 79, 102, 112, 116, 158
hyperbaric-oxygen chamber 93–4
hypertension 88
hypnosis 246

IDC Research 71
illness, movement to prevent 88, 89–90
immune system 80, 150, 155, 203, 206
imposter syndrome 173, 174–5
incidental exercise 94
Income Center for Trade 186
inflammation 74, 80, 93, 94, 113, 149,
    153, 162
infrared-sauna therapy 93
injury prevention, when exercising 92–4
inner critic 72, 144, 175
insecurity, feelings of 173–4
Insight Timer (app) 128
insomnia 9, 106, 117–20
Instagram 33, 187
insulin 162
intentions, setting of 21, 77–8, 83, 98
interruptions, dealing with 220–2
intrinsic motivation 64–5
iron deficiency 18, 120
irritable bowel syndrome 80, 150

Jackson, Lauren 92
Johnson & Johnson 7, 214
journals 17–19
Joy of Missing Out (JOMO) 177

kindness, random acts of 76, 143
Knight, Rob 156
Kondo, Marie 144
Korb, Alex 75

labelling, of emotions 233
lactobacillus 80
Larkin, Barry 243
Larkin, Gavin 243
larks 107
learning 60–1, 90
Leipzig, Adam 48
letters, of gratitude 74–5
The Life-Changing Magic of Tidying Up
    (Kondo) 144
life's work 48–9
light therapy boxes 108
limbic system 24
limiting beliefs 54–5, 69, 85–8
list-making 223
loneliness 172–3
longevity 188
love hormones 34
loving-kindness 142–4, 173, 175–6
low-VOC furnishings 110
lux scores 81

MacLean, Paul 24
magnesium 110, 113, 120
magnesium-salt tanks 93
major histocompatibility complex genes
    155
massage guns 95
mattress pads 110
Mayo Clinic 205
McMorrow, James Vincent 8
McRaven, William 78
meal plans 159
measurable goals 53, 55–7
medical checks 19
medications 153, 246, 247–8, 249
meditation
    as a part of mindfulness 121–2
    as part of a spiritual practice 62
    before sleep 114
    being consistent 125
    benefits of practising 122–3
    creating a vibe 125–6
    defined 124
    effect on the brain 83, 90, 123, 144
    finding and using apps 126, 127–8
    for emotional hangovers 183
    for empathy overload 181
    how to meditate 125–7, 129

Founder and Director of EQ MINDS, Chelsea Pottenger is one of Australia's most popular corporate wellness presenters and a woman on a mission to reset the corporate agenda. An accredited mindfulness and meditation coach and Mental Health Ambassador for R U OK? and Gidget Foundation Australia, she works with the world's biggest brands including Google, eBay and Estée Lauder, training more than 90,000 professionals every year to take charge of their mental wellbeing.

•

EQ MINDS is a wellness platform created to educate and empower people to prioritise and care for their mental health. It has become a destination frequented by busy minds seeking tools and resources to bring calm, nourish the mind and optimise mental health and wellbeing to improve quality of life.